WARTY TOWELS

FAWLTY TOWERS

JOHN CLEESE

FAWLTY TOWERS

FAWLTS & ALL

Headline

First published in 2025 by
HEADLINE PUBLISHING GROUP

1

Cataloguing in Publication Data is available
from the British Library

Hardback ISBN HB 978 1 0354 3321 6

Designed by Mike Jones

Illustrations by May Van Millingen,
Richard Smith and Chris Thompson

Typeset in Minion Pro, Axiforma and Bookman-Demi
Printed and bound in Italy by L.E.G.O. S.p.A.

Photo credits: BBC Picture Library, Getty Images,
Getty Images / Radio Times, Alamy, Shutterstock,
Shutterstock / ITV, Mirrorpix, Bayliss Media,
Mike Jones and the collection of John Cleese

HEADLINE PUBLISHING GROUP
An Hachette UK Company
Carmelite House
50 Victoria Embankment
London EC4Y 0DZ

www.headline.co.uk
www.hachette.co.uk

Acknowledgements:
With thanks to Derek Handley, Richard Norris,
Sarah Hart, Peter Kindred, Andrew Pixley,
CJay Ranger, Lucy Ansbro,
Graham McCann, Paul Farrar.

FSC
www.fsc.org

MIX
Paper | Supporting
responsible forestry
FSC® C023419

CONTENTS

FOREWORD BY GRAHAM McCANN — 8

RESERVATIONS

1 EARLY DAYS AND INSPIRATIONS — 14

2 ESCAPING PYTHON . . . WITH AN INVITATION FROM JIMMY — 24

3 ESTABLISHING A COMEDY — 32

4 CREATING CHARACTERS — 44

5 ENTER: JHD — 52

6 MAKING THE PILOT — 58
   A TOUCH OF CLASS — 74

7 INTERLUDE: MAKING A SITCOM — 80

FIRST SITTING

8 . . . AND FIVE MORE! — 86
   THE BUILDERS — 90
   THE WEDDING PARTY — 100
   THE HOTEL INSPECTORS — 106
   GOURMET NIGHT — 112
   THE GERMANS — 118

9 REACTION TO THE FIRST SERIES — 126

SECOND SITTING

10 BACK FOR MORE — 136
   COMMUNICATION PROBLEMS — 142
   THE PSYCHIATRIST — 148
   WALDORF SALAD — 156
   THE KIPPER AND THE CORPSE — 164
   THE ANNIVERSARY — 172
   BASIL THE RAT — 178

11 REACTION TO THE SECOND SERIES — 186

CHECKING OUT

12 MOPPING UP! — 192

13 BASIL'S LONG SHADOW? — 204

14 TAKING FAWLTY TO THE STAGE — 210

15 A LIFE CALLING TO LAUGHTER — 218

AFTERWORD BY CONNIE BOOTH — 222

ABOUT THE AUTHOR — 224

MAY WE WELCOME YOU TO FAWLTY TOWERS.

WE TRUST YOUR STAY WILL BE AN ENJOYABLE AND A GRACIOUS ONE.

In Basil, especially, we have a comic icon for the ages, a figure to stand alongside the likes of Falstaff, Pooter, Hancock and all the rest of those famously flawed few. When we look at him, as at them, we see, whether we like it or not, an aspect of ourselves staring straight back at us, a mirror of our mind and manners.

Emerson once remarked of the English: 'The Englishman finds no relief from reflection, except in reflection. When he wishes for amusement, he goes to work. His hilarity is like an attack of fever.' That's so Basil.

Santayana once observed, 'Instinctively the Englishman is no missionary, no conqueror. He prefers the country to the town, and home to foreign parts. He is rather glad and relieved if only natives will remain natives and strangers strangers, and at a comfortable distance from himself.' That's so Basil.

Bagehot once wrote of the English that they 'never think if they can help it – that they invent devices to avoid it – that, however greedy of enjoyment in other ways, they decline, if possible, to enjoy themselves in this'. That's so Basil.

All of that is so Basil – and most, if not all, of that is so us too, albeit at our worst, in all of our impossibly hopeful, profoundly fearful, twitchily sceptical, ridiculously contradictory 'grown-up' guises and gambits. For fifty years and counting, 'Fawltyesque' has served as our common adjectival admonition and our shared salute of social recognition.

This brings us to one of the real pleasures and privileges of a foreword, which is the opportunity it affords us to be considerably more candid about the author's importance than he is ever likely to be himself. Of all the many features of *Fawlty Towers* that merit celebration, and yet arguably has not yet been celebrated quite as much as it deserves, is the writing partnership of John Cleese and Connie Booth.

What the two of them achieved together, in just twelve half-hour episodes, is surely at least as impressive, if not more so, than anything else that has been written, anywhere in the world, in the entire history of sitcoms – by one, two or even whole huge teams of gifted humourists. The plotting, the pacing, the quality of the characterisations, the blend of the verbal and the visual, the sheer holistic intelligence and intensity of it all, is simply second to none.

Countless others, with the best intentions, have tried to collect the same ingredients ('No cheese – it's celery, apples, walnuts, grapes. . .'; 'Right! Now come on!'). None of them, in spite of their best

efforts, have combined them all so well into something – with more than a touch of class as well as craft – so breathtakingly right.

It's been said (by Schopenhauer – never knowingly confused with a barrel of laughs, admittedly, but in this particular instance probably the sharpest tool in the box) that, while 'talent hits a target no one else can hit, genius hits a target no one else can see'. Well, what those two did, so many of us think, really was genius.

Which is why this book, by one of them, could not be more welcome. Here, in all the fascinating pages that follow, those of us who so love what we have seen, will be given a very special insight – straight from the moose's mouth – into what, until now, remained largely hidden: the rare invention, industry and experiences (even rarer than a packet of sliced hippopotamus in suitcase sauce) that helped bring all the magic to the screen.

I therefore could not be more confident that, by the time you've reached the end, you'll feel the same strong need as me to say: 'Thank you, John. Thank you so bloody much!'

It's been well worth the wait.

Graham McCann

RESERVATIONS

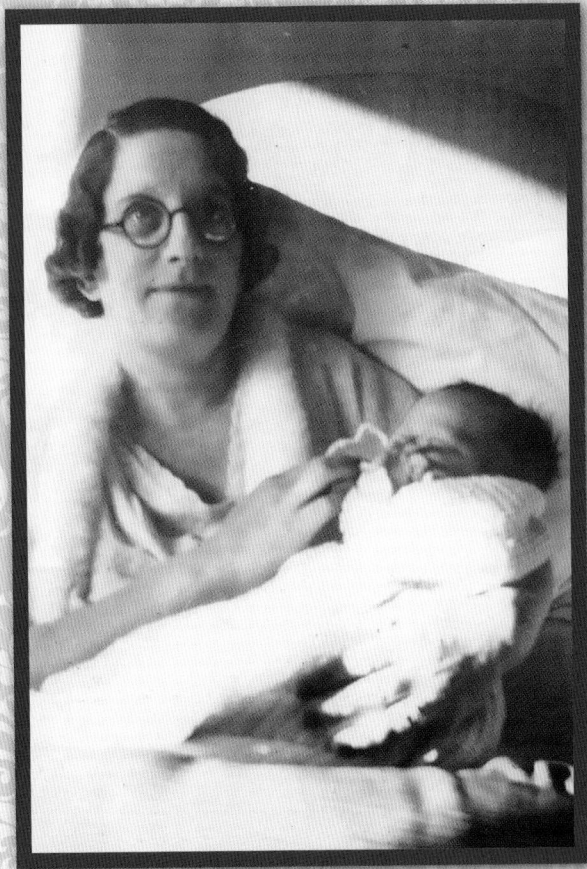

1940.

EARLY DAYS AND INSPIRATIONS

In a way it all began in Weston-super-Mare. I grew up there in the 1950s, learning all about little English seaside resorts. Nowhere near as posh as Torquay, of course, but with a certain orderly lower-class charm about it. The Westonians were an ever well-mannered, kind, friendly lot, whose main aim in life was to get safely into their graves without ever having been seriously embarrassed. Respectability was the name of the game, but respectability of a particularly lower middle-class kind.

My parents were from different levels within that class. My mother's father was an auctioneer, and her family had maids, so she was upper middle class. Dad, on the other hand, was the son of a solicitor's clerk in Bristol, called John Edwin Cheese, so he was lower middle-class. As the auctioneer regarded Dad as riff-raff, my parents had to elope to London to get married. They were later forgiven.

So, this class consciousness permeated my life in Weston. There was nothing cruel or harsh about it, just a constant preoccupation with using the right fork, or pronouncing the word 'garage' with an 'ah!' sound at the end, or watching the BBC and not ITV.

WESTON-SUPER-MARE

So, Basil Fawlty's preoccupation with class was something I understood. The moment a guest arrives, Basil instinctively calibrates their position in the class system and takes up the appropriate attitude to that position, whether it is fawning, condescension, or outright contempt. In each of these modes he is attempting to present himself as grander than he is. Even when he's grovelling, he's trying to show that he himself is a member of the class to which he is grovelling – his vocabulary and body language show he is sophisticated enough to recognise superior beings when he sees them.

Above: A 1950s postcard of Weston-super-Mare.

Opposite page: Me as a baby, toddler and boy with my mother, Muriel, my father, Reg, and teddy.

Below: Weston-super-Mare's coat of arms, as pictured on an old cigarette card.

When dealing with folk from the lower middle class he in fact inhabits, he slips momentarily into something resembling courtesy and continues to do so as long as they play their cards right. But when dealing with the working class, he becomes Lord of the Manor, behaving with an absent-minded dismissiveness that reminds riff-raff of their position in society.

Basil's other main motivation is fear – mostly, of course, of Sybil. But not exclusively, since he is alarmed by people who can harm his hotel's reputation: writers for hotel guides, food inspectors, influential guests. Connie and I used mistaken identity a lot, because it is always funny when someone behaves in a specific way to a person only to discover it's the wrong sort of behaviour. The change of gears is funniest when it's very smooth. And mistaken identity reminds me of how much our own behaviour is transactional – or manipulative.

But, in a way, *Fawlty Towers* also began when my parents used to take me each year to the same hotel in Bournemouth, for there I was able to see for the first time how a hotel worked. I knew how my school worked, and how my family functioned (after a fashion), but this was my first experience of watching grown-ups dealing with each other.

One of the great advantages of setting a sitcom in a hotel is that almost all of the viewers know how hotels are supposed to work. You don't have to spend half of the first programme explaining the norms.

What I noticed in that Bournemouth hotel was that there was a backstage, and a front stage. The frontstage consisted of the lobby, reception, the restaurant and bar – everywhere the guests would expect to go. Everything on the front stage was calm, organised and efficient. Backstage wasn't. Every problem, squabble, crisis and panic took place there, out of sight – what a great source for humour. At any time something has to be covered up, you have the makings of a farce. The other advantage of a hotel setting is that any kind of guest can turn up at any time – and be gone again by the start of the next episode.

The first inkling of Basil's personality came from an incident at my beloved prep school, St Peter's, on a summer evening in 1953. I learned something that I have never forgotten. There was a boy in my maths class called David Rogers. I didn't use his first name, because in those days calling a boy by his Christian name would have been considered evidence of carnal intent.

Rogers and I were taught maths by Mr Bartlett. He was a very good teacher, the sort of unambitious Oxford intellectual, with fastidious and classical taste, that I became familiar with in later years. As we were in awe of him, we desperately – desperately – wanted to please him with our work. If he was not pleased, he would declare that we had started a war with him, and he would behave like a rejected lover (I now realise) and we would all feel absolutely terrible and want to die.

Below: A delightful strip of photo booth photos of me aged 9 ... already displaying a range of comedy faces, from mildly confused to amused, via quizzical!

This particular evening, we were doing a geometry 'prep' for him, which involved using compasses to draw geometrical 'proofs'. I began to notice that Rogers, at the next desk, was not having a good time. He looked panicky and sweaty, because every time he tried to draw a circle, the sharp point of his compass would slip and the pencil completing the circle would slip too, and ruin the circle he had almost drawn.

This sequence of events repeated itself for some time, with Rogers' pencil slipping, and Rogers furiously rubbing out the almost-circle, until he had done it so many times that the page in his exercise book was looking like an impasto of a heavily ploughed field. Rogers meanwhile was oscillating between rage at the compass and terror at Bartlett's impending judgement, and he was emitting tiny squeaks of panic and fury as

he attracted more and more attention. Most of us thought he had gone completely mad.

Then suddenly, an icy calm came over him. He stood up, walked very purposefully over to the waste-paper basket, pulled a penknife out of his pocket and started very deliberately to sharpen the metal point of the compass. There was something about the steely determination with which he attempted to sharpen a metal point, combined with the carefully controlled ice-cold savagery he affected while doing it, that remains one of the funniest things I have ever seen.

So maybe it follows naturally that when I was trying to make people laugh at Basil, I created situations where his suppressed anger affects his behaviour to everyone else. It's not his anger that's funny. It's the fact that he can never express it properly, and that bottling it all up distorts all the rest of his emotional life!

What is odd, in retrospect, is that before Connie and I created Basil, I had a practice run at writing his part.

In the early 70s I used to pay regular visits to the Westside Health Club on Kensington High Street in London. I was particularly fond of one of the instructors there, one Bill Williams, who was from a family of sports trainers, who had all spent their lives getting boxers and swimmers and gymnasts super-fit. Bill was particularly good at varying workouts, and he had a number of older clients who thrived under his tuition.

One day, I made a mistake. I told Bill that if he ever wanted to open a small club of his own, I'd be interested in backing him. Of course, within six weeks he had found one . . . It was in Brighton, where, as he pointed out, there were lots of retired folk, who were much better customers, as they needed individual sessions.

So, in June 1970, our health club opened in Brighton. And six weeks later, Bill was dead. Just like that.

Not a great start for a health club.

The poor man, who was tough as they come, suddenly felt stomach pains. In hospital they opened him up and quickly sewed him up again. Stomach cancer. Bad stomach cancer. So, they sent him home to die.

Lovely man . . .

I never said goodbye to him, because his business partner, Dennis, apparently wanted to be sure Bill was stone-cold before he updated me on business prospects (and immediately scarpered with the thousand pounds I had lent him).

And now we get to the point of this story.

I had to pay off a number of builders, equipment salesmen and justifiably disappointed new club members. To do this, I approached an old friend who commissioned sitcoms for Thames Television: Humphrey Barclay. Humphrey had directed me in the Cambridge Footlights Revue of 1963, which got me into show business, and then into over a hundred episodes of the radio show *I'm Sorry I'll Read That Again* with Tim Brooke-Taylor and Bill Oddie. A couple of years earlier, he had asked Graham Chapman and I to write the pilot episode of London Weekend Television's *Doctor in the House*. Since Gra had been a medical student at St Bartholomew's Hospital, the job was a bit of a doddle, and the series took off splendidly.

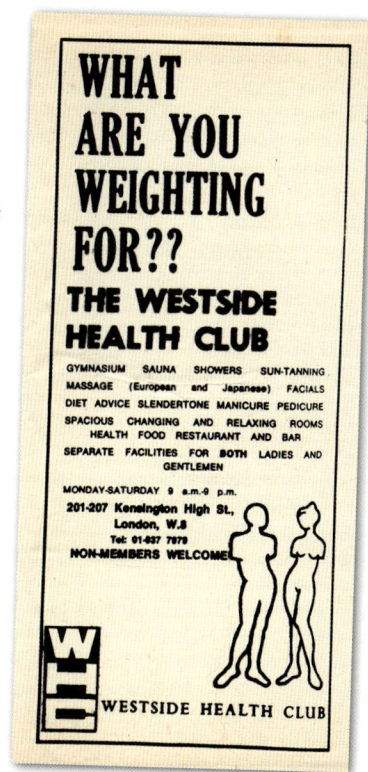

WHAT ARE YOU WEIGHTING FOR??
THE WESTSIDE HEALTH CLUB
GYMNASIUM   SAUNA   SHOWERS   SUN-TANNING
MASSAGE (European and Japanese)   FACIALS
DIET ADVICE SLENDERTONE MANICURE PEDICURE
SPACIOUS CHANGING AND RELAXING ROOMS
HEALTH FOOD RESTAURANT AND BAR
SEPARATE FACILITIES FOR BOTH LADIES AND GENTLEMEN
MONDAY-SATURDAY 9 a.m.-9 p.m.
201-207 Kensington High St., London, W.8
Tel: 01-937 7878
NON-MEMBERS WELCOME!
WESTSIDE HEALTH CLUB

Above: An advert for the Westside Health Club from the Friday, 12 March 1971 edition of the *Marylebone Mercury*.

Below left: The title card and credit for me and Graham Chapman from the first episode of *Doctor in the House*: 'Why do you want to be a Doctor?'

Below: Producer Humphrey Barclay on location for *Do Not Adjust Your Set* in 1968.

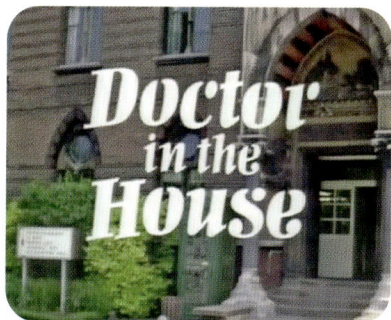

Many of the episodes were written by Graeme Garden and Bill Oddie; the other Graeme was a qualified doctor too.

So, I said to Humphrey, 'Can I write a few *Doctor* episodes for you?'

And Humphrey said, 'With Graham?'

And I said, 'No, on my own. I need the money.'

And Humphrey said, 'How about six?'

That's how we used to do business in the old days, before TV executives invented 'commissioning editors'. So, in 1970, I wrote six episodes of *Doctor at Large,* the spin-off of *Doctor in the House,* on my own, which did not please Gra. All writing partnerships can get a bit like marriages: 'I hear you've been writing with someone else?'

'It was just . . . a fling.'

Of those six episodes I can remember just two. One, called 'Mr Moon', featured John Le Mesurier, whom I had always adored, until he fucked up the whole show because he couldn't remember his lines. I adored him a bit less after that.

The other one I recall was called 'No Ill Feeling!' In this episode, the usual highly likeable gang of Barry Evans, Robin Nedwell, George Layton and George Davies were to stay at a hotel.

I modelled this hotel on a memorable one that the Pythons had stayed at in Torquay during location filming a year before: The Gleneagles. I used my recollection of that hotel's owner, Donald Sinclair, to create the character of Mr Clifford, played by Timothy Bateson.

On these pages, I have chosen some parts of 'No Ill Feeling!' to investigate how closely Mr Clifford's character tallied with Mr Fawlty's, four years later. You can watch the whole thing on YouTube. Incidentally, the character of an extremely irritating guest, played by the late, great Roy Kinnear, was echoed four years later by the superb Bernard Cribbins in 'The Hotel Inspectors', who also finishes the episode covered with food.

After the recording, Humphrey Barclay told me:

'There's a series in that hotel!' I remember thinking, 'Typical producer – always looking for a series!' I had no idea how right he was . . .

7.25 Doctor at Large

BARRY EVANS
George Layton
Geoffrey Davies in

No Ill Feeling!
BY JOHN CLEESE
with ROY KINNEAR

Upton takes a new job in general practice with Collier's uncle, Dr. Griffin. He is put up at a local hotel and encounters the resident funny-man Mr. Davidson—the life and soul of the party!

Michael Upton	Barry Evans
Paul Collier	George Layton
Dr. Griffin	Erian Oulton
Mr. Clifford	Timothy Bateson
Mrs. Clifford	Eunice Black
First old lady	Lucy Griffiths
Second old lady	Ailsa Grahame
Third old lady	Betty Hare
Mr. Davidson	Roy Kinnear
Dick Stuart-Clark	Geoffrey Davies

DESIGNER RODNEY CAMMISH : DIRECTOR ALAN WALLIS : EXECUTIV : PRODUCER HUMPHREY BARCLAY

London Weekend Television Production

Above: A promotional postcard for Gleneagles Hotel from the 1960s.
Above right: Proprietors, Donald and Beatrice Sinclair.

So, what was it about Gleneagles and its proprietors, Donald and Beatrice Sinclair, that had stuck in my mind so clearly?

I arrived in Torquay, Devon on the afternoon of Sunday, 10 May 1970, the day before location filming began for the second series of *Monty Python* (for sequences as the announcer on Broadsands Beach, if you must know!). I and all the Pythons and Connie Booth (we were married at the time) were booked into the Gleneagles Hotel on Asheldon Road in the Wellswood district.

Donald Sinclair was a former naval officer, and he had a temperament and manner that established him in my mind as the rudest man I'd ever come across in my life.

Below: *Monty Python* title card; filming on Broadsands Beach.

As Michael Palin described him in one of his diaries: 'He seemed to view us from the start as a colossal inconvenience.'

My clearest memory was of a Python group dinner on the first evening. I was mildly amused at the way Sinclair was stalking around the dining room, looking rather commanding but never actually doing anything. The Pythons were all at a long table, and as he strolled past, he suddenly stopped and stared at Terry Gilliam. Terry was eating his steak in the American fashion. He cut up all the meat, discarded his knife, and taking the fork in his right hand, speared the meat with it. He became aware of Sinclair's scrutiny and looked up at him. Sinclair said, with stern disapproval, 'We do not eat like that in this country,' and walked off . . .

I don't think I can convey just how extraordinary that was. In my entire life, I have never seen a restaurant manager reprove a guest's table manners. And doing so by picking Terry out from a group of his companions and telling him off in a loud and clear voice was utterly breathtaking. It was, above all, so wonderfully gratuitous. What was he hoping to achieve? He could not have done anything more inappropriate if he had struck Terry on the head with the flambéed pineapple. Nobody spoke. We looked at each other with a 'Did that actually happen?' look, familiar to us all from *Candid Camera*.

My own encounter was no less bizarre. I walked into the lobby and saw Sinclair sitting at the reception desk, staring into space. Suddenly he saw me coming and spun around, turning his back on me, pretending he was busy with some paperwork. I came up to the desk and waited politely. And waited . . . and waited.

It was impossible to believe that he did not know I was there. But he continued to pretend he was busy. I decided that he was hoping I would just go away. Or . . . could he just possibly think that I had left?

I cleared my throat tentatively and he whipped around to face me with an exasperated 'Oh, what?!', as though my intrusion was the last straw, the 150th time he had been interrupted in the last ten minutes.

I was slightly taken back.

'What do you want?' he shouted.

'Er . . . Could you call me a taxi?'

Incredulity. Clearly he thought I was unhinged.

Long silence.

'Call . . . you . . . a . . . taxi?' It was as though I had asked him for a dance.

'Yes,' I said, 'a taxi.'

Silence.

'Can you?'

'I suppose so'. And he dialed a taxi.

I was astonished that I had won.

The hotel was so awful that most of the Pythons moved to the five-star Imperial Hotel after a couple of days, leaving only Eric Idle, Connie and me, at the mercy of Basil's prototype. Why did we continue to stay there? Sheer laziness . . . And phenomenal luck . . .

One morning Eric left a bag behind when he went off to work. On returning that night, he asked Sinclair where the bag was.

'Behind the wall,' he replied, pointing out of the front door, at a wall on the other side of the swimming pool.

Eric was bamboozled.

'Why did you . . . ?'

'What is it now?'

'Why did you put it out there?' Pause.

'We thought it might be a bomb.'

'A bomb??!'

These were the days before the IRA had started letting off bombs in London. The last bomb had probably been during the Blitz.

For once, Sinclair seemed to think he needed to explain.

'Well . . . We've had a lot of staff problems recently.'

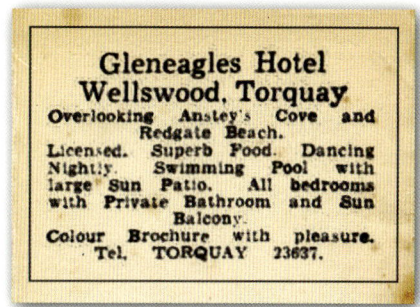

Above: A 1970 newspaper advert for the Gleneagles Hotel.

Below: A glossy colour advertisement for the Gleneagles Hotel from the early 1970s.

2.

ESCAPING PYTHON...WITH AN INVITATION FROM JIMMY

I wrote my six episodes of *Doctor at Large* in 1970, about a year after we'd done the first series of *Monty Python*.

I never wrote any more episodes, because at this point *Python* pretty much took over my life. What had at first been a TV series that took roughly six months to write and perform, now sprouted records, and books, and then . . . tours!

Slowly I found myself hemmed in by the procession of *Python* projects. I had loved the first series and had enjoyed most of the second, but by the third series in 1972, a lot of things were beginning to grate.

Firstly, I wanted to write stuff that was not in the *Python* style. I'd written a lot of sketches since 1966, and I wanted to try my hand at longer formats. I was fascinated by learning about plotting.

Secondly, Graham had, out of the blue,

become a problem. Within a few months there were days when, in the afternoon, he couldn't remember what we had written in the morning. It also affected his acting, and he was a really fine actor – until he couldn't remember his lines.

There was one sketch that had to be abandoned in front of the studio audience because he simply couldn't get it right and we were running out of recording time.

Opposite page: Strolling in one of the *Monty Python* 'Ministry of Silly Walks' sketches.

Below: Monty Python in 1969: left to right, Terry Jones, Graham Chapman, me, Eric Idle, Terry Gilliam and Michael Palin.

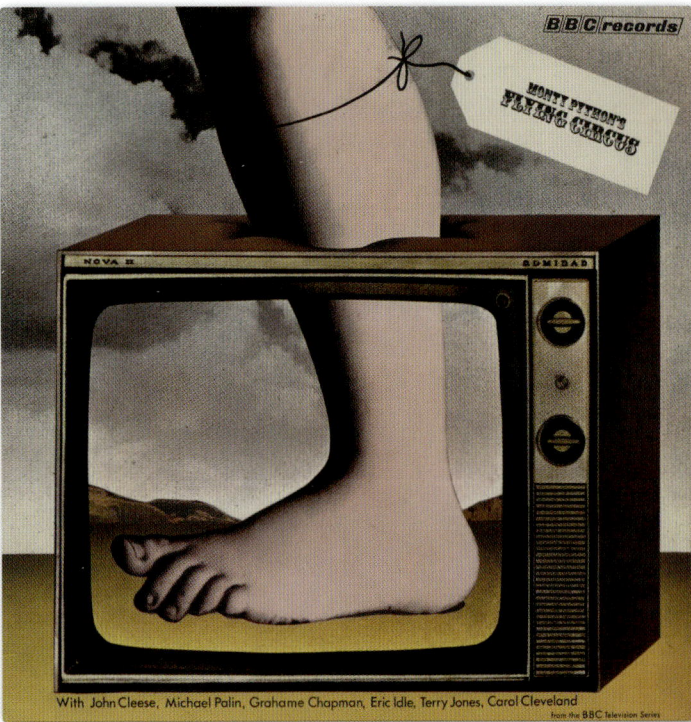

With John Cleese, Michael Palin, Grahame Chapman, Eric Idle, Terry Jones, Carol Cleveland
from the BBC Television Series

And the other Pythons regarded old Gra as my problem. Nobody else wanted to share writing duties with him.

Thirdly, I was getting tired of the endless arguments with Terry Jones. Normally there were disagreements about a script. I found it easy to work with Michael and Eric. Graham flitted in and out of script discussions, but presented no problem. Terry Gilliam attended very few script meetings; his work came later when we told him how many animations the script needed, and how long, and where the starting point should come.

But then there was Terry Jones . . .

Most writers feel strongly about some points, and less strongly about others, so that there's room for discussion and compromise. Terry felt strongly about everything. There was no hill he was not prepared to die on. No molehill either . . .

I remember on one occasion when he and I argued about what seemed to me a very important decision, and as our tussle continued, the others began to find my arguments more persuasive, and as the light began to fail, dear Terry finally conceded, and I experienced a moment of exhilaration that, finally, the Pythons had got it right!

The next morning we were back at Terry's house, and he was making us all coffee, when I heard something that froze my blood – 'I was thinking last night . .' Terry said, in the high-pitched whine that always heralded an impassioned display of Celtic self-confidence. 'And I reeeeally feel . . . ', and we were off again, regurgitating yesterday's debate word for word. Terry Jones always believed that the way to win his point was by becoming even more impassioned, rather than improving on his arguments. And, after two series, it had begun to grate on me.

The other reason I was tired of *Python* was that we were beginning to repeat our ideas. The first series included some really special and original humour. The second series was pretty good too, but towards the end I felt – though not passionately – that we were becoming a bit predictable.

For all these reasons I was able to slow down the stampede towards a third series. In my heart of hearts, I didn't really want to do another one, but I felt guilty about letting the others down. This

was compounded by my agent, David Wilkinson, telling me that the BBC would not commission the series if I was not in it. So, I argued to do a shorter series. As Terry Gilliam put it, I 'came to heel'!

But the new half-series came and went, and nothing improved, and I caved in again and agreed to do the other half and finally had to tell the others that I did not want to do any more *Python* TV shows.

Mike and Eric took it in their stride, but Gra and Terry Jones were angry. Terry Gilliam wanted to direct films, so I don't think he minded.

So anyway . . . my sanity was saved, and my only immediate concern was my bank manager.

Python was never that well paid. Back in 1969, for the first series I was paid £280 per episode for performing, plus an additional fee for writing. In total, each of us earned around £2,000–£3,000 for the entire series – which kept us busy for about six months. We paid income tax of around 90 per cent on that, so none of us were perusing yacht catalogues.

Measly though these sums seem now, I did realise that leaving *Python* would mean taking a cut in income.

Above: In entirely appropriate attire during filming of the opening show of *Monty Python's Flying Circus*, Walton-on-Thames, 21 August 1970. Spot the other Python...

Below: Michael Palin and me in the little-known 'Dead Parrot' sketch from the first series of *Monty Python's Flying Circus*.

I'd always told the Pythons that my dislike of the TV demands did not extend to film, which I found much more interesting, especially as film presented us with writing challenges very different from three-minute sketches.

So, at the beginning of 1973, we started writing *Monty Python and the Holy Grail*. This took us a very long time as we had no idea what we were doing, but by 1974, we were able to start shooting, which brought me some much-needed cash. Now that we were film stars, we were paid proper fees: £4,000 each . . . although, before leaving for filming in Scotland, the producers told us they could only pay us £2,000, and they hoped to be able to cough up the balance later.

Shortly after *Holy Grail* was shot, I was pleased to get a call inviting me to a lunch to discuss my future, with the BBC Head of Comedy, my old friend Jimmy Gilbert.

Jimmy had been the producer/director of *The Frost Report*, in which I first appeared on British television, in 1966. I'd never done television before, but at David Frost's invitation I found myself performing to an audience of 14 million, LIVE!!!, every Thursday. I've never been so scared in my life, but the people around me – David, Ronnie Barker, Ronnie Corbett, Nicky Henson, Bernard Thompson and Jimmy himself – were kind and reassuring and got me through my early screen fright.

Jimmy also presided at the weekly script conference, where Marty Feldman (the script editor!), John Law, Barry Cryer, David Nobbs, Dick

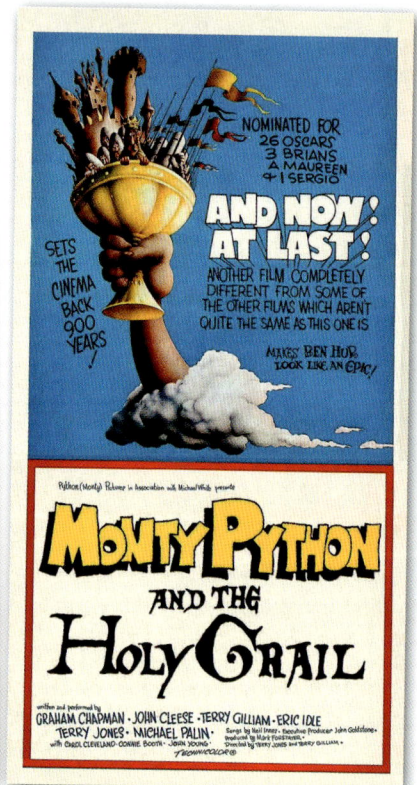

Vosburgh, Frank Muir, Dennis Norden and five Monty-Pythons-to-be, put together the next week's script.

Jimmy was the ideal host. With his soft-spoken, elegant Glaswegian accent, he nudged and coaxed us each week towards a finished script. Highly experienced, his occasional interventions were respected without question. The Python members would sometimes suggest something whacky, or zany, or off-the-wall, and sometimes these ideas brought gales of laughter from all the writers, but Jimmy would grin and say, 'Sorry, boys, but they won't get it in Bradford,' and it was instantly dropped and forgotten (later perhaps to re-emerge in *Monty Python*). Jimmy was one of the most admirable men I ever met. He was so good at his job and so fundamentally kind that he was an ideal Head of Comedy, in the days when such executives had risen through the ranks and had actually made many programmes themselves.

Below: With Ronnie Barker and Ronnie Corbett in *The Frost Report*'s 'class sketch', first broadcast on 7 April 1966.

Below right: Jimmy
Gilbert in his office at
BBC Television Centre.

Opposite page: With
Connie at the opening
night of *Harvey* at the
Prince of Wales Theatre
on 9 April 1975.

So anyway . . . Jimmy and I lunched at Cibo in Holland Park. Conversation flowed so easily that when Jimmy asked me if there was anything I'd like to do post-*Python* at the BBC, I simply said, 'Yes, I'd like to do something with Connie.' Jimmy asked me, 'Do you know what?' 'No. . .' I said. 'Well, why don't you go home and talk with Connie, and then call me and tell me, and I'll commission it?' And then we finished lunch.

Again, that's how things were done at a time when the BBC was making the best comedies in the world, before bureaucrats introduced committees and commissioning editors who had never actually made any programmes.

So I went home and talked to Connie. We felt that all the man–woman comedy was being done very well at the time by John Fortune and Eleanor Bron, who were starring in a TV series called *Where Was Spring?* So, there was no point in going there . . . and then one of us suggested doing a comedy about a badly run hotel, like the one we had stayed at, Gleneagles, four years earlier.

I called Jimmy and said, 'Connie and I would like to do a comedy set in a hotel, based on one we once stayed at when we were filming for *Monty Python*', and the BBC Head of Comedy said, 'OK. I'll commission it.'

Just like that.

And so, we went to work on putting together a pilot programme for the new series. At this point in my life, I had done a fair amount of writing, mostly with Graham. There were all the sketches for *The Frost Report*, *At Last the 1948 Show*, and *Monty Python*, a number of 30-minute sitcoms including *Doctor at Large*, a Sheila Hancock special, a Ronnie Barker special, an American special called *How to Irritate People* and three film scripts for Peter Sellers (*Rentasleuth*, *The Magic Christian* and *The Rise and Rise of Michael Rimmer*).

I had written one pilot for a new series (also with Gra) but that was for the already established *Doctors* series. This new programme would really be something completely different . . .

Jimmy Gilbert
Head of Comedy

BBC Comedy of the 60s and 70s would have been very different without the careful stewardship of Cecil James Gilbert.

Edinburgh-born Jimmy fell in love with performing at school, but the outbreak of war set aside any dreams of performance and the RAF beckoned.

After the war, Jimmy enrolled into RADA with the hope of entering the film industry as a director. Parallel with his studies, Jimmy also performed and wrote for theatre, writing the satire-based musical *Grab Me a Gondola,* which proved a great success, and led to him being offered a role in the BBC, initially focused within music programming. Rising through the ranks, he was soon identified as having an affinity for managing talent within the pressures of the studio.

Along with David Frost, Jimmy developed *The Frost Report,* and in the process put together Ronnie Barker and Ronnie Corbett, as well as several of the *Python* team.

As a director, Jimmy set the tone for the first series of *The Two Ronnies, Whatever Happened to the Likely Lads?* and *Last of the Summer Wine.* Later as Head of Comedy, Jimmy was able to green light dozens of series now considered classics. This usually meant hours in agonising meetings, which tended to lobotomise people's funny bones; Jimmy however still managed to keep his.

Going freelance in the early 1980s, Jimmy produced comedies for Thames Television, before going on to enjoy a well-earned retirement after his time in the television trenches.

3.

ESTABLISHING A COMEDY

In what ways did writing a pilot differ from one of the ordinary series episodes I had written in the past? The first thing, obviously, is that you need to spend most of your script introducing the main characters. This means you simply don't have enough time to create a very funny show – the plot needs to be a simple one. A very funny show would need to be more complex.

The second thing is to introduce the audience to the environment in which the characters live. If we had set the show in an undertaker's or food production company, we would have had to show whatever daily life was like there, what was normal and what was unexpected. We didn't have that problem with a hotel: everyone's been in one and knows how they're supposed to work. So, the very conventional setting of a hotel worked well for us.

The next essential ingredient was to establish the style of the comedy. Each show has its own level of reality. Some are much more naturalistic: *Friends, Steptoe and Son, The Office, Porridge*. Some get slightly less real: *Dad's Army, Are You Being Served?* Some are broader still: *'Allo 'Allo!* and *Only Fools and Horses*. Some of the best depart a long way from reality: *Blackadder*.

It doesn't matter which style each show chooses, provided only that it does not stray from that level of reality. If it does, everything collapses. The audience stops understanding how seriously to take the characters' behaviour. Motivations become random. No one knows what to believe and the audience loses its bearings and switches off.

Over the next six pages, we'll look at the pilot episode of *Fawlty Towers* and how we established it all.

FAWLTY TOWERS:

By John Cleese and Connie Booth

A Touch of Class

1

We begin with Basil taking a booking (establishing the routine of a hotel).

4

Old ladies appear (establishing their place in the scheme of things).

5

Guest complains about lack of alarm call (establishes that the hotel is not well run).

7

Basil and Sybil bicker (establishes that Basil is a snob, hoping to get a better class of guest, setting up his interaction with Lord Melbury. Sybil is more interested in the money, heralding continuous clashes about priorities).

8

Danny arrives (establishing Basil's automatic dislike for men who are young, casually dressed and a bit sexy. This aversion later makes Basil more stubborn about recognising the truth about Melbury).

2 Basil and Sybil bicker (establishing their relationship, with Sybil dominant, Basil on the defensive but doing most of the work).

3 Basil tells Manuel about the butter (establishing a pattern of miscommunication between them).

6 Basil talks to the Major (establishes the Major as a permanent resident, whom we will be seeing more of. Also confirms Basil's lack of interest in average guests. Establishes a guest's attempt to get Basil's attention, so he can be used as the punchline of the show).

9 Danny speaks fluent Spanish to Manuel (establishes more strongly Basil's attitude to Danny).

10 Basil and Sybil bicker about the painting and the menu (their ritual arguments about Basil's next job have been established, and can be a source of humour).

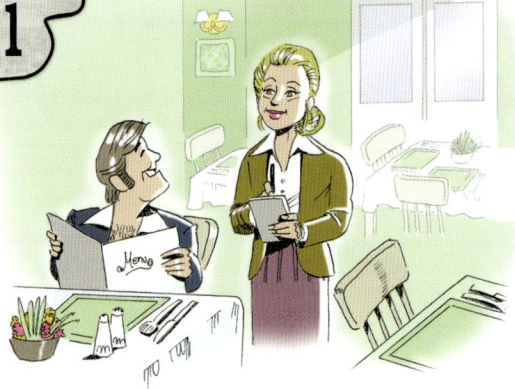

11 Danny orders food from Polly and sees her sketches (establishing an acquaintanceship that facilitates their collaboration in Melbury's arrest).

13 Basil takes Melbury's 'valuables' for safe-keeping and leads him to the dining room (establishing the valuables for Basil's later disappointment, and getting fun from Basil's obsequious behaviour and contemptuous treatment of regular guests).

16 Sybil criticises Basil and orders him about. Basil asks Polly to get £200 from the bank. (Fun from Basil's relentless humiliation and then setting up the ending. Pure plot!)

12 Basil is on the phone when Melbury arrives. Basil treats him with disdain until he realises Melbury is a Lord. Then he fawns, appallingly. (Having established Basil's social snobbery, we can get fun out of it, from the instantaneous switch from casual rudeness to over-the-top self-abasement.)

14 Melbury misses his chair (fun from Melbury sitting on the floor due to Basil's anxiety and him immediately blaming Manuel).

15 Melbury asks Basil to cash a cheque for £200 (fun from Basil being honoured in this way).

17 In town, Polly goes back, sees Danny who explains that he has come to catch Melbury. (Plot, plot, plot. Hard to get any fun out of this, so kept as short as possible!)

18 Back at the hotel, Basil is hanging a picture (the quiet before the storm).

19

Wareing asks for a drink (setting up the punchline).

20

Melbury arrives, sees coins in the cabinet and offers to have them valued (setting up the later confrontation between Basil and Melbury).

23

Sybil arrives and listens (anticipated fun as we close in on Basil's demise).

24

Sybil goes to the safe and opens the case to reveal bricks (the good thing about the bricks is that they settle the matter instantly. Fun as Basil's penny finally drops very, very slowly. Fun as he checks the bricks).

27

The posh guests leave in disgust (Basil denounces them, calling them snobs and reversing his normal view of the upper classes).

21

*Polly runs outside and signals
to Danny (plot, plot, plot).*

22

*Polly runs to tell Basil that Melbury is a trickster,
Basil ridicules her (fun that Basil's class
snobbery totally blocks his mental processes).*

25

*Two more guests arrive –
posh ones (setting up ending).*

26

*Melbury
arrives back
at reception.
Basil now
treats him with
mock-humorous
contempt …
Chase as
Melbury runs
but is caught
(denouement).*

28

*Basil returns to
the lobby and
starts hanging
the picture.
Wareing is
still waiting
for his drink.
(Punchline,
reminding us
that this is
Basil's life!)*

**THE
END**

39

As you see, dear reader, a sitcom pilot has three requirements:

1. Establishing things about character and situation that will not change in later episodes.

2. Making plot points to tell the story of this particular episode.

3. The funny bits.

Obviously, you want as many of the three as possible. But this does not mean that a simple plot leaves more room for fun, just because it's a very simple plot. 'A Touch of Class' had limited comic possibilities simply because of its simplicity. As Connie and I developed plots with two or even three storylines, the episodes became funnier by the end of the second series.

Below (and pages 32–3): Connie and I photographed for a lifestyle magazine feature on our writing process, pictured in our Kensington home, the height of 1970s style and class!

The trouble is that establishing plot points isn't funny. Also, an audience can usually spot plot. And once they have spotted it, they can begin to guess how the story is going to turn out, which robs it of the essential requirement: surprise!

So Connie and I realised that the way to counteract that was to find a way to make the plot lines funny, so they didn't stand out so obviously from the deliberately funny stuff.

So we always tried to hide plot points, by making them part of a humorous sequence, or at least by establishing them in an emotional exchange where the characters are angry with each other or upset about something. Then they don't stand out and give the story away.

And sometimes we could make the plot ingenious enough to be intrinsically funny. That's what I love about some of the classic French farces, especially the ones written by Georges Feydeau at the end of the 19th century. They are so fiendishly clever that the audience laughs with delight. I shall never forget when I saw *A Flea in Her Ear* at the National Theatre, in 1966, with Albert Finney, Geraldine McEwan and Edward Hardwicke, directed by Jacques Charon of the Comedie Française. It was the best night of my play-going existence, when I realised that great farcical comedy could be accompanied by fiendishly clever plotting – an orgasmic combination of belly laughter and intellectual delight.

There's only one problem with this kind of farce: it's the hardest kind of acting, so it is fairly rare to see it done really well. It is often done badly, causing naïve watchers to equate fantastically

Farces: an education...

Farce originated in medieval France, from humorous interludes that brought levity to serious mystery and morality plays. The word farce comes from the French '*farcir*', which means to stuff or to fill. The main components of farce are a flawed protagonist (who is usually acting on a false presumption, but who opts to cover up his mistake rather than come clean – much like Basil), physical comedy and slapstick, mistaken identity, miscommunication and confusion.

The characters are often trapped in a single physical location: in *A Flea in Her Ear* much of the action takes place in a hotel called Le Coq d'Or (The Golden Cock). In that particular play, the plot starts off with a woman, Raymonde, deciding to test her husband Chandebise's fidelity by sending him a letter – ostensibly written by an admirer, but actually by her friend Lucienne - inviting him to an assignation. Then assorted characters assemble at the hotel for all sorts of different, related and unrelated reasons – romance, celebration, jealousy. There's a gun, a character who can't speak clearly so is constantly misunderstood (just like Manuel!) and the comedy is relentlessly fast-paced, with incidents piling up on each other to increase the muddle – and the humour – exponentially.

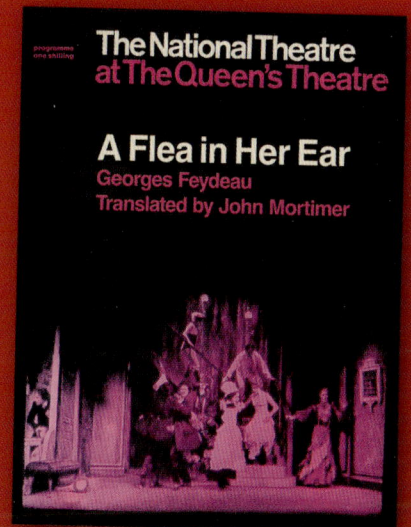

programme
one shilling

The National Theatre
at The Queen's Theatre

A Flea in Her Ear
Georges Feydeau
Translated by John Mortimer

bad farce with gross overacting, clumsy physical comedy, playing entirely for laughs, telegraphing jokes, and a complete lack of believability.

Noel Coward famously disparaged acting as 'knowing the lines and not bumping into the furniture'. Great straight acting requires making interesting choices and convincing the audience of the authenticity of the character's emotions. Great comedy, however, involves all of the above, PLUS COMEDY TECHNIQUE.

Above: The programme from the National Theatre's 1966 production of *A Flea in Her Ear* – the best night of my play-going existence!

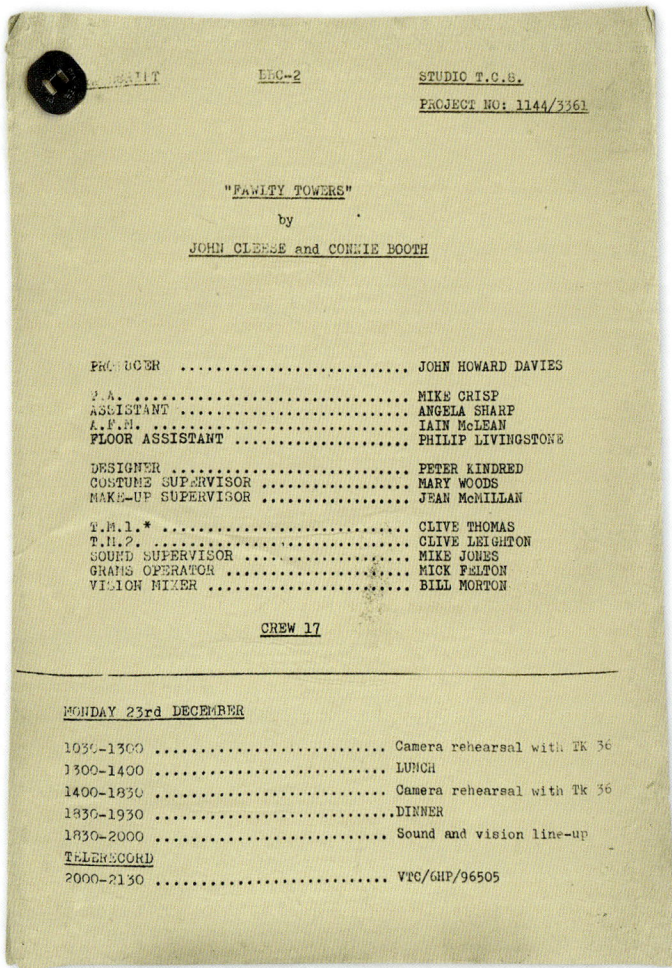

"FAWLTY TOWERS"

by

JOHN CLEESE and CONNIE BOOTH

PRODUCER	JOHN HOWARD DAVIES
P.A.	MIKE CRISP
ASSISTANT	ANGELA SHARP
A.F.M.	IAIN McLEAN
FLOOR ASSISTANT	PHILIP LIVINGSTONE
DESIGNER	PETER KINDRED
COSTUME SUPERVISOR	MARY WOODS
MAKE-UP SUPERVISOR	JEAN McMILLAN
T.M.1.*	CLIVE THOMAS
T.M.2.	CLIVE LEIGHTON
SOUND SUPERVISOR	MIKE JONES
GRAMS OPERATOR	MICK FELTON
VISION MIXER	BILL MORTON

CREW 17

MONDAY 23rd DECEMBER

1030-1300	Camera rehearsal with TK 36
1300-1400	LUNCH
1400-1830	Camera rehearsal with TK 36
1830-1930	DINNER
1830-2000	Sound and vision line-up
TELERECORD	
2000-2130	VTC/6HP/96505

Above and opposite page: Cover and interior pages from the very first *Fawlty* script – look at those timings for that brutal day of recording – and it was all on the day before Christmas Eve 1974!

Opposite page, top: Another shot of Connie and I in our Kensington home.

All actors who can do drama and comedy equally well will tell you comedy is the harder. I once had a long conversation with actor Michael Gambon, who convinced me of this idea.

This is why a number of very fine dramatic actors fail when they try to make people laugh.

Nevertheless, the unsophisticated believe that serious drama – which is normally the expression of negative emotion – is more important than being amused by the pettiness of the human condition.

If this does not convince you, think of how many more great dramas there are, compared with great comedies. It must be because they are easier to create.

End of lecture.

Where was I? Oh, yes.

There is a relatively mundane reason why *Fawlty Towers* was better than most other sitcoms.

Well, people are always surprised that there were only twelve episodes. Why?

Because so much action happens in them. Why?

Because Connie and I took much longer to write them.

Most writers will knock out a sitcom episode in ten days. At that pace, you only have to write three minutes of material each day. That's not much. But you are unlikely to come up with more than a couple of really good ideas.

When we were writing *Fawlty Towers*, the average BBC sitcom script had 65 pages. The *Fawlty Towers* scripts were about 140 pages – about twice as many.

That was because there were many more humorous moments in the *Fawlty Towers* scripts. This is why viewers can watch the episodes many, many times.

Connie and I deliberately set aside six weeks to write each episode. We were not more creative than other writers. We simply gave ourselves much, much more time.

We used to spend over two weeks just working out the plot, before we wrote any dialogue. But the dialogue then flowed easily because, with the plot in place, we knew what each character was trying to achieve, and whom they were going to have to talk to next.

CAST LIST

JOHN CLEESE	–	Basil Fawlty
PRUNELLA SCALES	–	Sybil Fawlty
ANDREW SACHS	–	Manuel
CONNIE BOOTH	–	Polly
MICHAEL GWYNN	–	Lord Melbury
BALLARD BERKELEY	–	Major Gowen
ROBIN ELLIS	–	Danny Brown
MARTIN WILDECK	–	Sir Richard Morris
LIONEL WHEELER	–	Mr. Watson
TERENCE CONOLEY	–	Mr. Wareing
DAVID SIMEON	–	Mr. Mackenzie

WALK-ONS

GARRY RICH	–	Newspaper Boy
JULIE MELION	–	Mrs. Watson
ANNETTE PETERS	–	Mrs. Wareing
OSCAR PECK	–	Master Wareing
PAT SYMONS	–	Lady Morris
GILLY FLOWER	–	Miss Tibbs
RENEE ROBERTS	–	Miss Gatsby
CLAIRE RUSSELL	–	Mrs. Mackenzie
DENNIS PLENTY	–	P.C.
IAN ELLIOT	–	P.C.
DAVID WATERMAN	–	C.I.D. Officer
PAT MILNER	–	C.I.D. Officer

CAMS	(on TK)	ACTION	SOUND
		SCENE 1.	
2.	MIX TO 2	RECEPTION.	
	MLS COUNTER	INT. LOBBY OF HOTEL.	
	CRAB R TO		
	MLS BASIL		
		THE LOBBY OF FAWLTY TOWERS HOTEL.	
		AT THE RECEPTION DESK BASIL	
		FAWLTY IS AT THE TELEPHONE	

BASIL:
... One double room without bath

for the 16th, 17th and 18th...

yes and if you'd be so good

as to confirm by letter...

thank you so much, goodbye.

SYBIL ENTERS
HOLD 2S

(HE PUTS THE RECEIVER DOWN AND
NOTES SOMETHING IN THE RESERVATIONS
BOOK WHILE TAKING A SIP FROM
A CUP OF TEA ON THE TOP OF THE
COUNTER. SYBIL HAS ENTERED
FROM THE OFFICE BEHIND RECEPTION
AND PUTS SOME PAPERS DOWN;
SHE THEN MOVES BASIL'S SAUCER
DWON FROM THE TOP OF THE COUNTER ON
TO THE DESK.

(1 next)

SYBIL:
Have you made up the bill for

room Twelve Basil.

BASIL:
I haven't yet, no.

-1-

CREATING CHARACTERS

When Connie and I sat down to write the pilot for what would become *Fawlty Towers*, we knew we had a main character, and a domineering wife. I was keen to have a hotel employee who spoke very little English. This was because the number of non-English waiters in London restaurants had sharply increased in the late 60s, as restaurant owners suddenly discovered they didn't cost much. So, it was a fact that in the 1970s, you were pleased when, after ordering your meal, what eventually arrived at your table contained more than 50 per cent of what you'd actually ordered.

Also, I have always found people not understanding each other funny, particularly if the misunderstanding gets convoluted.

Basil: Manuel! There – is – too – much – butter – on – those – trays.

Manuel: Que?

Basil: There is too much butter on those trays. *(he points to each tray in turn)*

Manuel: No, no, no, Señor!

Basil: What?

Manuel: Not 'on – those – trays'. No sir – 'uno dos tres.' Uno . . . dos . . . tres . . .

Basil: No, no. Hay mucho burro alli!

Manuel: Que?

Basil: Hay . . . mucho . . . burro . . . alli!

Manuel: Ah, mantequilla!

Basil: What? Que?

Manuel: Mantequilla. Burro is . . . is . . . *(brays like a donkey)*

Basil: What?

Manuel: Burro . . .
(does more donkey imitations)

Basil: Manuel, por favor . . .

Manuel: Si, si . . .

Sybil: *(coming back in)*
What's the matter,
Basil?

Basil: Nothing, dear,
I'm just dealing with it.

Manuel: *(to Sybil)*
He speak good . . .
how do you say . . . ?

Sybil: English!

Basil: Mantequilla . . .
solamente . . . dos . . .

Manuel: Dos?

Sybil: *(to Basil)*
Don't look at me.
You're the one
who's supposed
to be able to
speak it.

*Basil angrily
grabs the
excess butter
from the trays.*

Basil: Two pieces! Two
each! Arriba, arriba!!

So, at the beginning of the
pilot episode, in the first couple
of minutes we establish Manuel's
confused relationship with Basil.

At the same time, we establish that
none of the confusion is Manuel's
fault, as Basil has clearly lied to Sybil
about his ability to speak Spanish. This
is enormously important emotionally
and is crucial to the development
of Manuel's character.

Andrew Sachs / Manuel

'I know noooothing!' Manuel, the Spanish ambassador
to Torquay! *Fawlty Towers'* hapless waiter with a limited
understanding of the English language, but a heart of
gold . . . and from the other side of the camera, one of the
finest comedy creations ever, thanks in no small part to the
superb performance of the incredible Andrew Sachs.

Andy was born in Berlin in 1930 as the son of Jewish and
Austrian parents. To escape the Nazis, the family moved to
Britain in 1938 and settled in Kilburn.

An early role as a schoolboy in the very first Ealing comedy,
Hue and Cry, left a lasting impression on Andy, and
whilst he had every intention of pursuing a career
in shipping management, the pull of blossoming
radio dramas and repertory theatre came
calling, and he never looked back. With an
amazing spatial awareness and a gift for
voices, both theatre and television couldn't
get enough of him.

Andy's faultless performance as Manuel
would open many doors – least of all, three
pop singles he released in character!
Straight after the first series aired, he
would charm cinema audiences in
1978's *Revenge of the Pink Panther*,
and in the same year he would play
a waiter in *What's Up Nurse!*

Andy's wife, Melody Lang, would
appear in the second-series
Fawlty episode 'Basil the Rat' as
Mrs Taylor (a brilliantly confused
dining room guest).

Parallel with his acting, Andy
turned his talents to writing,
penning several well-thought-of
BBC radio plays, including *The
Revenge*, a ground-breaking
half-hour play totally without
dialogue!

In later years, Andy
notched up lovely roles
in soaps *Coronation Street*
and *EastEnders* and
had a beautiful part in
actor Dustin Hoffman's
directorial debut,
Quartet, in 2012.

So we must be assured that Manuel suffers no real emotional pain. As Chaplin knew, a kick in the pants is nothing to get very upset about. Unless you are an extreme woke believer, in which case your lack of a sense of humour will have killed your sense of proportion.

Connie and I shared an almost identical sense of humour. For example, when we met in 1964, we found we both revered the actor Jonathan Winters. I'd only just discovered him a few months before, when I saw him in a wonderful knockabout comedy film called *It's a Mad, Mad, Mad, Mad World*. Finding we both adored him was similar to the stories of couples who discovered on their first date they both liked *Monty Python*.

The other man we both found outstandingly funny was Basil Fawlty.

I think that building a fictional character is the same process in writing as it is in acting. If I have to play a new character, I will rummage around, trying this voice, or that gesture, until suddenly, without explanation, I do something that quite surprisingly feels right. Then you build on that to find something else that feels right. Then you build on that, experimenting until you find something else that feels right too. This goes on, and these individual moments multiply, until something like a personality coalesces. At this point you begin to feel more and more sure whether new inventions feel right or not.

But with Basil, we had something very real to start with: Mr Donald Sinclair from the Gleneagles Hotel.

Manuel must never do anything aggressive, no matter what happens to him, as he accepts mistreatment as part of his career path as a waiter, and he hopes to learn from it. He never ceases to be helpful and optimistic, and if Basil chastises him, obviously he deserves it, even if he doesn't quite understand why.

If Manuel ever became resentful it would change everything. We would become concerned for him, and we'd stop laughing. So, his optimism never leaves him, or the whole emotional tone of the show would change. The philosopher Henri Bergson said that any laughter requires 'a momentary anesthesia of the heart', and comedians have to make sure that moment is very short. We can laugh at Jerry the mouse running Tom the cat over with a steamroller, because it's an animation, but if Tom emitted a cry of pain, suddenly we would be reminded of the reality of being crushed by a steamroller and our amusement would freeze.

Connie Booth / Polly

The beating heart of Fawlty Towers, who holds it all together, Polly Sherman lit up 1970s Torquay with her sketchbook in hand. And much like her creation, the talented actress and writer Connie Booth also made *Fawlty Towers* the series possible.

Born in Indianapolis to an actress mother and stockbroker father, Connie and her family moved to New York State in the 1950s, where the thriving acting community and host of visiting productions from the Big Apple drew her in.

After studying drama in the city, Connie soon found work, from fringe productions to work as a Broadway understudy across a wide range of plays and shows. She soon built upon her natural skills as an actor and developed a faultless knack for comic timing.

A chance meeting with a touring comedy troupe from England changed the course of Connie's life when she met John Cleese and they married in February 1968.

Relocating to England, Connie appeared with John in dozens of episodes of *Monty Python's Flying Circus* and the first two *Python* films (playing a vast array of parts and characters) before developing and co-writing both series of *Fawlty Towers* together.

Away from *Fawlty*, Connie became a highly sought-after TV guest performer with her natural elegance a perfect fit for period dramas (such as *Dickens of London*, *Little Lord Fauntleroy* and *The Buccaneers*), but she was also equally magnificent in contemporary work, stealing scenes in a memorable *Bergerac* story and the acclaimed 1982 BBC drama *The Story of Ruth*.

Stage work also remained an incredibly important part of Connie's life, and among a host of roles, her starring performance in the West End production of *Little Lies* was universally praised.

In the mid-90s, Connie changed career completely, and after five years studying at the University of London, she successfully moved away from acting work and into a rewarding time working in psychotherapy.

Connie and I were still carrying pictures of him in our minds from four years previously – it was hard to forget a hotelier who really felt that he could run a hotel properly if only it wasn't for the guests. Nothing you asked him to do was too little trouble.

We retained from our Torquay experience the idea that Basil's wife, whom we named Sybil, definitely wore the trousers. In a way, Basil was the classic hen-pecked husband, but we knew that my size would help to disguise that cliché.

And there is something inherently funny about a person being frightened by someone much smaller than themselves. I noticed later that young children would understand *Fawlty Towers* several years before they could get *Monty Python*, and I decided it was because the series was

basically about who was frightened of whom. Children are good at that.

The one big addition we made to our version of Sinclair was to make him obsessed with his place in the British class system, in the same way that Americans revere anyone with a lot of money regardless of how it was acquired. (A truth that led to one of my favourite sayings: 'If you want to know what God thinks of money, look at who he gives it to.')

Basil regards the British upper class as effortlessly superior human beings. Even knowing that real toffs are all a bit slow on the uptake and find their highest form of accomplishment in the large-scale slaughter of God's creations (pheasants, grouse, salmon, hares, stags, you name it) he still thinks of them as visitors from a higher

Prunella Scales
Sybil Fawlty

'I know . . . I know . . . I know . . . Oh, I know!' – an icon of television comedy, a little piranha fish with a laugh that sounds like someone machine-gunning a seal, it can only be Sybil Fawlty! And she could have only been played by the faultless Prunella Scales.

Pru was born a Surrey girl, but the outbreak of war saw her family relocate to Devon. As a daughter of an actress (Pru's mother Catherine was a RADA and rep theatre vet), acting was firmly in the family blood. So her natural affinity for performance led her to winning a two-year scholarship to the Old Vic in 1949.

Starting out in stage management, Pru soon won parts and impressive notes for her range and comedic rhythm. Film casting agents would quickly fall for Pru, with parts in *Room at the Top* and *Waltz of the Toreadors* bringing her to the attention of the BBC, and her casting in the massively successful 1960s sitcom *Marriage Lines*.

Pru never let small-screen fame affect her, and she continued to be a joyful jobbing actor, delighting audiences across stage, radio and television. She would even bring an

unforgettable magic to a series of Tesco ads in the 90s.

Pru's mantelpiece narrowly escaped several well-deserved gongs. She was nominated at the Laurence Olivier Awards in 1980 for the fantastic *Make and Break* (which co-starred Leonard Rossiter) and in 1990 for Alan Bennett's *Single Spies*. In another Alan Bennett television play, *A Question of Attribution*, she was nominated for a BAFTA for her sublime performance as Queen Elizabeth II.

In 1982, Pru was cast in Radio 4's *After Henry*, Simon Brett's touching series about a 42-year-old widow. A TV version with much of the same cast was later developed by ITV and was a massive hit.

In later years, Pru, together with her husband, fellow actor Timothy West, delighted millions with their beautiful, life-affirming series, *Great Canal Journeys*.

dimension, who deserve boot-licking of the highest quality.

At the other end of the food chain are the riff-raff, some of whom have never sat in chairs before. Basil spends minimal time with them, unless they threaten his authority, in which case he will use his well-practised sarcasm on them to push them back down to where they belong.

Next, Connie and I had to find the right role for her, and we came up with Polly. I knew what a wonderful comic actress Connie was. The first time I saw her on stage, in 1965, she was performing in a farce called *Never Too Late* in 'summer stock' theatre, playing opposite the legendary Bert Lahr, who was world renowned as the Cowardly Lion in *The Wizard of Oz*. He was primarily a farce actor, but Connie stood

toe to toe and gave as good as she got! I remember I felt very proud.

It was important that Polly bring some clarity and sanity to the chaos around her. We decided she needed to be a student working part-time at Fawlty Towers, because if she was a full-time employee, it would've been harder for her to keep her emotional distance.

Below: The glamorous Sybil applies another layer of nail varnish to her claws!

An early critic said that Polly was 'Laertes to Basil's Hamlet'. I eventually found out what he meant, which was that it was very useful for us as writers to have one character to whom Basil could confide his plans and motivations, so that the audience would understand what was going on.

Polly had to be middle class, and that, along with her status as a part-time employee, meant she therefore could be trusted, in Basil's eyes, to keep secrets from Sybil ('Dragonfly', for example).

Polly's point of view meant she could also sympathise with Basil's desire to avoid Sybil's wrath and occasionally help Basil to try and avoid it. She could also be Manuel's mentor and guardian.

I don't remember why we came up with a Major, but by the end of the second series, we were laughing more at him than any of the other characters or, I should say, 'laughing more *with* him'.

You see, laughter is always critical. We simply don't laugh at people who are kind, generous, wise and who behave appropriately. As an American agent once said, 'Show me a sitcom about St Francis of Assisi, and I'll show you a bummer'.

When the Pythons first discussed how we were going to create a comedy set at the time of Christ, we instinctively knew that nothing was funny about Jesus! What we laugh at is greed, lust, stupidity, aggressiveness, pomposity, vulgarity, self-importance, dishonesty and any behaviour that falls below normal standards of moral behaviour.

Extreme opinion claims that because laughter is critical, it must be unkind.

No. Jokes are unkind if they are intended to hurt people's feelings and make them feel bad about themselves. Such jokes are wrong, and we should not make them.

Affectionate jokes remind us that we can do better! Henri Bergson says that we laugh at people who behave like machines. But if people's behaviour is appropriate, they are not funny.

We can learn a lot from laughter, provided only that it is automatic.

And so, we love the Major, even as we laugh at him.

We can even have affection for curmudgeons like the characters Alf Garnett and Archie Bunker, and comedian W. C. Fields. (A man who hates dogs and children can't be all bad.)

And Basil. It escaped my notice for years that his initials B. F. meant, for my father's generation, 'Bloody Fool', which was the rudest description that an English gentleman was allowed. These days he would be called an 'asshole'.

But although Basil is an awful human being, we quite like him! Why? Because he makes us laugh. I know from experience, if you make people laugh, they feel affection for you.

So, that gave us the hard-core of the cast.

Ballard Berkeley
Major Gowen

'Papers arrived yet, Fawlty?' The unforgettable bumbling magnificence of the Major is a reassuring presence across all episodes of *Fawlty Towers*. For actor Ballard Berkeley, after decades of performances on stage and screen, his small-screen immortality as the Major capped off a long career.

Ballard Blascheck was born in Royal Tunbridge Wells in 1904. A young devotee to both cricket and treading the boards, Ballard made his professional stage debut in 1928 (using the more English 'Berkeley' as his stage surname).

Repertory theatre and West End parts between the wars soon became his bread and butter with an enviable roster of film parts (for which his commanding frame and good looks won him many!). These ranged from 1930s musical extravaganza, *London Melody*, to the 1939 comedy-mystery, *The Gang's All Here*. Ballard was a true matinee idol of the time, who inhabited dozens of memorable character roles in both supporting and main features.

During the Second World War, Ballard served as a Metropolitan Police special constable on the London streets during the very worst days of the Blitz, receiving Defence and Long Service medals for his duty.

As the Blitz subsided in late 1941, the British Film Industry recommenced production and Ballard enjoyed a role in Noël Coward's patriotic war film *In Which We Serve*, where he played an Engineer Commander. After the war, the silver screen continued to be a firm source of employment for Ballard – a notable part in Alfred Hitchcock's thriller *Stage Fright* in 1950, where Ballard played a sergeant, set the tone for the next two decades where he played a range of well-appointed butlers and officers.

Fawlty came into Ballard's life at the age of 70, and his incredible portrayal of the Major opened the floodgates for many other comedic senior citizens, from *To the Manor Born* and *Terry and June* to *Are You Being Served?* A cheeky spot of casting in Dick Clement and Ian La Frenais's 1983 comedy film *Bullshot* even saw Ballard cast as a Hotel Guest!

His most notable role post-*Fawlty* was as Guy Penrose, father of Julia McKenzie's protagonist in the ITV comedy *Fresh Fields*, appearing in ten episodes.

5.

ENTER: JHD

Before Connie and I had got very much further, we got the most important phone call of the entire series.

It was from Jimmy Gilbert, and he was telling us that the *Fawlty Towers* director was going to be John Howard Davies.

I could not have been more delighted . . .

I knew Johnny very well, as he had directed the first six *Monty Python*

Below: John Howard Davies (JHD) photographed whilst on duty as a BBC production assistant in February 1966.

Opposite page: JHD (with a sea of scripts on his desk!) in his Television Centre office in August 1974.

episodes five years earlier! I had a great liking and respect for him – more so than most of the other Pythons. He had made the mistake of trying to get Graham Chapman to behave more professionally (like turning up on time) and so Gra resented him deeply. He also attempted to take charge of the production, which was a source of annoyance to Terry Jones. Michael, of course, got on with him well.

There were a lot of reasons I respected Johnny. First, he never tried to bullshit me. I always experience people bullshitting me as vaguely insulting. It means, 'I am not going to tell you the truth for reasons I prefer to keep hidden. So instead, I shall tell you something irrelevant and misleading which will deceive you, because you are stupider than me.' (Ian McNaughton, who succeeded Johnny as director of *Monty Python*, would always bullshit me. If he told me that the rushes were particularly good, you could bet the farm there was something wrong with them.)

Second, Johnny was a very good judge of acting. He could make expert suggestions, but in a very gentle and friendly way, so that he never seemed a 'clever dick'. This also meant he was terribly good at casting. He introduced us to Carol Cleveland, who appeared in thirty Monty Python episodes and all the films. But now he was on *Fawlty Towers*, his extraordinarily good taste led us to Prunella Scales and Ballard Berkeley – priceless choices for the entire series. But more of this later.

There was an astonishing reason for this ability of his.

John Howard Davies had been a huge child star. At the age of seven (!) he'd been chosen by England's finest film director, David Lean, to play the part of Oliver, the boy who asked for 'more' in *Oliver Twist* (1948). Straight after that he played the central role in *The Rocking Horse Winner*

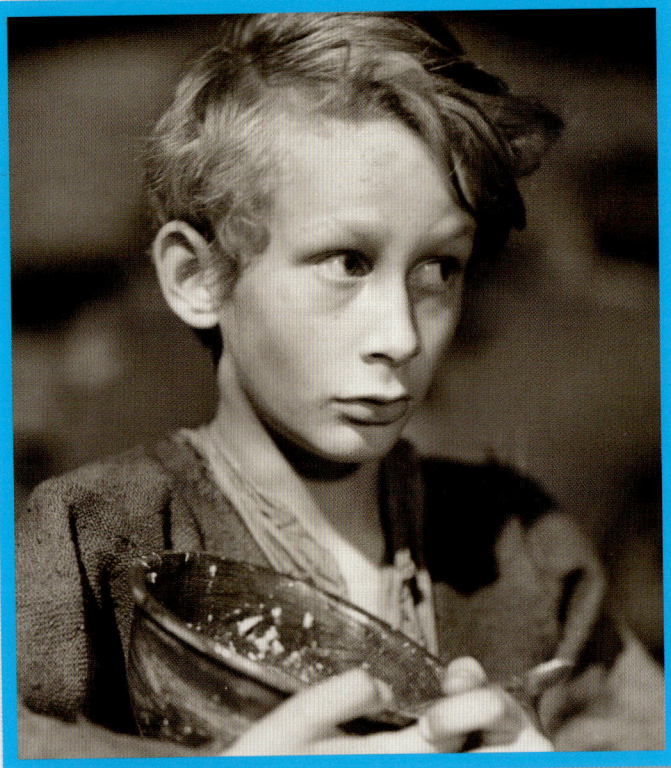

Below: A very young JHD as Oliver in Rank's 1948 film *Oliver Twist*.

(1949), which I went to see at the Odeon Weston-super-Mare when I was nine. It's a very creepy film about a boy who can forecast racehorse winners if he rides his rocking horse with sufficient frenzy. And then he played Tom Brown in *Tom Brown's Schooldays* (1951). By the age of twelve, he was a big star in the UK.

So, he went to school at Haileybury and then joined the Navy!

He used to say that he wasn't a good enough actor to become a proper one, and wasn't good-looking enough to become a star.

Yes, he was a modest chap.

After the Navy, inevitably he became a carpet salesman, and then a clerk, and then – equally inevitably – emigrated to Australia, where he got married and drifted towards the theatre, as a stage manager, and finally . . . back to acting again.

Maybe show business was more in his blood than he realised. His father Jack Davies was a successful comedy writer at Elstree Studios, and his mother Dorothy Davies was a novelist.

I had always noticed that Johnny was very sensitive to people's emotions, and I once talked to him about that. He told me that he attributed it to his parents' rather tumultuous marriage, and his consequent need for an early-warning system. His parents were married a long time, and his mother once told him, 'It's never been easy, but every day I could count on three good laughs.'

No wonder JHD (as he was known) was so good at comedy.

The other thing I liked about him was that he was not Scottish.

John Howard Davies / Director and Producer

The actor, director and producer extraordinaire, JHD was a vital cog in the *Fawlty Towers* machine.

It seems highly fitting for a child star so closely associated with a line about 'wanting more', that JHD found himself a fantastic second and third helping of career behind the camera working at the BBC and ITV.

JHD's non-*Fawlty* BBC Comedy highlights include directing all thirty episodes of *The Good Life*, the seventh series of *Steptoe and Son* and the first twenty episodes of *The Goodies*.

In 1985, JHD took up a position at Thames Television (where Jimmy Gilbert had also moved to) and he heralded in several new comedy series for ITV. Each of these new comedies would feature the stars JHD cast in *The Good Life*! Penelope Keith and Richard Briers (*All in Good Faith* for Briers and *Executive Stress, No Job for a Lady* and *Law and Disorder* for Keith!). JHD also teamed up again with *Fawlty Towers* alumni Prunella Scales and Joan Sanderson for the comedy *After Henry*.

Come the 1990s, JHD continued to add to his sitcom CV by overseeing *Mr Bean* and *The Vicar of Dibley*.

Away from his television work, JHD also happened to be a champion target shooter, appearing in the final of the 1994 Queen's Prize and representing Wales in the Commonwealth Shooting Championships on several occasions.

I had been pounced on and monopolised by Scottish directors from the moment in 1963 that I started in English (Sorry! *British*) show business. First Charles Maxwell at BBC Light Entertainment Radio. Then Jimmy Gilbert, then Ian Fordyce on *At Last the 1948 Show*, Joe McGrath, Ian McNaughton . . . all of them refugees from north of the Border, who'd come south, married our women and stolen the jobs of less talented English directors. All of them profoundly proud of their Scottish heritage (while refusing to actually live there). I finally made a film with Charlie Crichton, who looked and sounded 100 per cent English. Then, one evening, under the influence of Scotch, he admitted his Caledonian bloodline. There was no way one could have known, for he seemed about as Scottish as a cucumber sandwich . . .

I digress.

My great delight was that John Howard Davies, at least, was not Scottish . . . He was Welsh.

So, when Connie and I finally sat down with him and started to prepare for the first episode of *Fawlty Towers* (or 'John Cleese Pilot' as it was imaginatively titled on BBC paperwork), his instincts were almost always spot-on.

Starting with the casting. Connie and I had been enchanted by Alan Ayckbourn's *Norman Conquests*. This trilogy of plays, which played on different nights during the London run in 1974, were so extraordinarily brilliant that I still feel in awe of them. Not just for the genius of the writing, but for the pitch-perfect performances from the cast, five of whom I'd never seen before.

And the scene that was for me the most brilliant of all was where Michael Gambon, as a totally literal-minded veterinary surgeon, was trying to have a conversation with another actress I didn't know, Bridget Turner.

So, we suggested to Johnny that we should approach Bridget and ask her if she would like to play Sybil. And we did, and she, very politely, passed.

Connie and I were both rather shaken. Fortunately, JHD withheld the information that she hadn't found it funny, because our confidence was still rather brittle.

So JHD suggested Prunella Scales, whose work I knew quite well (especially for the 1961 sitcom *Marriage Lines* with Richard Briers) and, thank goodness, she accepted!

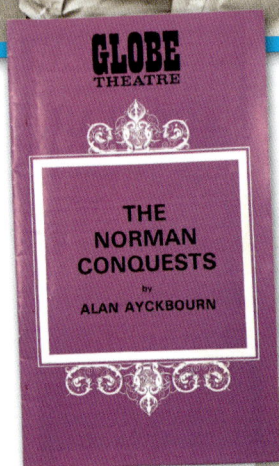

Take a look at these names . . . Michael Gambon, Penelope Keith, Felicity Kendal, Mark Kingston, Bridget Turner, and a talented newcomer, Tom Courtenay. They were breathtakingly funny. Imagine discovering Gambon, Keith and Kendal in the same evening.

Above: Tom Courtenay, Felicity Kendal, Bridget Turner and Penelope Keith, the stars of *The Norman Conquests* trilogy by Alan Ayckbourn, pictured at the Globe Theatre in August 1974. Bridget Turner was the woman who almost played Sybil!

Right: . . . and the magnificent Prunella Scales, the woman who *made* Sybil! Pictured here with Richard Briers in their *Marriage Lines* guises of George and Kate Starling.

I had already decided that I wanted Andrew Sachs to play Manuel. I'd seen a brilliant farce performance of his in Alan Bennett's *Habeas Corpus*. He played a piano tuner, who, before he started work, did some finger loosening exercises watched by the formidable Margaret Courtney. She was expecting someone to arrive to fit a special brassiere for her, so Andrew's warm-up got her rather excited.

That was in 1973. In 1974 I asked him to play the part of a musician in a short film I made with Connie that summer called *Romance with a Double Bass*; a sweet little comedy based on a short story by Chekhov.

What I prized about Andy (as we called him) was that he was so good at physical comedy, which is the hardest kind of comedy to get right, especially if you only have five days' rehearsal. Andy was keen to play the part but worried about having to do a Spanish accent. He asked if he could do a German accent (he was born in Berlin of German-Jewish parents) but I told him that Manuel's behaviour was never going to be very Teutonic. So, we agreed we'd have a Spanish accent coach there at all times. And of course he mastered it. ('Que?' is always going to be funnier than 'Was?')

JHD then came up with Ballard Berkeley. Ballard was in his 70s and had made the transition from being a 1930s matinee idol to a successful character actor, and then, when his age meant there were fewer roles around, he was to enjoy a resurgence of fame as the Major. He was the perfect English gentleman in every way, and, consequently, mad about cricket. As was I.

One day I was rehearsing a scene with Prunella when I spotted Ballard behind her, dancing up and down and signalling, with his fingers, the number six. This meant of course that the sixth Australian wicket had just fallen at Lord's. He was so overjoyed he couldn't wait till we'd finished the scene.

He was the Major incarnate. All he had to do was to add the addled bit.

JHD chose the old ladies. They came as a pair so they could chatter away and reproduce old-lady bird noises.

Above: Some shots from our short film, *Romance with a Double Bass*, where we first worked with the brilliant Andy Sachs.

Below: Three familiar faces from the series before they ever visited Fawlty Towers; Ballard Berkeley, Gilly Flower (modelling hats for Kembray) and Renee Roberts.

6.
MAKING THE PILOT

After we'd made the casting decisions, JHD went off and did all the things directors do. First, with the help of production designer Peter Kindred, he found the building that was to serve as the exterior of Fawlty Towers hotel. It was the headquarters of the Wooburn Grange Country Club, in Wooburn Green in Buckinghamshire, just a 40-minute drive from the BBC TV Centre.

Strangely, the exterior, perfect for the hotel, hid a surprisingly grotty interior. It consisted of red plastic tables and counters, oddly positioned slot machines, a ubiquitous smell of stale beer, and garish red menus advertising 'chicken-in-a-basket' and Babycham.

We never saw the clientele because we stopped filming before they arrived, but we all sensed they were a dodgy crowd. This was confirmed when we arrived to shoot for the second series and were told that someone had just been murdered with a shotgun there.

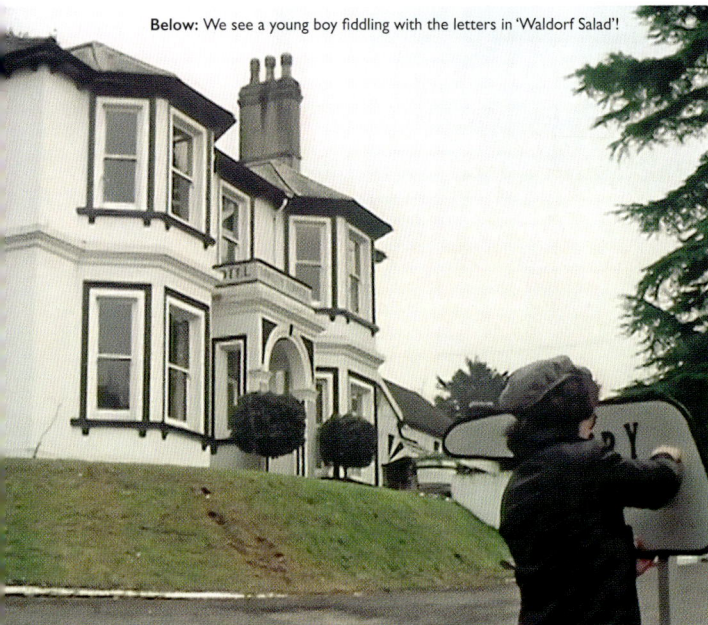

Below: We see a young boy fiddling with the letters in 'Waldorf Salad'!

And a few years after we filmed there, it was burned to the ground, never to be seen again. Except on television.

But we had a huge slice of luck there. JHD's production assistant, Ian McLean, showed us that the sign reading 'Fawlty Towers' was not pre-printed. It was a simple white surface to which we could attach individual letters. Ian suggested we could do anagrams and the whole team gathered round, coming up with some real beauties: Watery Fowls, Farty Towels and . . . Flowery Twats, which doesn't quite work. But who cares? Neither does Forty Weasels.

Lovely little bonus jokes, created almost by accident because the makers of the sign didn't finish the job. I love being lucky.

    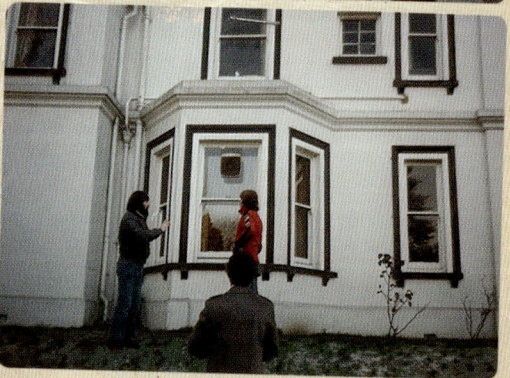

EXTERIOR. FRONT ENTRANCE. JAN. 79.

SIDE WINDOWS. (BEDROOMS ETC).

Wooburn Grange Country Club

The little country club located in Bourne End, Buckinghamshire, will be forever etched into the minds of viewers as Fawlty Towers, but it was only technically the hotel for a total of seven days!

On Monday, 16 December 1974, all of the exterior shots of the series' pilot story, 'A Touch of Class', were filmed, including the very first title card.

When the full series was commissioned the following year, the crew returned to the Grange for two days from Monday, 21 July (with the first day used to film scenes for 'The Builders' and 'The Germans' and the second to film scenes for 'Gourmet Night').

Four years later, the second series crew returned to Wooburn for two days' filming from Tuesday, 30 January 1979. Here the new anagram sign shots were filmed, and the evening of the first day was spent filming Basil and Manuel's night-time escapades with the ladder for 'The Psychiatrist'. The following day, filming was completed for 'Waldorf Salad', 'The Kipper and the Corpse' and 'The Anniversary'.

Wooburn became Fawlty Towers for the final time on Tuesday, 27 February 1979, for two days' filming. This was initially planned to shoot the exterior work for just 'Basil the Rat', but as actor Julian Holloway was no longer available for the studio recording of 'The Anniversary' (following a BBC strike putting back the studio scenes), the brief establishing scene for that story needed to be re-shot with new actor Ken Campbell.

Eagle-eyed viewers might have noticed that during these second series appearances, the curved metal sign 'WOOBURN GRANGE COUNTRY CLUB' is visible at the bottom of the hotel's drive . . .

The Grange's association with the series was capitalised on when it briefly became the nightclub 'Basil's' in the early 1980s. The listed building was subsequently left derelict and was destroyed by a fire in March 1991. A few years later, a housing estate was built on the site.

In quiet and secluded situation amid the lovely BUCKINGHAMSHIRE COUNTRYSIDE, BETWEEN
BEACONSFIELD AND MARLOW
about a mile from the River Thames.

This beautifully appointed freehold Country Residence

THE GRANGE, WOOBURN GREEN, BOURNE END

On 2 floors: oak panelled lounge and hall leading to oak staircase, double drawing room 28 ft. by 17ft opening into a delightful winter garden 36 ft. by 34 ft. with Bougainvillaea, etc., amusing genuine chinese room, spacious dining room in the Adams style oak floored throughout, convenient and modern kitchen, etc.

5 bedrooms (3 en suite with bath), 2 staff bedrooms and bath in separate wing. Double garage with gardeners cottage. Automatic oil-fired central heating throughout the whole comprising:

An exceptionally choice property which must be seen to be appreciated.

For Sale privately or by Auction OCTOBER 3 next.

Solicitors: Messrs. BOULTON, SONS & SANDEMAN, 7, Mackenzie Street, Slough, Bucks. Illustrated brochure from the Auctioneers: HAMPTON & SONS, 6, Arlington Street, St. James's, S.W.1.

The Wooburn Grange Country Club

exists for the pleasurable relaxation and entertainment of all those who seek club facilities, superb cuisine and, above all, the unmatchable atmosphere synonymous with excellence, interest, quality and comfort.

Wooburn Grange also provides Chemin de Fer and Roulette facilities under the direction of Monsieur Robert Megos Valentini of Monte Carlo.

Come and see for yourselves! Limited Membership still available by applying to:

The Membership Committee, Wooburn Grange Country Club, Bourne End, Bucks

Telephone: BOURNE END 1645

5

Top right: Advertisement for the 1956 sale of the club which appeared in *Country Life* and other newspapers.

Far left: By the early 1970s, the Wooburn Grange Country Club was well established and offering various types of membership.

Above: The sad sight of the Wooburn Grange Country Club after a fire destroyed much of the building in March 1991.

TV LOUNGE

PRIVATE

DINING ROOM

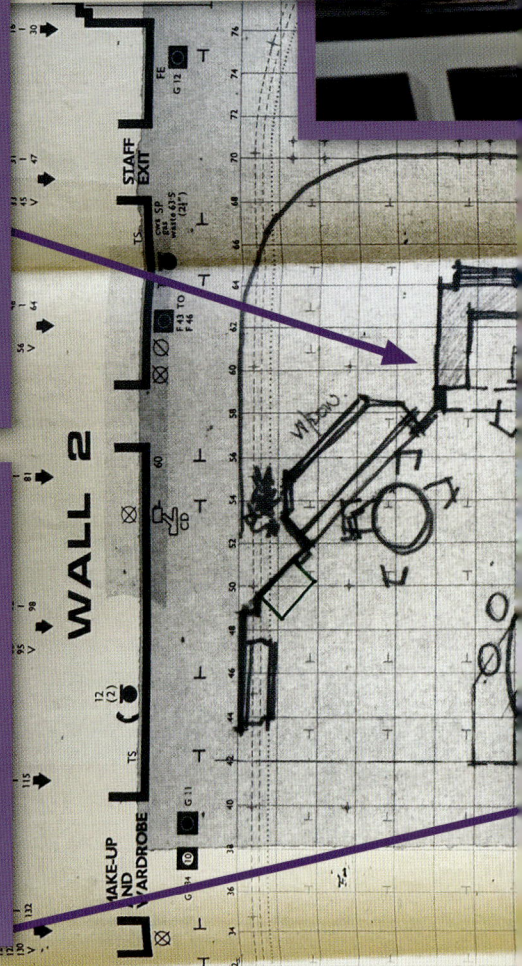

WALL 2

STAFF EXIT

FE

MAKE-UP AND WARDROBE

PRIVATE

The design for the studio set was worked out by Peter Kindred, who came up with a very clever and simple layout that relied on the fact that in television shows, upper floors don't have to be on the upper floor. When they were needed, upper floors were built behind our main set, usually on the other side of the bar.

In the West End stage production ingeniously planned by the director CJay Ranger, the set is remarkably similar, except that a bedroom was built above the ground floor set to accommodate Mrs Richards' scene (from 'Communication Problems').

Far left: Designer Peter Kindred's original sketch for the lobby and set photos from our first series.

Below: ... and Peter's original studio floor plans for our first episode ... The studio audience would be looking in from the bottom of the page.

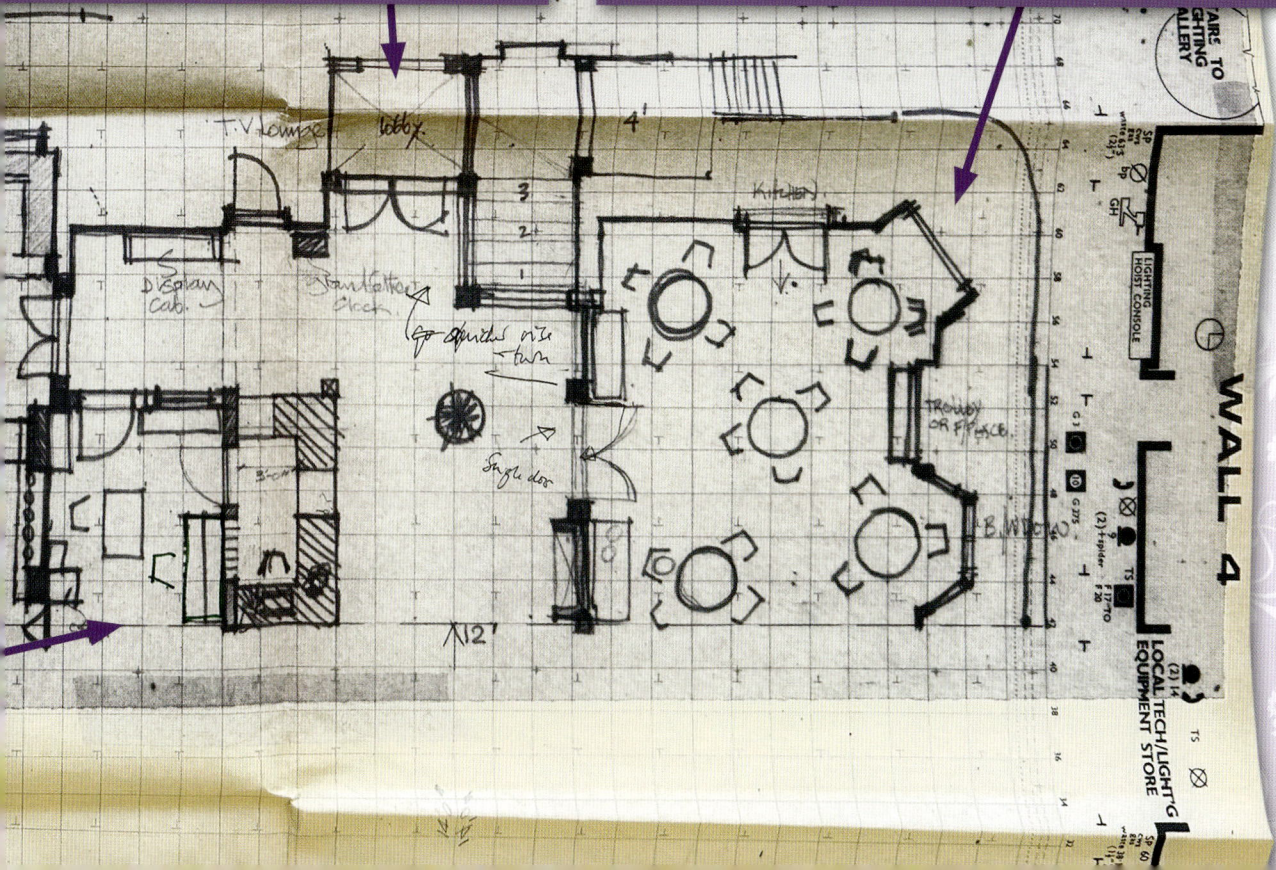

Peter Kindred / Production Design

After designing for the likes of *Z Cars* and introducing the Cybermen into *Doctor Who*, Peter Kindred was the BBC Production Designer tasked in 1974 with taking the sets described on the scripted page and making them a reality:

'Shortly after John Cleese had got the green light to write the pilot, we started looking for an exterior location that could believably match the scale of what we could do in the studio . . . as well as somewhere we could easily get to for filming! After a time, I found a rather nice little country club in Bourne End. It was a sweet little place, not very big but it was just perfect.

'I already had an idea how the hotel should work as far as the studio floor should go, but obviously we had to tie in roughly with the exterior and suggest the shape of the location. If you were coming up the steps and going into the hotel, it had to look as though it was the same place. Obviously, the real location influenced what happened in the studio, but funnily enough, I never actually went inside the club. I made up the shape of the sets from the exterior only.

'It was of course an audience show, so the seating took up an awful lot of the studio. We had a gap for the cameras and then we had the sets. They worked a little bit like a theatre show, all stretched out so the audience could see all the rooms. We'd often have the sets for the bedrooms behind the other sets. The hospital room in 'The Germans' was built just the other side of the *Fawlty Towers* bar set, for example!

'As a way of making it appear that characters were going upstairs, I decided we'd echo all those old guest houses which had weird interior arrangements of staircases which go up, get to a small landing and come down again. By having the cast members go up two or three stairs to a platform, and then going down three stairs, it suggested they had gone upstairs and around a corner again.

'I can remember on that first series we had a warm-up man, and he did a lot of chicken impersonations with his arms going up and down . . . Well, after about two episodes, John decided he couldn't stand him, so he decided to take over the warm-up duties, which was much better. He did all his brilliant *Monty Python* walks to get the audience going.

'I enjoyed doing *Fawlty Towers*, it was quite jolly. We obviously had no idea what it would become.'

Opposite page, top: The upper corridor set (built in the studio behind the bar set), which became the perfect place for numerous farcical moments throughout the series.

Opposite page, right: Our kitchen set.

Above: Two of the bedroom sets – these were both extensively redressed to work as many different rooms.

Below: A moment from our very first episode which captures the state of Sybil and Basil's marriage perfectly!

So, with JHD and the team preparing everything for the recording, Connie and I did a final polish on the script and sent it off to Jimmy Gilbert. When I visited him to get his comments, he was apparently rather bothered.

'John,' he said, 'why are these two together?'

I nearly laughed. I realised that this considerate, kind, beautifully mannered man had obviously been in a perfect marriage for forty-odd years and was slightly shocked to learn of the bickering combat zone Connie and I had created for Sybil and Basil.

I thought carefully and gently asked him, 'Jimmy . . . do you know why . . . any of your married friends . . . are together?'

He took a long time to answer. 'No, not really.'

So that was the first hurdle cleared.

Like the BBC producer who said to historian Bettany Hughes, 'Nobody's interested in history any more, and nobody watches history on television.'

This was before *World at War*, *Vikings*, *Lucy Worsley Investigates* and *Horrible Histories* – to name a few!

How can you be so sure of yourself? Only if you have no idea that you have no idea what you are doing.

It's the triumph of ego over reality. You want to demonstrate to others that you are so experienced and intelligent that you can lay down the law, and they can rely on the fact that you are a superior kind of human being.

Like many critics, incidentally.

It has always puzzled me that people who can't write dialogue, can't direct it, and can't act it, are put in judgement over people who can.

But I digress . . .

To return to Ian Main.

What annoys me is not that Ian Main was wrong, but that he was so adamant about his opinion. Had he said that a couple of the characters 'might be a bit clichéd', it might have given pause for thought to the director, the writers and the actors. If he'd queried whether some of the situations were stereotypical, apart from showing that he didn't understand that pilot episodes need to be kept simpler than subsequent episodes, it might nevertheless have stimulated the writers to see if there was some truth in his idea.

Below: Recording the pilot, 'A Touch of Class', at long last! With a duo of BBC studio cameras pointing at us... It looks like this caught us between scenes – myself, Michael Gwynn (as Lord Melbury) and Andy appear to be somewhat out of character!

Dennis Wilson / Music

For millions of viewers around the world, Dennis Wilson's distinctive *Fawlty Towers* theme tune instantly sets the scene for the wonderful entertainment audiences are about to enjoy. The cascading, elegant refrain sounds on the verge of delicately unravelling – perfectly echoing Basil's disposition and life in the hotel in general.

This is something which fellow TV composer Paul Farrer considers part of the music's hidden genius: 'The purpose of theme music, more than anything else, is to invite you into the world. If you take the *Fawlty Towers* theme at surface-level, it's got this tightly wound, repressed English tea-shopness, as genteel as a paper doily. But actually, it's a bit clever. It's a string quartet, which is all about restriction, and this reflects the limited set. You could also see the four instruments as reflecting the interweaving

chaos of the four central characters.

'It's got that gritted-teeth niceness that's presenting itself as being delightful. The theme has a beautiful precision that is just slightly off,' notes Farrer.

Dennis Wilson was a talented Leicester-born pianist, composer and arranger with extensive experience in film and television. When he was appointed to compose the music for *Fawlty Towers*, he had recently written the theme for ITV's hit sitcom *Rising Damp*. Funnily enough, back in 1961, he had composed the music for Prunella Scales' big breakthrough comedy, *Marriage Lines*.

For the recording of the pilot episode of the series, Dennis was also commissioned to compose 30 seconds of incidental music in the same style as the series' theme.

This music would be used to soundtrack Polly's trip to the bank in the episode and would prove to be unique to 'A Touch of Class', with incidental music in subsequent episodes limited to very brief stings of the main theme used as a segue between scenes.

But no, he announced, 'I cannot see this series being anything other than a disaster.'

Suppose the script had been written by two young writers. Would they have left the profession, not knowing that this pompous prick had absolutely no idea what he was talking about?

But Main was not alone. A friend of mine, a BBC director called Iain Johnstone, who had produced the famous televised debate about *Life of Brian* (when Michael Palin and I prevailed against author and Christian Malcolm Muggeridge and the Bishop of Southwark), told me another story. He

said he'd been sitting in the BBC bar, when he overheard three light entertainment producers discussing the *Fawlty* pilot script. They were saying how poor it was, and that it was incomprehensible that I had left *Monty Python* to do this.

Prunella Scales, too, recalled that she had a meeting with a very senior BBC producer who held the same view. But of course, nobody told Connie and I at the time!

We knew only that JHD claimed to have fallen out of bed laughing when he first read it, and then Pru and Andy both really liked it.

Above: *Piano Romance* – a lovely album of instrumental standards Dennis recorded for His Master's Voice in 1956, shortly after he joined the BBC Show Band – an association with the corporation which eventually led him to being given the job of creating the music for *Fawlty*. I never had the pleasure of meeting Dennis (all of that side of the production was handled remotely in those days) but what he did was absolutely perfect. He captured the faded gentility of what we were trying to create.

PLEASE FAMILIARISE YOURSELVES WITH
OUR FACILITIES SO YOU DON'T HAVE
TO ASK US WHERE THINGS ARE.
WE HOPE YOU ENJOY YOUR STAY.

DRAWING ROOM

OPEN DOOR SEEN IN 'A TOUCH OF CLASS',
INTERIOR SEEN IN 'THE BUILDERS', THEN
DOOR COVERED UP BY MR O'REILLY!

BAR

WALLS WERE GIVEN A RED
MAKE-OVER FOR SERIES TWO!

OFFICE

Fawlty Towers is located at 16 Elwood Avenue in Torquay ('The Builders'). The visiting inspectors in 'The Hotel Inspectors' mention that the hotel has 26 rooms, including 12 with private bathrooms . . . but Sybil mentions in 'A Touch of Class' that '22 rooms is the limit!' – perhaps suggesting that the inspectors' figure includes the staff rooms as well. Confusingly, Basil and Sybil's first bedroom (seen in 'The Wedding Party') is opposite a door with 'Room 58' on it!

The dining room shifts a yard or two away from the front of the hotel after 'A Touch of Class', allowing an extra door to the kitchen to be added in 'The Builders'.

LOBBY

KITCHEN
HEAVILY MODIFIED FOR SERIES TWO!

THE DINING ROOM

POLLY'S BEDROOM
'THE BUILDERS'

MANUEL'S BEDROOM
'BASIL THE RAT'

ROOM 10
'THE WEDDING PARTY'

ROOM 22
'COMMUNICATION PROBLEMS'

ROOM 8
'THE ANNIVERSARY'

BASIL AND SYBIL'S ROOM
'THE PSYCHIATRIST'
'THE ANNIVERSARY'

FAWLTY TOWERS
HOTEL PLAN

OUR UPPER ROOMS HAVE BEEN THE SUBJECT OF MANY REFINEMENTS, MODIFICATIONS AND RE-NUMBERING OVER THE YEARS – DON'T ASK WHY.

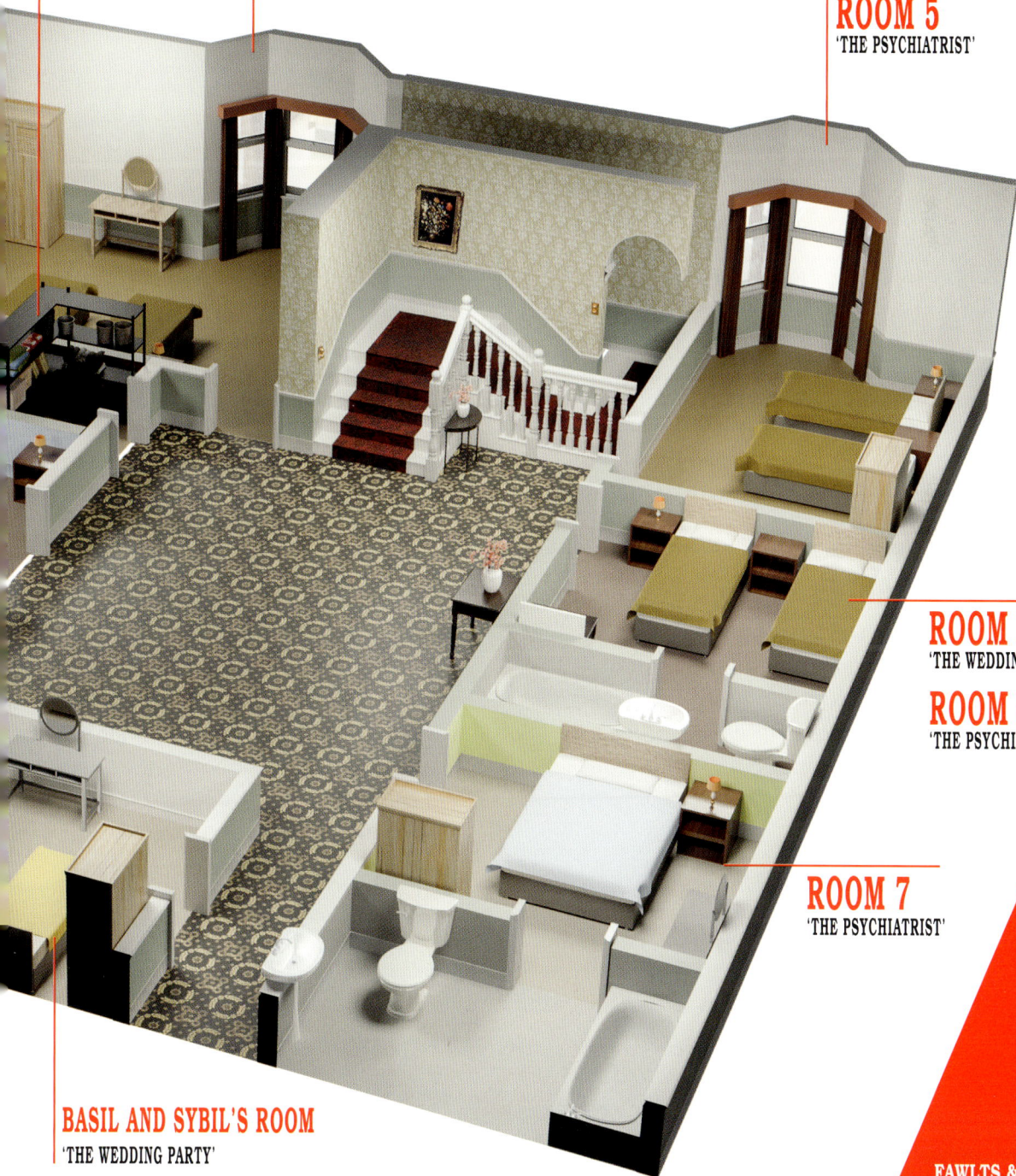

STORAGE CUPBOARD
'THE PSYCHIATRIST'

ROOM 16
'THE WEDDING PARTY'
'THE KIPPER AND THE CORPSE'
(DOOR COVERED UP IN 'THE PSYCHIATRIST'
AND 'THE ANNIVERSARY'!)

ROOM 18
'COMMUNICATION PROBLEMS'

ROOM 14
'THE WEDDING PARTY'

ROOM 5
'THE PSYCHIATRIST'

ROOM 12
'THE WEDDING PARTY'

ROOM 6
'THE PSYCHIATRIST'

ROOM 7
'THE PSYCHIATRIST'

BASIL AND SYBIL'S ROOM
'THE WEDDING PARTY'

A TOUCH OF CLASS

74 FAWLTY TOWERS

Above: Pru and I with the brilliant Michael Gwynn as Lord Melbury, in a scene that instantly reveals Basil's view of the class system. Incidentally, the name of Melbury came from Melbury Road near where I lived at the time in Kensington.

By the way, these *Radio Times* still photos were always taken during our camera rehearsals (which took place the afternoon before the Sunday evening recording), so sometimes the costumes can vary slightly from what made it to the screen!

And so, in the middle of December 1974, we started rehearsing the very first show, 'A Touch of Class'.

The odd thing is that I remember so little about the rehearsal period or the recording!

This must be because it was uneventful.

Obviously, that was because of the sheer competence of all the people around me. With JHD organising us and with a cast of people of great skill and experience, everything ran so smoothly it did not feel like a first show.

I do remember being delighted by Michael Gwynn as Lord Melbury, and realising again just how good at casting JHD was.

We rehearsed for a week at the 'Acton Hilton', as everyone called

the BBC rehearsal block in North Acton, where one could step into the lift and find oneself next to the best 'talent' working in England. The rehearsal rooms were large and airy, with the walls and the set marked out on the floor in coloured tape. There were tables and chairs, and various props, all of them quite different to the ones we'd have on Sunday for the actual recording.

We always recorded on a Sunday, because that meant we could cast the cream of the actors who were performing every other night of the week in the West End theatres. During the week, rehearsals started fairly late in the day to make sure the actors got a good night's sleep after the adrenaline from their stage shows had subsided.

On Sunday, we turned up at the BBC TV Centre near White City. I don't remember feeling very nervous, probably because

I'd recorded over forty *Monty Pythons* in the studios there, and everything seemed very familiar. Connie had done a few *Python* shows there too. We spent the day rehearsing with the cameras. In those days, a show would have four huge TV cameras, and a vision mixer would sit in the control room next to the director with four buttons and a script in front of him. Once the show started, he would push Button 1 if he wanted to record the picture he was getting from Camera 1, and so on. A tremendously demanding job, requiring the clarity and quick-wittedness of an air traffic controller. If he'd pressed the wrong button, he'd be recording the wrong camera's shot, and we'd have to do that bit again. Thank God they were so good, because we only had two hours to record the whole show.

An odd thing just happened as I was writing this!

I experienced a flashback – a moment of recall from the recording. I remember when I, as Basil, picked up the picture and carried it across the lobby to hang it up. And (probably because there was no dialogue), I thought to myself, 'This is going well. It's going to be all right.' What a lovely thought to have in the middle of a pilot – cheerful and relaxing. My comic timing is always best when I'm relaxed.

And that was the general feeling after the recording was over. Everyone was satisfied and felt quietly confident. We'd not let ourselves down. It was OK!

If at that moment someone had told me that one day this show would get better viewing figures than *Monty Python*, I would have laughed in their face. No way, José!!

And most important of all, when he saw the recording, Jimmy Gilbert was happy with it. We met, and he told me there and then that he was commissioning a series of six. Connie and I were overjoyed. And then he gave me an outstandingly bad piece of advice: 'But John, you're going to have to have them out of the hotel more.'

Above: Basil's job of hanging the painting became a wonderful recurring device in our first episode.

Below: Basil was not impressed by the unrefined Danny Brown (played by Robin Ellis), who turns out to be an undercover policeman. When the pilot became a series, we got Robin back to redo his scene with Connie in the dining room, as we had decided it would offer more comedy and plot potential for Polly to be an art student, rather than a philosophy one.

Robin Ellis / Danny Brown

'More riffraff!' Basil thought, another example of the slipping standards of modern society . . . But Danny Brown was actually an undercover man from CID on the lookout for a con man posing as aristocracy!

For most viewers, Robin Ellis will always be a cockney undercover cop, but when he walked onto the *Fawlty* set,

Robin was an RSC and West End stage veteran.

Shortly after his role in *Fawlty* was finally broadcast (some ten months after it was made), Robin became a household name as Ross Poldark in the BBC's *Poldark*. Soon after, both big and small-screen parts flooded in, including a role in the reimagined *Poldark* in 2015.

In later years, the multi-talented Robin has written a number of hugely successful cookery books.

Wrong. Wrong. WRONG. Not Ian-Main-wrong, but fucking close!!

We're talking about farce, right? Not comedy of manners, or satire, or observational comedy, or surreal comedy or parody, but farce. Thus, keeping as much of *Fawlty* inside the pressure-cooker of the hotel – with its networks of doors and side rooms – was essential.

And the essence of farce is that its protagonist has done something that he has to keep hidden, or he (it's almost always a man) will suffer a horrendous loss of face. So, he has to conceal something, but each lie fails and forces him to adopt a new deceit, which in turn is revealed, so he has to . . . and so on.

The reason that great farce is funnier than other forms of comedy is that the farcical mode produces two allied phenomena: pace and emotional intensity.

Here's the reason pace is important. Getting the first laugh is harder than getting subsequent ones. It's like the first lesson that salesmen learn. If they can get the first sale, it's much, much easier to get another one.

So pace is vital to farce, because if you can get an audience laughing, you can get them on a roll. And the reason that farce is always allied with physical comedy is that if you are making verbal jokes in a theatre, you have to wait for an audience to quieten down, or they won't be able to hear the next joke. This inevitably slows everything down. Whereas if you add jokes that are only visual, you can keep the audience laughing.

In TV comedy, we could avoid any slowing down because the actors all had a

Michael Gwynn
Lord Melbury

As *Fawlty Towers'* first notable guest actor, both in front and behind the camera, Michael Gwynn's deliciously nonchalant Lord Melbury perfectly exposes Basil's adoration for the upper classes . . . which ultimately causes our hotelier to come a cropper!

Michael was born in Bath in 1916, and any hopes for an acting career had to be set aside for duty during the war, where he served in East Africa as a Major.

Both stage and screen soon beckoned after hostilities ended, with Michael's natural presence winning him plenty of work, including a starring part in 1960s cult classic *Village of the Damned*. He also found time to appear in two 1963 epic feature films, *Jason and the Argonauts* and *Cleopatra*!

After guest starring in dozens of the popular ITV series (including *Danger Man*, *The Saint* and *Randall and Hopkirk*), Michael proved his sitcom chops with an unforgettable turn in *Some Mothers Do 'Ave 'Em* in 1973 as Wing Commander Day.

Other than his memorable stint as Melbury in *Fawlty Towers*, Michael is best remembered for his work with Hammer Films, including 1958's *The Revenge of Frankenstein* and 1970's *Scars of Dracula*. His chiselled, dignified demeanour was perfectly suited for dramatic big-screen horror.

Michael sadly passed away just a year after 'A Touch of Class' aired, no doubt denying audiences dozens of wonderful performances.

microphone 18 inches above their heads, so the audience at home could hear the dialogue over the sound of the studio audience's laughing. The thing that we had to persuade guest actors to do was to ignore the studio audience's laughter! And surprisingly, our actors were able to change a lifetime habit very easily by simply reverting to rehearsal-room timing.

The other requisite of farce is emotional intensity. This is why a great comedy actor can raise the roof.

You see, all actors have to accomplish two things: they have to make interesting choices, and they have to act those choices convincingly; that is, make them emotionally believable.

A comedy actor has to do both of these and then, as I said on page 42, add comedy technique. Some very good straight actors can't do this, whereas the top comedy actors can always act straight roles (surprisingly). Convincingly.

The reason for this is that great comedy acting is more difficult and demanding. As Henry Irving, said on his deathbed, when asked if dying was difficult: 'No, dying is easy, comedy is hard.'

This truism has escaped the notice of most people, except for great comedy actors, of course.

Where was I?

Oh yes. So, a great comedy protagonist in a farce will make each revelation of his mendacity more painful, and the audience becomes utterly convinced that he continues to make bad choices because of his increasingly frantic state of mind.

'A Touch of Class'

SERIES 1 EPISODE 1

Recorded: 23 December 1974 (TC8)

First transmission: 19 September 1975

Guest stars: Michael Gwynn (Lord Melbury), Robin Ellis (Danny Brown), Martin Wyldeck (Sir Richard Morris), David Simeon (Mr Mackenzie), Terence Conoley (Mr Wareing), Lionel Wheeler (Mr Watson)

Uncredited: Garry Rich (Newspaper Boy), Julie Mellon (Mrs Watson), Annette Peters (Mrs Wareing), Oscar Peck (Master Wareing), Pat Symons (Lady Morris), Claire Russell (Mrs Mackenzie), Dennis Plenty, Ian Elliot (PCs), David Waterman, Pat Milner (CID Officers)

A favourite quote of mine comes from Daniel Goleman in *Emotional Intelligence*: 'Stress makes you stupid.' Everyone knows that the more frenzied you become, the more your capacity for logical reasoning goes off the cliff! We can see this in my favourite moment from this episode, illustrated on page 79, where Basil simply cannot believe that the bricks he has been told are valuables are in fact . . . bricks.

Below: Connie sets up the plot on location in Cookham High Street in Berkshire. This was shot in mid-December 1974 – meaning some viewers spotted Christmas decorations in the shop windows! This exterior sequence was filmed in a very different way to anything else in the series . . . it feels more like a BBC drama.

Above: Basil gives Lord Melbury – who the audience now know is a con man – his envelope of money . . .

Below: Action! The mask falls off and Basil goes after Melbury!

Right: 'You snobs! You stupid, stuck-up, toffee-nosed, half-witted, upper-class piles of . . . pus!'

Far right: 'A gin and orange . . .' What a way to finish with Terence Conoley's wonderfully delivered drinks order!

So, our farce protagonist's bad choices land him in even more disastrous situations, leading to greater frenzy and even worse plans for escape. A downward spiral that lies at the heart of every farce.

That's why I cry with laughter at farces like *The Lady from Maxim's*, Peter Shaffer's *Black Comedy*, Alan Ayckbourn's *Bedroom Farce*, Michael Frayn's *Noises Off*, Richard Bean's *One Man, Two Guvnors*, Ben Travis's *Rocky Nook* and Ray Cooney's *Move Over Mrs Markham*.

The puzzle for me has always been the vague disdain with which the literary classes treat farce. In fact, when I once said that being very funny is much harder than being very clever, several of them didn't like that at all. The left hemisphere's hold over British education has a lot to answer for.

Which is not to say that there isn't a lot of very bad farce around.

But that's not the point.

'LET'S HAVE A LOOK AT THESE VALUABLES . . .'

7.

INTERLUDE: MAKING A SITCOM

This is the moment, I think, when I should explain a little more about the comparatively difficult procedure of making a BBC sitcom. The process was:

Day 1: Assemble the cast in the rehearsal room and read through the script. The cast have questions, and we try to answer them. There may be a few tweaks to the script, but not many, because Connie and I had polished it carefully, so we don't have to lose valuable rehearsal time. Then, after lunch, we start 'putting it on its feet' – that is, figuring out all the moves and especially all the comedy 'business' – the physical comedy – which always takes more working out and practising than just getting the words right. The script is about 140 pages, so we hope to have settled the moves for the first 70 pages before we pack it in.

Day 2: We hope to have finished the other 70 pages by lunch, so that in the afternoon we do a 'stagger-through' with everyone holding the script in one hand and trying to remember all the moves we've worked out.

Day 3: Another couple of 'stagger-throughs' before lunch, with the cast beginning to do some scenes 'off the script', which makes the moves a lot more natural. After lunch, we start more work on the more difficult scenes, where there's a lot of dialogue or physical comedy – 'business'.

Day 4: One day this week, we have a compulsory day off.

Day 5: We now have one whole day to rehearse – to run it again and again. And, if possible, again.

Day 6: Is a very odd day because all the cameras and sound men, vision mixers, lighting folk and other technicians arrive and watch the cast run through the whole show, in complete silence! Because they're not listening to the words at all. They're watching as they hold floor plans and figure out how the cameras are going to move, and which shot will be on which camera as they suck on their pipes. One or two of them do not have pipes, as they have been granted a special dispensation. And the cast do the whole show, stopping and starting again, desperately trying not to get depressed about the complete lack of reaction from fifteen technicians.

All of whom might as well be Icelandic. More about that later.

And the technicians finally leave, and after the smoke has cleared and we can see each other again, we have final notes and make our way home while trying to cheer each other up. You see, performing comedy to radio silence does no favours to your ego.

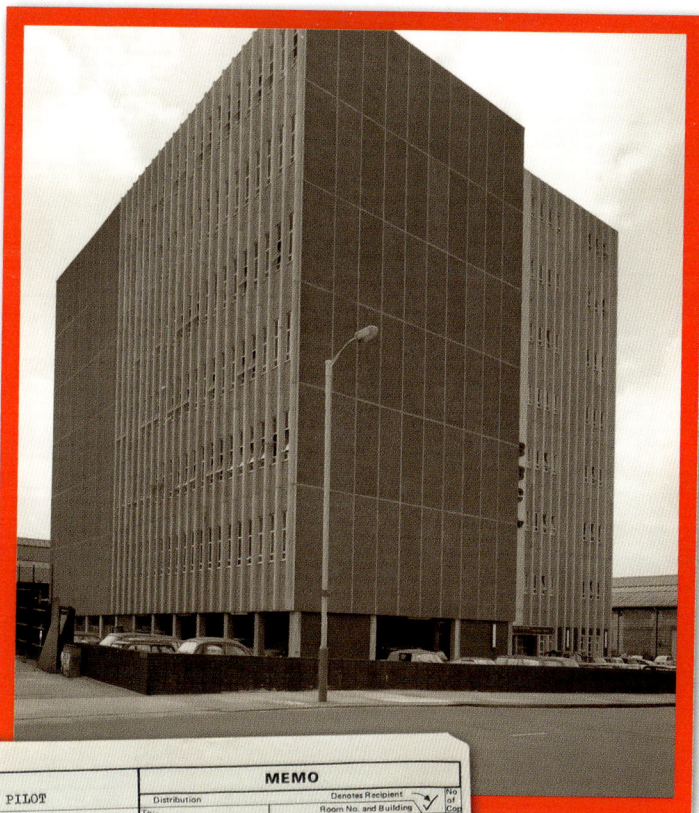

Above and below: The exterior of the Acton Rehearsal Block – the BBC's purpose-built six-floor rehearsal space, complete with a canteen on top, where you could bump into anyone from a Two Ronnie to a Doctor Who.

Left: JHD's memo to book rehearsal space for our first episode.

10.00 a.m. – Camera rehearsal. A very slow process where the cast painstakingly work our way through the script, stopping and starting all the time. This allows the cameramen to learn which of their shots will be recorded by the vision mixer onto the tape of the show. JHD and the cameramen are able to discuss the framing of each shot, whether the cameras will be still or moving, where a camera would have to move to for its next shot. The cast rehearse each section at the pace they will use in the actual recording, so that everyone involved with the cameras can get used to the pace of the show.

Day 7: The day in the TV studio when we recorded the show! The *Fawlty Towers* episodes were always taped on a Sunday, as I explained, so that guest artists would be available even if they were appearing in the West End.

09.30 a.m. – Arrive at BBC TV Centre at White City. Find dressing room, get coffee, go to the allotted TVC studio.

1.00 p.m. – Lunch or rest.

2.00 p.m. – Finish camera rehearsal. Notes for all the technicians. Break.

3.30 p.m. – First stagger-through of the whole show, stopping and restarting every time we made a mistake.

5.00 p.m. – Proper Dress Rehearsal, with full dress and everything done exactly as per the show.

6.00 p.m. – Break for early dinner and getting nervous.

6.30 p.m. – Audience arrives.

7.00 p.m. – Audience is welcomed by the warm-up man, who explains what happens during the recording, and tells some 'jokes'.

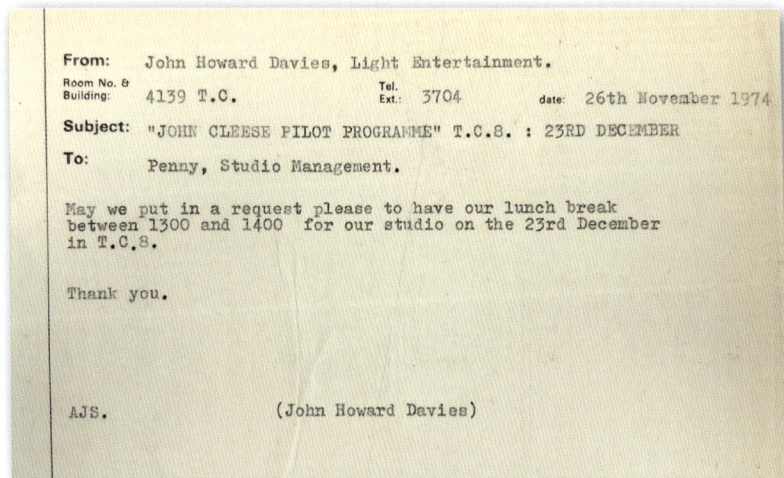

```
From:     John Howard Davies, Light Entertainment.
Room No. &
Building:  4139 T.C.          Tel.
                              Ext.:  3704      date:  26th November 1974

Subject:  "JOHN CLEESE PILOT PROGRAMME" T.C.8. : 23RD DECEMBER

To:       Penny, Studio Management.

May we put in a request please to have our lunch break
between 1300 and 1400  for our studio on the 23rd December
in T.C.8.

Thank you.


AJS.              (John Howard Davies)
```

7.20 p.m. – Make-up and wardrobe check.

7.45 p.m. – Get more nervous.

8.00 p.m. – Start recording show. Not a moment to lose, as we have only two hours to record, with all the set and costume changes … and mistakes!

10.00 p.m. – Recording ends and cameras are switched off. No chance of an extra five minutes, so if we'd failed to finish on time, the audience at home would suddenly see a blank screen.

All in all, a pretty demanding day, although, if the audience enjoyed it, so did we. In the theatre, a first night is always a nerve-wracking experience. In TV, every show is a first night! Later, in repose, it struck me that the reason so many TV shows aren't that brilliant is that just getting the show done is a huge achievement in itself. If it happened to be a good show, that was kind of a bonus. Getting the fucking thing done at all was the real achievement.

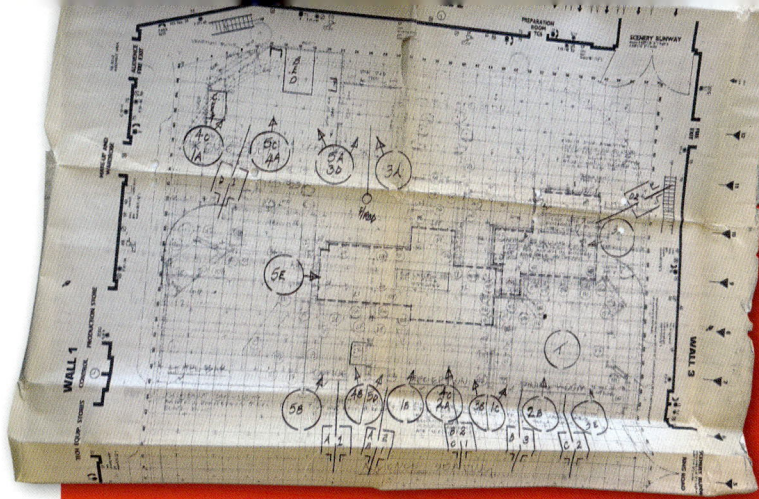

Camera Movements

Amazingly, learning all the lines and blocking out a carefully written script wasn't all that was required to make an episode of *Fawlty Towers*.

In the era of analogue television you couldn't just point lots of cameras and record every angle, then pick and choose which shot you wanted to use in the edit at a later date.

Despite having four cameras on set, sitcoms at the time could only record to one tape (as those tape machines were incredibly expensive!). Which particular camera's feed that went down on tape was determined by the director and the vision mixer in the studio gallery, where footage from all the cameras appeared on a wall in front of them.

Obviously those decisions couldn't be made on the hop, so lots of very clever (and terribly dull!) planning and camera rehearsal beforehand was required.

Enter, the camera script – the technical template for the whole show. These versions of a script were printed on yellow paper and broke down dialogue and shots. Here the script could be choreographed, almost like a ballet, with the actors, cameras and also sound crew (with their booms held almost like fishing rods) all synchronised together.

Special versions of studio floor plans were marked up as well, denoting the route each numbered camera had to move around.

FIRST SITTING

8.

...AND FIVE MORE!

Connie and I were now able to sit down and write another five episodes. We didn't plan them, we just waited until we got an idea we really liked, and then, very carefully, we developed the plot. This was why we took so much time, because good comedy ideas don't come frequently, so the longer we played with the plot ideas, the richer the plot became. This made the dialogue much easier to invent, when, after two weeks of plotting, we started on the actual script. If you have a series of comic situations, you don't have to think up a lot of jokes – just making

the scenes flow believably will be enough. Any jokes you come up with are a bonus, as the scenes are amusing enough already.

But executives very seldom really comprehend the creative process, so they don't allow writers enough time to conjure up really good, funny plots.

So, the writers have to rush to agree the plot, which means it will lack enough good comedy ideas.

Then, because the plots themselves aren't really funny, the writers have to come up with lots of jokes, which do not arise from the plot.

This unrewarding process is enforced by BBC light entertainment economics. I think that if I encouraged executives to pay writers more, they'd have more time to be creative. The executives' main objection would be that the writers wouldn't work so hard. Of course, they might simply enjoy the writing process more, which would in turn make for a more playful and original script.

My favourite story about the everlasting battle between execs and writers is about Sam Goldwyn in his early days in Hollywood. Writers had to turn up every morning and go to their typewriters in a special building for them, wittily entitled 'The Writers' Block'. There, they would make coffee, sit down, and start thinking.

But first, they checked that their lookout was in place. This person had to

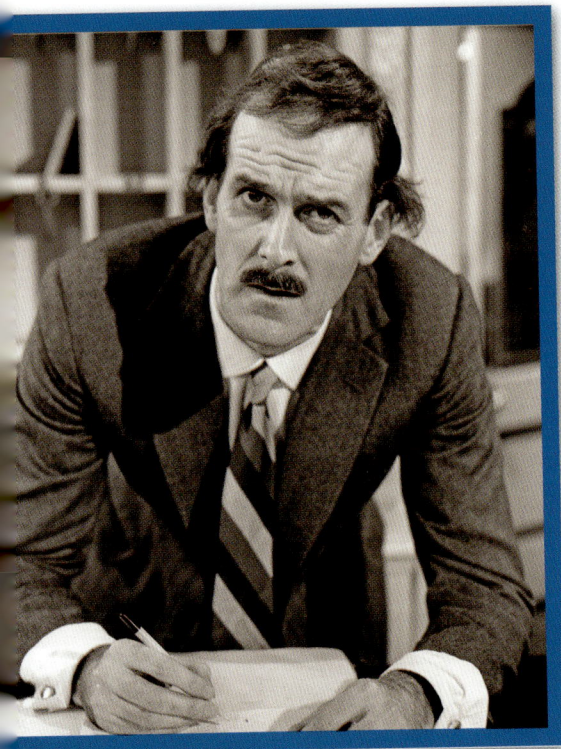

Above: Reunited on set for a camera rehearsal of 'The Builders' ... (Furiously working BBC script man pictured on the far left!)

Left: The pains of writing!

Opposite page: Two pages from my copy of our second *Fawlty* episode, 'The Builders'.

sit at the top corner of their block, and sound the alarm whenever Sam Goldwyn was seen. Sam used to sneak up so he could check that the writers were working hard enough.

The moment the alarm went off, the writers inserted a new sheet in their machines and started typing up any old rubbish that amused them, and that cacophonous metallic clattering would continue until the alarm sounded again, meaning that Sam was satisfied with the level of their industry and had left.

Below: Fawlty Towers' resident duo of glamorous Edwardian sirens! Miss Abitha Tibbs (Gilly Flower) and Miss Ursula Angina Gatsby (Renee Roberts) – our wonderful old ladies.

At which the writers would throw away what they'd typed and would revert to their real work: thinking.

So, Connie and I were taking six weeks to write every episode. This is unheard of. Most writers take a maximum of ten days. I'd like to thank those companies who, by asking me to make TV and radio commercials for them, subsidised the first series of *Fawlty Towers*: General Accident, Texaco, Sony.

Sometimes if we got stuck, we'd move on to another episode and then return to the previous one refreshed. I'd already discovered that if you work on something, the unconscious part of your brain will continue to work on it while you move on to something else.

But although we were not consciously working on a plan, if you look at the next five shows, they do seem to have a kind of logic to them:

• 'The Builders' is about Basil's obsession – class – and his consequent disdain for his ordinary guests.

• 'The Wedding Party' shows Basil's attitude to sex and how his uptight views cause him to see sexuality where there is none, giving everyone the correct impression that he is really obsessed with it.

• 'The Hotel Inspectors' reveals Basil's main fear (aside from Sybil) that his hotel will be publicly criticised as second rate, with a resulting loss of status.

Gilly Flower and Renee Roberts
Miss Abitha Tibbs & Miss Ursula Angina Gatsby

A reassuring presence in the hotel for all 12 episodes, the delightful Gilly Flower and Renee Roberts brought the elegant dotty duo Miss Tibbs and Miss Gatsby to life.

Gilly Flower was a bit of a BBC casting dream, and throughout the 60s and 70s notched up multiple TV appearances. Interestingly, before turning to acting, she was a hat model!

Renee Roberts had previously popped up in one of Graham Chapman's solo *Doctor at Large* episodes in 1971, as well as a BBC *Play for Today* and a *Doctor Who*.

Miss Tibbs would of course enjoy a moment of actual plot when she sees the dead body in *The Kipper and the Corpse* and is duly knocked out in the confusion.

The ladies would later enjoy another scene together in a 1983 episode of fellow BBC comedy *Only Fools and Horses*! In the story 'Homesick', Gilly and Renee were cast together as two orange-buying customers in a market scene. Although only ever listed as '1st and 2nd Old Lady' in the script, an excitable *Radio Times* billing listed them as Miss Tibbs and Miss Gatsby! So who knows, perhaps they ended up in Peckham and quickly developed a cockney twang?

• 'Gourmet Night' takes us back to his obsession with class.

• 'The Germans' has two themes: the misunderstanding of the fire drill, and later, how after a bang on the head, Basil cannot escape from his 1945 prejudices, and consequently loses it with the Germans, causing such chaos that a doctor arrives to take him back to hospital.

Within these individual themes, though, the humour emerged all the time from:

1. Basil always striving unsuccessfully to conceal something (as we've established, the basis of farce).

2. Miscommunication, which I always find funny and huge fun to write. The longer it can be extended, the better.

3. Mistaken identity, which causes Basil to switch his attitude to a guest in the blink of an eye.

4. Ingenious lying, where changing the cover story becomes more creative, and unbelievable. The speed at which each lie is replaced delights the audience.

5. Basil's disproportionate fear of Sybil, which he tries to disguise through sarcasm, but which is very real.

6. Sybil's lifestyle: gossiping, taking it easy, always ordering Basil about, eating chocolates in bed – but still fundamentally keeping the hotel running.

Above: The pains of writing! Connie was simply magnificent as Polly, and the best possible writing partner.

7. Manuel's unquestioning respect for Basil, and his dedication to his job, despite his lack of any real success.

8. The Major living happily in a world of his own, uncontaminated by reality.

Polly doesn't have a particularly comic personality because she's the sensible one and only gets involved in the general madness when she gets caught up helping Basil to conceal his lies (See 'Dragonfly!' in 'Communication Problems!').

Let's now look at each of these episodes, to see what lessons we can learn, especially how the plot creates the situation that can be funny.

THE BUILDERS

'The Builders' was the second episode we recorded and didn't have as complicated a plot as some of the later episodes. Let's run through how the key elements of the plot are set up in the first scene.

1. We start at the reception desk where Polly gives a key to a guest and takes a phone call giving the hotel address to a delivery driver for a garden gnome. We remind the audience of Polly's competence.

2. Because only Manuel is around when the gnome arrives, we set up its delivery now, so it does not seem out of the blue when it happens.

3. Basil and Sybil are preparing to depart on their weekend away to Paignton with friends. This establishes that they are both away for the weekend, but staying somewhere that is not far from Torquay, so that they can drive back easily if they need to.

4. Polly tells Sybil about the delivery of the gnome. Sybil gives her number and reminds her that Mr Stubbs (the builder) is coming. We learn that Mr Stubbs has been hired by Sybil to come and do construction work at the hotel: a door is being installed at the bottom of the stairs that will lead straight through into the kitchen.

5. Manuel is practising English: 'I will het your vill.' Polly helps: 'I will get your bill.' This tells a new audience that Manuel's English is not good.

6. Sybil asks Manuel to put her golf shoes into her suitcase. This request to put the shoes in the case will later be very important.

7. Miss Tibbs and Miss Gatsby chide Basil about going away and leaving them. He tells them about the works in the hotel: this is necessary, as it adds details about the upcoming events.

Now the phone rings. It's O'Reilly (an Irish builder). Sybil answers and passes it to Basil, who pretends it's about finally fixing the garden wall (lie #1). Sybil thinks Stubbs (reliable builder) is fixing the interior, so this exchange is all-important. Basil knows Sybil doesn't trust O'Reilly, so he talks about imaginary work in order that Sybil will not realise that he has hired O'Reilly to do the major construction on the doors in the hotel.

Basil and Sybil argue about O'Reilly (cheap, cock-up artist) vs. Stubbs (expensive, professional job). The mention of O'Reilly leads naturally into an argument which makes clear Basil's and Sybil's attitude to Stubbs and O'Reilly and Basil's belief in trying to do anything on the cheap.

Sybil mentions Basil's dress style and asks him to be agreeable this weekend.

Friends arrive in their car. This enables us to get Sybil out of the hotel so that Basil can brief Polly about O'Reilly. Basil speaks to Polly about the work that O'Reilly's men are going to do. This makes it clear that it's O'Reilly that is doing the

construction, and not Stubbs, and that Polly will be supervising the work. Basil explains that Sybil doesn't know, and Polly says she won't tell her. Basil thanks her for her loyalty to him. Now we have set up the typical farce plotline: something has to be concealed.

Basil and Sybil leave. Too late, Manuel remembers the golf shoes. This is important as it gives Sybil a reason to return later to get them before she can play golf.

Above: Hatching the plot! Sybil berates Basil about the differences between O'Reilly and Stubbs . . .

Below: 'Oh, Mr Fawlty! Ursula and I think you're a very naughty boy . . . Leaving us all alone!' Connie and I added a nice little reference to our original hotel inspiration in this scene, as Basil reminds Miss Tibbs and Miss Gatsby that because of the building works they will be having their dinner at the 'Gleneagles Hotel'.

a large garden gnome. Confusing conversation between Bennion and Manuel . . . Manuel puts the gnome behind the desk, out of sight.

Remember, the gnome has nothing to do with the plot. It's introduced as it gives a couple of later scenes some extra absurdity and it gives us a punchline at the very end. O'Reilly's men arrive (Lurphy, Jones, and Kerr). Another confusing conversation between them and Manuel. He goes to wake Polly but is unable to. (This is a plot weakness. Why can't he wake her?) Manuel returns to the lobby. Talks to the men about knowing what to do. They claim to know. Basil calls, and Manuel tells him Polly is busy and that the men are there. And the confusion between Manuel and O'Reilly sets up why the builders get it so wrong.

Time lapse: There's a break in continuity here, to allow for time to pass.

Back in the lobby, Manuel and Polly are talking, and she tells him she's tired and going for a siesta, and to wake her when the workmen arrive. She leaves. Very important!

Polly's not there when O'Reilly and his men arrive because she knows what they are supposed to do, so they can go ahead with their cock-up without being supervised. Manuel goes behind the reception desk as he is 'now in charge'. The delivery driver, Bennion, arrives with

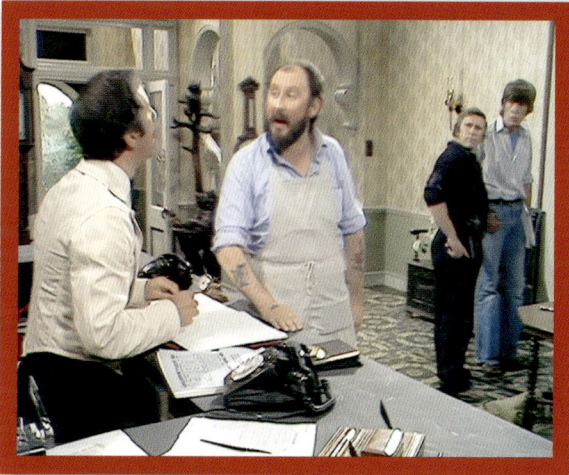

'The Builders'

Recorded: 3 August 1975 (TC3)

First transmission:
26 September 1975

Guest stars: David Kelly (O'Reilly), James Appleby (Stubbs), George Lee (Delivery Man), Michael Cronin (Lurphy), Michael Halsey (Jones), Barney Dorman (Kerr)

Uncredited: Pat Gorman (Hotel Guest), Judy Roger (Sybil's Friend).

**SERIES 1
EPISODE 2**

Another time lapse. Next morning, Basil returns, alone. He looks at the wall by the stairs. There is no new kitchen door. The door now leads to the staircase. He finds the dining room door has disappeared. Basil takes it in. The key moment of the plot:

what will Basil do now, to hide this from Sybil and get the hotel lobby restored before she sees it? Polly appears. Basil grabs Polly. She says she fell asleep and Manuel didn't wake her, but it's not his fault. As usual, Polly defends Manuel as she thinks of a plan to help Basil. She says it's really Basil's fault for hiring O'Reilly.

Above left: 'You Orelly men!' Manuel talks to the three builders sent by O'Reilly – Lurphy (Michael Cronin), Kerr (Barney Dorman) and Jones (Michael Halsey).

Below: 'Polly! What have you done with my hotel!' – Basil grabs Polly's ear in shocked confusion as he tries to understand what happened with his clear building instructions . . .

Basil sarcastically chastises himself. Polly slaps Basil to knock sense into him. She tells him to call O'Reilly. A sensible next step, keeping the plot developing. Basil runs to the phone, trips over the gnome and then tries to strangle it. The appearance of the gnome at a moment of crisis makes the scene more ridiculous. Basil calls O'Reilly but is interrupted by the sight of Manuel who can't find the door to the dining room. Basil asks Manuel to show the Major to the dining room through the kitchen. Wonderful comic possibilities as they try to find the door that is usually there while Basil's fury builds. Basil resumes his call with O'Reilly and tells him to put the hotel back in its original condition.

There is now a third time lapse.

One hour later, O'Reilly arrives on his own (his men won't work on Sundays). He says it will take two and a half hours to fix. This is to tell the audience that the whole disaster may be manageable. It takes the temperature down so that we can warm it up again. O'Reilly tells Basil he worries too much. By making O'Reilly a cheerful devil-may-care charmer, (which would not normally be considered plot), his calm is accentuated by the contrast with Basil's life-threatening anxiety.

Sybil returns early, to collect her golfing shoes. She sees O'Reilly's van and storms towards the hotel. Sybil's surprise return, now triggers the climactic scene. O'Reilly hides. Basil tries to head Sybil off and take her for a walk. She refuses, enters the lobby and he shows her the construction fiasco. Basil attempts a cover-up, saying this has been done by Stubbs (lie #2). Sybil asks why O'Reilly is parked outside. Basil has forgotten about the van and now claims O'Reilly is there to fix 'Stubbs's mistake'. This is his third lie.

Sybil says that Stubbs should fix his own mistake. Basil says that O'Reilly came because it's Sunday (lie #4). He tried calling Stubbs at work and home just a few minutes ago. The phone rings, Basil answers, says its Stubbs' office (lie #5) and passes the phone to a dubious Sybil. She starts to speak, hands the phone back to Basil and goes into the living room where Polly is on another extension pretending to be Stubbs' office.

So, the latest cover-up is exposed. Sybil rants at Basil about his lies and how bad

O'Reilly is. Sybil finally explodes. Basil has run out of lies. O'Reilly comes out of hiding from the bar and tries to placate Sybil. Once again, his attempt to charm bites the dust. She screams at O'Reilly,

Above: Basil introduces Manuel to the new wall he never wanted.

Below: O'Reilly (David Kelly) looks at the new wall his lads built, with Basil in disbelief.

attacks both him and Basil with a golfing umbrella, and phones up Stubbs, who agrees he will come in the morning. Sybil picks up her golf shoes and says she is going to Audrey's and won't be back until tomorrow. She sees the gnome and first suggests Basil puts him in the garden and then decides to put him in charge as he's cheaper than Basil and would do a better job. Sybil leaves. Basil is completely humiliated. Now the plot

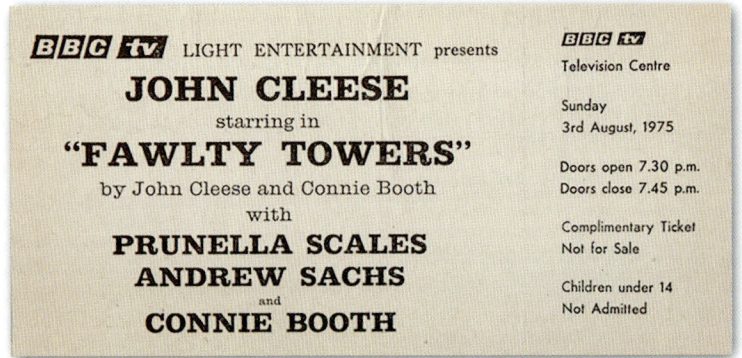

BBC tv LIGHT ENTERTAINMENT presents
JOHN CLEESE
starring in
"FAWLTY TOWERS"
by John Cleese and Connie Booth
with
PRUNELLA SCALES
ANDREW SACHS
and
CONNIE BOOTH

BBC tv
Television Centre

Sunday
3rd August, 1975

Doors open 7.30 p.m.
Doors close 7.45 p.m.

Complimentary Ticket
Not for Sale

Children under 14
Not Admitted

David Kelly
O'Reilly

The hapless builder O'Reilly didn't take Sybil Fawlty's simmering rage seriously in 'The Builders', and soon felt the wrath of her umbrella!

Dublin-born David Kelly started his career on the Irish stage before television came calling, with David cast in RTÉ's *O'Dea's Your Man* in 1964. This brought him to the attention of the BBC and by the late 60s he joined the cast of *Me Mammy* which was recorded in London's Television Centre.

Once in London, more comedy roles soon followed, seeing David pop up as a guest actor in dozens of series. He would later be cast as a regular in sitcoms *Robin's Nest* and *Slinger's*

Day – alongside a stint on *Emmerdale Farm*. A 1998 appearance as another 'Mr O'Reilly' in *Ballykissangel* may have had *Fawlty* viewers scratching their heads!

David capped off his career with two notable film roles – as Grandpa Joe in the 2005 film *Charlie and the Chocolate Factory*, and in 2007, as the guard at the wall in the popular fantasy *Stardust*.

has to kick in again. What can Basil do? O'Reilly starts to leave but Basil tells him he is going to fix the mess.

Time lapse.

Next morning – everything has been renovated and returned to its rightful place. Sybil returns and sees that everything has been fixed. Stubbs arrives and Sybil apologises as it appears to now be OK. Stubbs agrees that it is a good job. A moment when everything suddenly seems OK. Basil has won! He is gracious. Stubbs then discovers that the new door to the kitchen has been put into a supporting wall with no steel or concrete support. He explains that the whole building may fall down. He sets to work immediately. Basil collapses. Always better to have a moment of apparent triumph just before the final defeat. Basil, set on revenge, leaves the hotel carrying the gnome to go and see O'Reilly and adds that he may then go to Canada. This is my favourite moment in this episode. The plot is complete, but we need a smile at the end. And at the very end of a comedy, you can always get sillier provided there's nothing coming after it.

'The Builders' was recorded on Sunday, 3 August 1976, some eight months after we recorded the pilot episode. But despite this long time apart, getting back together to rehearse, and then to record, went as smoothly as we could have hoped.

Except for one thing. Throughout the two hours of recording, the audience was very muted. Comedy performers listen like hawks to the audience's reaction, and although we got all the laughs we were expecting, they weren't very big ones!

This puzzled me during the recording because I couldn't sense anything wrong with it. And the next day, seated in the editing suite with JHD, I still couldn't! The performances all seemed perfect, and we all felt we had a good show.

Then JHD was told the explanation. What was not right was the audience. You see, almost all comedy shows at the BBC were recorded in front of an audience of about 200 people. It was a principle that the laughter track on a show should come from a real audience, and not pre-recorded laughter from other shows.

So, there was a department at the Beeb whose job it was to provide these 200 people for each comedy programme.

On the evening that 'The Builders' was recorded, the unit had decided that a group of seventy visitors from the Icelandic Broadcasting Corporation should be included in the studio audience, even though they didn't speak much English.

And being Ticket Unit employees, they put our Icelandic friends in the first few rows, so that they had the best views.

It had apparently never occurred to the Ticket Unit personnel to ask their boss why these audiences were being brought there.

Perhaps they assumed they were there to make sure the actors didn't get lonely.

Maybe they thought it was good PR for the Beeb to show some ordinary folk how the BBC worked.

But it had clearly never occurred to them that these tickets were being given out because the audience was supposed to laugh – to provide laughter, that would help increase the amusement of the vast audiences at home.

Above: The moment Sybil realises what Basil has done . . . O'Reilly, not Stubbs, is doing their building work! A simple little location insert, which did the job beautifully. Top marks to the BBC art department for the suitably ramshackle O'Reilly sign!

For viewers paying attention, Connie and I subtly laid the groundwork for O'Reilly as an unreliable builder during Basil's phone call in our first episode, 'A Touch of Class'. This is the famous call which Basil abruptly ends when Melbury walks in.

Or . . . maybe a couple of them knew that laughter was part of the deal, but they assumed that it would occur spontaneously, even if the audience had no idea what was going on in front of them, nor what was being said.

I began to notice an odd phenomenon observable everywhere: a lot of people don't realise what the real purpose is of the job they are doing.

For example, years later I was playing a scene in *The Pink Panther 2*, where I was in a crowd of about thirty people at the opposite end from the camera. In other words, it was a wide shot.

And a wardrobe assistant was pestering me to change my shirt, because of a spot on my collar. I had to explain: I don't think the spot could be seen even if someone in the cinema audience had a telescope on him. This assistant had been working in movies for years.

And in the second series of *Fawlty Towers*, I was in a scene where Basil started shouting loudly. And just before I shouted, I saw the boom mic disappearing into the distance. I asked the boom operator why he was doing this, and he said:

'Well, you shout so loud, we get some distortion on the sound.'

So I pointed out that loud shouting helped the humour, whereas quieter, undistorted shouting wouldn't.

People lose sight of the wider purpose of the task when they focus solely and entirely on their own job.

So, the lack of audience reaction to 'The Builders' was due to us performing to a stony-faced horde of ex-Vikings, filling seats in the front, 35 per cent of the studio audience.

But, as I said, it was a perfectly decent show.

James Appleby Stubbs

To play Stubbs, the man who 'you may pay a little more for, but you get a really professional job', JHD cast James Appleby. A Lambeth-born actor, James took the dialogue and embodied the part of Stubbs beautifully as a competent contrast to David Kelly's lackadaisical O'Reilly.

In a similar fashion to his character in *Fawlty*, James Appleby was a stalwart of TV, where he was almost always cast as a policeman or a guard in everything from *Softly, Softly* to *Love Thy Neighbour*. He also did his duty on *Doctor Who* – playing two guards and a policeman over three different serials!

Straight after recording 'The Builders', James stepped into costume drama and appeared in the BBC's 1975 production of *North and South* as Pinfold, and continued to grace our screens well into the 1990s.

JOHN CLEESE'S TOP FAWLTY TOWERS MOMENTS

2

'I'M GOING TO SEE MR O'REILLY, DEAR.
THEN I THINK I MIGHT GO TO CANADA …'

THE WEDDING PARTY

The third episode, 'The Wedding Party', was more complicated, because we had a larger cast and more changes of scene.

The episode was entirely about sex – or at least, Basil's attitude to it, exploring the respectable point about sex that the ones that are most censorious about it are normally the ones most obsessed with it.

For example, there's that story about an old lady who complained to the police about a man in a house down the road exposing himself.

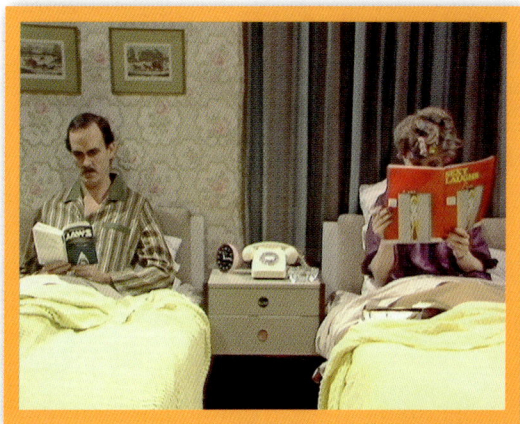

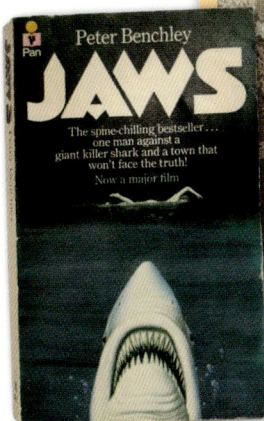

When the police officers visited, they looked carefully at where she was pointing.

'We can't see him,' they told her.

'Well,' she said, 'you have to get on top of the wardrobe and use the binoculars.'

So anyway . . .

The first few scenes of 'The Wedding Party' concern Sybil flirting with an attractive younger man, the appearance of the coquettish Mrs Peignoir, who charms Basil in a way to which he is not accustomed, and Polly kissing her boyfriend by the reception desk. Connie and I wrote all of this to place sexuality firmly in Basil's mind.

We are winding him up so that he will later overreact.

Then, an attractive couple, Jean and Alan, who are friends of Polly, arrive to confirm their room. They are tickled by his progressively more disapproving attitude, which winds him up a lot more. Then two more guests arrive, Mr and Mrs Lloyd.

From now on, Connie and I contrived a series of scenes where Basil saw or overheard behaviour that convinced him that all the guests and Polly were involved in sexual escapades on a Sodom and Gomorrah scale, with the result that he eventually confronts the whole wedding party and tells them to leave.

When he finally realises his mistake, he apologises in a frenzied speech, in which he tries to explain his extraordinary behaviour. In the eyes of the guests, he is clearly insane.

Much later, he is downstairs listening to music when a latecomer arrives. This is, to his surprise, Mrs Peignoir. She's tipsy and she flirts with him, knowing he is terrified of being seen. This continues as he opens a window in her room. Basil escapes to his bedroom, and there is a knock at the door. It's Mrs Peignoir, returning the tape recorder he left in her room. She teases him wickedly. He gets back to his bedroom but is terrified by another knock at the door.

Above left: An intimate look into the Fawltys' married life! Basil reading *Jaws* seemed highly appropriate, it contrasts brilliantly with Sybil casually smoking, reading her magazine (*Sexy Laughs*) with her hair in rollers.

Above: Sybil sends Basil to investigate some strange noises in the hotel hallways – which turn out to be a rather jolly Manuel, back from celebrating his birthday.

Opposite page top: Basil holds his tape recorder and smiles at the delightful Mrs Peignoir (Yvonne Gilan) . . . Connie and I had a little fun with the name 'Peignoir', as it is the French word for a sexy dressing-gown/nightdress garment. It perfectly aligns with the character's coquettishness.

Opposite page, bottom left: Basil is clearly not impressed by Alan (Trevor Adams) and Jean (April Walker) when they arrive at the hotel.

Above: Basil's worst fears about modern-day morality seem to be confirmed as he sees Mr Lloyd (Conrad Phillips) embrace Polly!

Right: Mrs Lloyd (Diana King) is alarmed by the sight of Manuel's legs appearing from a basket in the kitchen . . . More basket-based body humour will follow in the second series, in 'The Kipper and the Corpse', of course.

Trevor Adams
Alan Bruce

'The Wedding Party's snappily dressed ladies' man (whose electric razor is always hungry for batteries!) was played by RADA graduate Trevor Adams.

After a year of Shakespeare on the stage in Stratford-upon-Avon, Trevor fell into television just in time for the 60s to become the 70s, when young men with long hair were required everywhere! Trevor would make memorable guest appearances in *Dixon of Dock Green* and Granada TV's *Crown Court* . . . He also enjoyed a semi-regular role in *The Professionals*.

The year after his episode of *Fawlty*, Trevor was cast in *The Fall and Rise of Reginald Perrin*, as series regular Tony Webster – a character with a few similarities to Alan.

Trevor left the acting profession in the early 1980s when he moved to Norwich and successfully retrained as a solicitor – events even Basil would be impressed by!

Basil assumes it's Mrs Peignoir and pleads with her to leave him alone. Sybil reveals it's her. She tells him she heard a burglar downstairs. He runs down and sees a shadowy figure (Manuel, who's returned from his birthday celebration) and tries to knock him out with a frying pan. Manuel falls. And in the dark, Basil stumbles onto him. The lights go on, and the wedding party, just returning, stare at a trouserless Basil sitting on Manuel's recumbent figure with frying pan raised, which is my favourite moment in 'The Wedding Party'.

I watched this episode shortly before writing this, and I was surprised by how much I laughed. I was also surprised there were so many things that were not right!

I am proud of:

1. The acting of the young couple, Mrs Lloyd, Polly and Manuel – all excellent. Sybil is better than excellent – utterly superb. Basil bickering at the start and also reacting to Sybil's telling him he's made a fool of himself with the family.

2. Some of JHD's shooting, especially the way he moves the plot on by showing action in the background – very classy.

3. The scenes giving rise to Basil's suspicions are concisely written – just the right length.

I am disappointed by:

1. My acting in the first scenes with the young couple. I'm a bit too intense. Maybe Basil should be more disapproving and not quite so angry.

2. When I am talking to Sybil through the bedroom door, thinking she's Mrs Peignoir, I take too long to realise it's Sybil. I should have recognised her voice sooner.

'The Wedding Party'

(aka: 'Morality')

SERIES 1 EPISODE 3

Recorded: 10 August 1975 (TC8)

First transmission: 3 October 1975

Guest stars: Yvonne Gilan (Mrs Peignoir), Conrad Phillips (Mr Lloyd), Diana King (Mrs Lloyd), Alan Bruce (Trevor Adams), April Walker (Jean Wilson), Jay Neill (Bar Guest)

Uncredited: Mark Allington, John Wilder, Kathleen Heath (Hotel Guests)

Below: Basil attempts to talk himself out of his impromptu room search! With Jean (April Walker), Alan (Trevor Adams) and Mrs Lloyd (Diana King) sitting on the bed.

Below right: The wedding party arrive back at the hotel to face the alarming sight of Basil in his underpants, on top of Manuel and brandishing a saucepan … Cue an absolutely wonderful closing line: 'We've been to a wedding!'

3. The two moments when the actors have to hold up the dialogue while the studio audience applauds. We should have edited the applause out by going to a close-up.

4. Script weakness when Basil plays music while talking to Mrs Peignoir and then taking the tape recorder and leaving it in her room. She needs a reason to go to Basil's bedroom, but we should have thought of a better one. Playing the music is too unmotivated.

5. I find it unconvincing that Basil goes down to the lobby at the very end because Sybil says something about a burglar. Sybil should have seen a shadowy figure (Manuel) and hurried upstairs to summon Basil, and been more urgent knocking on the door.

6. The shooting of the very end, when the family arrive back at the hotel, is rather messy. We should have re-shot it. I fell clumsily on top of Manuel, so the sequence should have been sharper.

Perhaps JHD didn't re-shoot the ending because there wasn't enough time! It was quite a long show, and we had to be completely finished on the dot of ten o'clock because at that moment the cameras had to be switched off! (This was fatuous executive thinking of the worst, most rigid kind.)

Yvonne Gilan
Mrs Peignoir

'The Wedding Party' sees the glamorous and cultured French antique dealer Mrs Peignoir enjoy a two-night stay at the hotel . . . and crave the company of Basil Fawlty!

Scottish actress Yvonne Gilan brings a pitch-perfect French accent and natural charm to the part of Mrs Peignoir, drawing every ounce of humour out of every awkward encounter with Basil.

Yvonne was no stranger to comedy after starring in Alan Bennett's 1966 satirical comedy sketch show (and *Monty Python* influence), *On the Margin*, which also featured a pre-Sybil Prunella Scales.

Apart from comedy, Yvonne enjoyed dozens of memorable roles, from *Dixon of Dock Green* and *Crossroads* to *Shoestring*. The 1980s would see her juggle television appearances in the likes of *EastEnders* and *Vanity Fair* with big-screen outings. Notable film parts included both 1981's *Chariots of Fire* and later, Steven Spielberg's *Empire of the Sun* in 1987.

Away from acting, Yvonne wrote an award-winning screenplay for 1964 experimental film *The Peaches*, and in later years worked at the University of Oxford as a motivational speaker, eventually earning a fellowship.

'GOOD NIGHT! WE'VE BEEN TO A WEDDING!'

THE HOTEL INSPECTORS

The plot of Episode Four, 'The Hotel Inspectors', is a simple one: Sybil tells Basil that her friend Audrey says that there are a trio of hotel inspectors in town, whose recommendations can make or break a hotel. A particularly annoying guest, Mr Hutchinson, has already crossed swords with Basil when he makes a casual remark that Basil construes as meaning he is one of the inspectors. Basil immediately switches his behaviour from

insulting to fawning. He continues his self-abasement until Sybil, who has overheard Mr Hutchinson on a phone call, reveals that he is a spoon salesman. Basil resents Hutchinson for 'deceiving' him and becomes hostile.

Basil next decides that a guest called Mr Walt is the hotel inspector and starts bootlicking him. When Hutchinson starts complaining about the service, Basil tries to quieten him so that Walt will not hear. Basil claps his hand over Hutchinson's mouth so strongly that Hutchinson passes out and has to be carried away to recover.

Basil explains to Walt that Hutchinson is an old and valued customer who always behaves likes this, but Hutchinson returns and beats him up, before going upstairs.

Basil, terrified that Walt will write about all this in the inspectors' magazine, now pleads with Walt not to do so:

Basil: The only danger is that somebody will think that he isn't satisfied about something or the fighting is real and tell somebody. You won't mention it, will you? We'd love to offer you dinner here tonight as our guest to show our gratitude.

Opposite page: Wonderful scenes of misunderstanding at the hotel's reception, desk, as Basil and Sybil welcome Mr Hutchinson (Bernard Cribbins) and Mr Walt (James Cossins) to the hotel.

Above: 'This wine is corked' – this whole sequence with the wine was ad-libbed during recording. It was a joke from God!

Below: More brilliance from Bernard, as Mr Hutchinson is about to get special service . . .

Above: The glorious scene where Basil whimpers and begs Mr Walt not to give the hotel a bad review . . .

Basil: All right. £50, then.

Walt: Beg your pardon?

Basil: £50 not to mention it.

Walt: £50?

Basil: £60 not to write about it, articles, books, letters.

Walt: I'm afraid I really don't . . .

Basil: Please! It's taken us 12 years to build this place up. Don't put this in the book. We're finished if you . . . Please don't.

Walt: Book? What book?

Basil: The hotel guide. Sorry, I shouldn't have mentioned it. What have I done?

Walt: You've got me confused with someone else.

(Basil starts to whimper)

Walt: I've nothing to do with any hotel guide. I'm down here for the exhibition. I sell outboard motors. All right?

Walt: What?

Basil: Dinner tonight? Would you?

Walt: No, I can't tonight. Thank you.

Basil: Tomorrow night?

Walt: I shall be leaving tomorrow. I'm sorry.

James Cossins / Mr Walt

Mr Walt is, without doubt, the most stony-faced seller of outboard motors to ever visit Torquay! A no-nonsense man who appreciates his wine, it is only when faced with Basil's agonised pleading that Walt's fierce guard comes down!

With that effortless intense glare and trimmed moustache, it is no surprise that James Cossins served in the RAF before getting into acting. Leaving RADA and entering repertory theatre, James honed his craft on stage throughout the 50s and 60s and became a much-in-demand guest actor who could

be relied upon to play all manner of authority figures.

Small-screen highlights include guest turns in *Callan*, *The Good Life* and *All Creatures Great and Small*. One of his only regular roles was as Major Andrews in the first series of the Richard Briers comedy, *All in Good Faith*.

Much like *A Touch of Class*'s Michael Gwynn, James also played a memorable instructor frustrated by Frank Spencer, in *Some Mothers Do 'Ave 'Em* ('The P. R. Course').

On the cinema screen, James notched up credits in *The Man With The Golden Gun*, *How I Won the War* and *Gandhi*. Not bad going for an outboard motor salesman!

Basil: What? Outboard motors? You're not an inspector?

Walt: No.

Basil: Not on the side?

Walt: No.

Basil: Swear to God?

Walt: I tell you, I have nothing to do with it.

Basil: Oh, thank you. Thank you so much. I don't know how I could ever ... Thanks! Thanks!

Basil recovers, kisses Walt, and runs to the kitchen.

Three men now arrive who are clearly hotel inspectors. When Hutchinson comes down the stairs with his case, Basil and Manuel catch up with him, attack him with custard pies, and kick him out of the hotel. The three inspectors watch this in

'The Hotel Inspectors'

Recorded: 17 August 1975 (TC8)

First transmission: 10 October 1975

Guest stars: Bernard Cribbins (Mr Hutchinson), James Cossins (Mr Walt), Geoffrey Morris (John), Peter Brett (Brian)

Uncredited: Lewis Alexander (Chris).

SERIES 1
EPISODE 4

disbelief. When Basil returns to reception, he suddenly realises who they are, and they have just seen the assault on Mr Hutchinson. Basil screams! Black-out!!

Not only was the plot simple, all the action was confined to the reception area and the dining room. However, the difficult part was the number and complexity of short scenes in the dining area. Fortunately, we had two of the best comedy actors in England to help us. Bernard Cribbins, whom I had adored since before I was born, and Jimmy Cossins, fresh from his hilarious performance as the unforgettable driving instructor in Dick Clement's comedy thriller *Otley*.

Left and below: The three genuine hotel inspectors – led by Geoffrey Morris (John), Peter Brett (Brian, with the beard) and Lewis Alexander (Chris) – arrive at the hotel, much to Basil's alarm!

Bernard Cribbins
Mr Hutchinson

Of all the guests to stay at Fawlty Towers, none drove Basil Fawlty quite as close to the edge of madness as Mr Hutchinson, who was unceremoniously ejected from the hotel with a suitcase full of cream and a custard pie to the face!

Such a part called for a skilled performer who really knew their craft. As one of the most loved comedy actors of his generation, Bernard Cribbins was more than up to the job.

Born in Oldham, Lancashire in 1928, Bernard was drawn straight from school into his local theatre club and onwards to repertory theatre. With the constant turnaround of productions, 'rep' was the best kind of education for an actor and Cribbins prospered with his natural energy and comic timing winning him great praise.

By the late 1950s, his breathless knack for playing a lovable fool saw Cribbins become a fixture at the cinema, notably sharing the screen with Peter Sellers in *The Wrong Arm of the Law*. Other early film roles included two Carry On films and *Crooks in Cloisters*.

By the late 1960s, Bernard had built up a side career as a pop singer – taking advantage of his screen fame – with several charting novelty records to his name.

Another memorable film came in 1966 as Bernard co-starred in the big-screen *Doctor Who* outing, *Daleks' Invasion Earth 2150 A.D.*

When Bernard got the call to appear in 'The Hotel Inspectors', he was fresh from a run of 70s film hits (*The Railway Children* and the Alfred Hitchcock thriller *Frenzy*) and his own sketch series for ITV, *Cribbins*.

Away from drama and comedy, Bernard was also one of the most popular readers on the BBC children's show *Jackanory* and narrated the stop-motion animated series *The Wombles*.

In a career which spanned over eight decades, Bernard enjoyed a well-earned national treasure status and in the 2000s found a whole new audience in CBBC hit *Old Jack's Boat* and a return to *Doctor Who*.

The accuracy and skill of these great performers, plus, of course, Manuel, Polly and Sybil, meant that we were able to shoot all the misunderstandings and changes of attitudes, and switching of tables and plates of food, and rough-housing, and slapstick, and quick-fire repartee, in the paltry four and a half days' rehearsal and two hours in the recording studio that the BBC executives allowed us.

It was the episode that, so far, I was most proud of.

But of course, the very next day we were all sitting round a large, rather cheap table, reading the script for next week's show …

'PLEASE, SEÑOR, MR FAWLTY WANTS TO SAY ADIOS!'

GOURMET NIGHT

'Gourmet Night' features some of *Fawlty Towers*' most memorable moments: Basil thrashing his car, Polly, Manuel and Sybil doing cabaret, and 'Well, if you don't like duck . . . you're stuck.'

Again, the plot for 'Gourmet Night' was simple. Basil wants to organise a special dinner for Torquay sophisticates, and he hires a special chef for the occasion. On the big night, the chef becomes incapacitated, so Basil has to get the food from a Torquay restaurant run by a friend, André. Consequently, the menu suddenly becomes very restricted: 'Duck with orange. Duck with cherries. Duck surprise.'

'What's Duck surprise?'

'Well . . . That's Duck without orange or cherries.'

Basil now jumps in his car and races to his friend's restaurant, where he picks up the roast duck (with appropriate sauces) and speeds back to his hotel – where disaster strikes, in the form of the kitchen's swing door. The duck is dropped on the floor, Manuel gets his foot stuck in it, and Basil, knocked by the door, falls and squashes it. The duck is now unpresentable.

Basil races back to André's restaurant. We see the latest duck given to him, but as he is thanking André, a waiter takes it and puts another covered dish in its place. Basil takes that and hares off.

Meanwhile, back at the hotel, Manuel, Polly and Sybil try to pass the time for the increasingly bored and annoyed guests – Manuel plays the guitar, Polly sings and Sybil tells a couple of slightly off-colour jokes.

Meanwhile, Basil's car has stalled. He can't start it, so he shouts abuse and threats at it. Finally, in a fury, he gets out of the car, runs to get a branch, and then thrashes the car mercilessly.

Back at the hotel – more cabaret.

Then Basil is seen running up the drive of the hotel, just managing to balance the tray, up the steps, into the kitchen and through the door to the diners. He proclaims, 'Ladies and gentlemen, so sorry to have kept you waiting,' and lifts up the silver cover of the serving dish, revealing a nasty pink trifle. He hurriedly slams the cover back down and stands there, hoping for a miracle. Then he takes the cover off, and, putting both hands into the trifle, he feels around, in case the duck is lurking there.

This is my favourite moment in the whole of the first series of *Fawlty Towers*. When someone keeps on trying for success, even when the odds against it have become quite astronomical, there is something rather magnificent about uninterrupted optimism. (Rather like the line, 'Nobody's perfect', at the end of *Some Like It Hot*.)

Back to the dinner . . .

There is a stunned silence.

Basil asks cheerfully, 'Who's for trifle?'

A guest asks, 'What happened to the duck?'

Basil . . . 'Duck's off. Sorry!'

Black-out! (You can't top that.)

After this episode had been transmitted, I sensed something had changed. Thrashing the car had hit a nerve with the British public. Everyone was talking about it, with an enthusiasm and warmth that was new for *Fawlty Towers*. Absurdly large numbers of people shared their hatred of their cars with me, telling me that Basil's

rage was exactly how they had felt on similar occasions.

I felt proud we had offered such useful therapy to so many – that finally releasing years of pent-up fury had such a cathartic effect.

I think that many viewers felt an affection for Basil, even though he was basically a horrible human being, because they would have sometimes liked to behave like him. It was only overpowering English repression that kept them out of jail.

For those of you who are interested in comedy technique, there are two other lessons from 'Gourmet Night'.

The first is very basic.

The audience always wants to believe in what's happening, because the moment they start not believing is the moment when they stop having a good time.

Above: The regular Fawlty staff are joined by their guest chef, Kurt (Steve Plytas) . . .

Below: . . . but poor Kurt had a bit of a drink problem! For this scene we intended to actually show Kurt being sick. We carefully rehearsed it and recorded it, but decided to edit it out from the final broadcast. It was just a bit too graphic for our show.

Right: Basil runs out of André's restaurant with a very special silver platter under his arm . . .

I had learned right after Cambridge, when the 1963 Footlights Revue played in the West End for five months, that if you fuck up – suddenly drying up because you've forgotten your lines, or falling over by accident, or going missing when you should be entering the scene – you 'lose' the audience. They go silent, and disappointed because their belief in what's happening is destroyed. The spell is broken, and it takes ages – ages! – to win back their confidence, so they can start enjoying themselves again.

But there's another way to lose them, and then you never quite win them back,

and that's having something in the script that the audience doesn't believe, that they cannot accept as possible. Quite simply, the plot stops working!

At this moment the audience doesn't understand what's happening and they basically check out. They can never really believe in the story again, because they know something's not right.

And the way to guarantee this disaster is to have too many coincidences.

The audience will always accept one coincidence. They might – *just* – accept two. Three? Forget it. That's the sound of theatre seats springing upright.

Would the audience accept Basil's car breaking down exactly when he most needs it to work? Right out of the blue, on this day of all days?! No. It must not be a coincidence.

So, there are references throughout the script that the car is having problems and badly needs to be taken into the garage. Then, when it does break down, it's not right out of the blue. It's acceptable.

Say you write a character of a doctor who is the spitting image of the President of Transylvania, that's OK. The audience will buy that. But if the doctor's wife looks exactly like the President's wife . . . the audience thinks, 'Oh no! That's ridiculous. What kind of idiot do they think I am?'

André Maranne / André
Steve Plytas / Kurt

With the theme of 'Gourmet Night' established as a night of culinary greatness coming to Fawlty Towers, two new characters were called for.

It is Torquay restaurateur André who inspires Basil and Sybil to run their special night and hire his old friend Kurt.

André was played by the French-born British actor André Maranne, who also lent his name to his character. As an Anglo-French actor in Britain, André was very much in demand on film and TV. His most notable role was that of Sergeant François Chevalier in six Pink Panther films alongside Peter Sellers.

Greek actor Steve Plytas was cast as the enthusiastic chef who (as we see, for good reason!) – stays off the drink when he works.

Steve was another veteran performer who was much in demand for playing Greek characters in British-made films and TV series. He can be seen in literally everything: from James Bond films, to episodes of *Minder*, *The Two Ronnies* and *Batman*!

So, if you want something to happen at the end of a plot that might look too much of a coincidence, put a 'signpost' or two (carefully disguised) earlier in the plot. And this can be done in a slightly arbitrary way.

Dennis Norden once told me, 'If someone in the first scene of a film coughs once, that means they have a cough. If they cough twice, that means they're sick. If they cough three times, they're going to die.'

So, the 'signposts' need to be hidden if it's a whodunit. They need to be subtle if it's a comedy. If they're obvious, people will guess the ending, and you're dead. Unless you're making a Marvel film . . . And if it's a Bond film, where the signposts are intentionally invisible, you had best forget trying to follow the plot, and just enjoy the chases and special effects.

The other lesson from 'Gourmet Night' is that parallel storylines can help to advance an episode's plot more rapidly, and therefore more comedically, than a single story-line. The two separate stories are: Basil racing to and fro fetching ducks, and Sybil, Manuel and Polly trying to pass the time by doing cabaret for the guests.

By cutting between the two we can jump the story forward, keep the pressure up, and avoid relaxing the tempo.

You see, in comedy, pace is everything. A missed beat immediately takes the pressure off, and checks the necessary momentum.

'Gourmet Night'

SERIES 1 EPISODE 5

Recorded: 7 September 1975 (TC8)

First transmission: 17 October 1975

Guest stars: André Maranne (André), Steve Plytas (Kurt), Alan Cuthbertson (Colonel Hall), Ann Way (Mrs Hall), Richard Caldicott (Mr Twitchen), Betty Huntley-Wright (Mrs Twitchen), Jeffrey Segal (Mr Heath), Elizabeth Benson (Mrs Heath), Tony Page (Master Heath).

Uncredited: Steve Kelly (Lorry Driver), Michael Dalton (Waiter)

Below: Polly and Manuel do their utmost to entertain the gourmet guests Colonel Hall (Alan Cuthbertson) and Mrs Hall (Ann Way) whilst they wait for their duck . . .

Right: 'Well, don't say I haven't warned you!

'I've laid it on the line to you time and time again!

'Right! Well, this is it!

'I'm gonna give you a damn good thrashing!'

This scene has gone down in the history books and is one of the icons of the series. We actually filmed it all rather quickly with a load of other location work (see page 129), but I took a great deal of care finding a branch with *just* the right amount of bend – it made all the difference to the joke!

To return to my point from pages 75–6, the reason Jimmy Gilbert was so wrong when he told me 'You're going to have to get them out of the hotel more' is that staying in the hotel enabled the pressure on Basil to build up.

There were then only two ways that that pressure could easily ebb away.

One would be if the script failed to keep the story developing. Any time there's no forward momentum, the plot becomes static and you lose the audience's attention slightly. And then, terminally.

The other way is to have a lot of time lapses. A time lapse is like taking your foot off the accelerator. If you've managed to get the audience on a roll, you lose them partially every time you take a break. That's why the greatest laughter is generated by the best farces. They get us laughing and then keep us on a roll as the action unfolds, and unfolds and unfolds, and our innards endanger themselves.

So, Connie and I deliberately kept time lapses to an absolute minimum, which simply meant keeping the scenes as continuous as possible. This is much harder to write: you have to avoid just ending a scene and then starting on a new one. It requires much more thought to construct a plot where one scene glides effortlessly into another, with the action moving seamlessly into another room, or another actor joins a scene, or simultaneous action elsewhere switches the audience's attention to a different location. But a continuous flow of plot development will always build more audience hysteria than a staccato one.

Alan Cuthbertson
Colonel Hall

Stiff-upper-lipped, mustachioed men of a certain age seemed to be drawn to Torquay, but 'Gourmet Night's Colonel Hall was one of the most snobbish by far!

Another familiar face from dozens of films and TV shows, Alan Cuthbertson was almost exclusively cast as stern-faced British military characters, despite hailing from Perth, Australia!

After serving as a flight lieutenant with the Royal Australian Air Force in the Second World War, Alan emigrated to Britain and rediscovered his passion for acting, which he had enjoyed from an early age. Once in London, television soon came calling, snapping up Alan for appearances in cult favourites *The Avengers*, *The Champions* and *UFO*.

Alan would also become a regular character player on the hugely popular *Morecambe and Wise Show* and appear as the annoying neighbour Tarquin Spry in sitcom *Terry and June*.

In later years Alan appeared in the star-studded film *The Sea Wolves* and Michael Palin's autobiographical TV film *East of Ipswich*.

5 · JOHN CLEESE'S TOP FAWLTY TOWERS MOMENTS

'WELL, ER, WHO'S FOR TRIFLE?!'

THE GERMANS

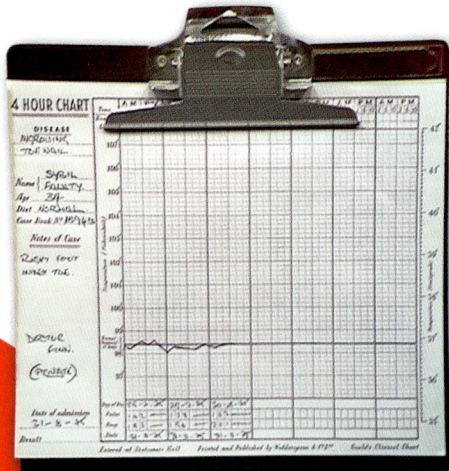

L et's consider the final show of the first series, 'The Germans'. This episode has always caused confusion, because it's not really one episode: it's more like two joined together. The first half is 'The Fire Drill'. And the Germans don't even arrive until that is concluded, with Basil being taken to hospital! The episode starts in hospital, too. Sybil is there for an operation on an in-grown toenail – just enough to keep her out of the hotel for the duration of the show. This is important, because if she was at the hotel, she would have taken control and Basil's catastrophic handling of the fire drill and the Germans' arrival would have been restrained.

The first scene establishes that Basil has a busy day ahead and that Sybil is going to keep reminding him of what he needs to do. This well-placed lack of confidence in his abilities winds Basil up, so that when Sybil interrupts his efforts by constantly phoning him when he gets back to the hotel, it makes him progressively more angry.

It is important to note that the whole plot happens during the course of just one day, and there are only three time-breaks in the whole 30 minutes: one to get Basil back from the hospital, another to get him back to the hospital and a third to get him back to the hotel again to greet the Germans. Otherwise, the action is continuous, so that the farcical pressure builds up uninterrupted.

The only reason that we have to get Basil back to the hospital is to emphasise that he's had a bad blow to the head! Because otherwise his subsequent behaviour towards the Germans would not have been believable, even for Basil! We bandage his head to remind the audience of this.

Now, when Basil first gets back to Fawlty Towers, he has one of those aimless chats with the Major when neither party ever gets a thought clearly communicated into the other party's mind. Connie and I loved writing these exchanges.

The Major: Evening, Fawlty. Hampshire won.

Basil: Did it? Oh, isn't that good, how splendid!

The Major: Oh, Fawlty, how's . . . um . . .

Basil: . . . My wife?

The Major: That's it, that's it.

Basil: Fine, absolutely fine. They're taking it out tomorrow morning.

The Major: Is she? Good.

Basil: Not her, the nail. They won't have operated until tomorrow.

The Major: What?

Basil: The nail. They're taking it out tomorrow.

The Major: How did she get a nail in her?

Basil: I thought I told you, Major, she's having her toenail out.

The Major: What, just one of them?

It's pretty clear from an exchange like this, that while Basil is merely very distracted, the Major is out to breakfast, lunch and

dinner, that he is not the sharpest knife in the drawer, is not playing with the full deck, is a couple of sandwiches short of a picnic, that he couldn't pour water out of a wellington boot with the instructions on the heel, and that the lights are on, but no one's home . . . you get my drift?

A minute or two later, the Major explains the difference between two outdated descriptive racial terms. Words that set the media on fire.

Now these words were not uttered by the Prime Minister to Parliament at PMQs, or by the Archbishop of Canterbury during the Coronation ceremony. They were spoken by a character in a comedy show who has patently lost his marbles.

What many people do not comprehend, including some of the BBC's top brass, is this: there are two ways of making fun of someone.

Below: Talking with the Major, big red fire alarm button in view, (which can also be seen in the preceding episode, 'Gourmet Night' – which we recorded *after* 'The Germans' – keep up!).

The first is that you use humorous or insulting insults about them (for example, the way I have just written disparagingly about the Major's cognitive abilities).

The second is that you take the view you want to make fun of . . . And you put that view in the mouth of someone who is incontestably barmy, stupid and ridiculous. In this way, you say: 'These views could only be held by an idiot.' Capisce?

But a certain class of person simply doesn't understand this. When they hear Alf Garnett sounding off, they don't understand that Johnny Speight is making fun of Alf's views, by putting them in the mouth of someone laughable.

These simpletons apparently believe that Connie and I

were propagating far-right propaganda. Because the class of person that I'm talking about suffers from a mental block I called literal-mindedness. That is, they believe that what a person says means exactly what their words say, because they are incapable of comprehending IRONY. They really do not understand that when a person speaks ironically, they mean the opposite of the words they are saying. And the literal-minded don't get irony, (or sarcasm, or metaphor, or comic exaggeration, or a host of other possible interpretations).

Can you imagine what it would be like to miss the meaning of a lot of what people are saying to you? Of course, it doesn't bother the literal-minded. Because they can only comprehend one of all the possible meanings. So they know that their interpretation must be right, as there simply aren't any others! And our mistake is to take these literal-minded people's opinions seriously. It's like asking someone who is colour-blind to construct a colour chart.

Here endeth the sermon.

Now . . . While Basil and the Major were exchanging messages apparently sympathetic to the Nazis, Polly is looking for her German

phrase book. This reminds the audience of their impending visit and allows the Major to express his view of the Germans, in totally unironic terms.

'Bunch of Krauts, that's what they all are! Bad eggs!' Imagine the uproar at Broadcasting House if Connie and I had written this about Czechs, or Paraguayans or Indonesians or even Scots! We would never have worked again.

Basil now starts work on his list of duties, preparing to put up the moose's head. He places a chair, gets the moose, stands on the chair, and . . . the phone rings.

I am very proud of the next bit.

He looks around and calls for Polly.

Nothing. He waits. Nothing.

So he has to get down and take the moose to reception and pick up the phone. And we, the audience, know who is on the other end. But it's still funny . . .

> **Basil:** I was just doing it, you stupid woman! I just put it down to come here to be reminded by you to do what I'm already doing! I mean, what's the point of reminding me to do what I'm already doing . . . I mean, what is the bloody point??! I'm doing it, aren't I?!

He's right, of course, which makes his indignation even funnier. When he finishes, he leaves the moose head on the reception desk and goes to get a hammer – and Manuel goes behind the desk and rummages about while practising his English. The Major enters and thinks the moose is talking to him. And this is what I love about English farce. We are able to believe – just like the Major believes that the moose is actually talking to him. Many Americans now decide, it's too silly.

'The Germans'

(aka 'The Fire Drill')

Recorded: 31 August 1975 (TC6)

First transmission: 24 October 1975

Guest stars: Claire Davenport (Mrs Wilson), Brenda Cowling (Sister), Louis Mahoney (Doctor), John Lawrence (Mr Sharp), Iris Fry (Mrs Sharp), Willy Bowman, Nick Kane, Lisa Bergmayr, Dan Gillan (German Guests)

Uncredited: Della MacCrea, Martine Holland (Nurses), Ron Musgrove (Doctor), Steve Kelly (Ambulance Driver), Thelma Horrocks, Barbara Bermel (German Women), Michael Mungarvan (Hospital Orderly), Diana Holt, Derek Southern (Hotel Guests Couple).

SERIES 1 EPISODE 6

But the English, who are not generally as literal-minded as Midwesterners, can relax and relish the utter, UTTER silliness of the situation. At the Apollo, I can watch the audience at this moment and many of them are quite hysterical. It makes me feel very happy – as though I've done something useful.

And now we get into the fire drill, which is just ten minutes of cumulative misunderstandings, which for me is the funniest thing we ever wrote. It's based on two simple ideas:

One, that the hotel has two bells: a fire alarm bell, and a burglar alarm bell.

Below: 'Please, Mr. Fawlty, is fire!' – Andy doing some incredible business with flames! Poor Andy suffered second-degree chemical burns during the shot that followed this one (out in reception, whilst looking out of the kitchen door). The chemicals which helped to create the smoke soaked into his clothing. The BBC paid him £700 compensation for the accident.

Two, that during the fire drill, an actual fire starts, and so Basil starts treating the actual fire as though it was just a drill.

So, first the burglar alarm goes off by accident, and Basil has to explain to all the guests who are reacting to what they think is the fire bell, that, it's a different bell, and that the drill hasn't started yet, but they don't understand, so he sounds the fire bell so that they'll recognise it when he rings it, but they now think the drill has started . . . and on and on until Manuel runs up to tell him that there is a real fire in the kitchen but Basil tells him it's not a real fire, just the drill, and when Manuel argues Basil pushes him back into the fire in the kitchen and jams the door shut and then realises there

Above right: Now admitted to hospital with concussion, Basil becomes a patient of Doctor Finn.

is a real fire and has to tell the guests, and there's panic and Basil gets knocked out.

This mammoth misunderstanding fest lasts for nine minutes and I'm proud we managed to prolong it for such an extended period, without ever repeating the same joke. The only bad bit is right at the end when Basil gets knocked out. It's poorly done, and very unconvincing, with Basil straightening up and banging his head on a frying pan that Manuel is holding. A weak idea and we should have come up with something better. In the stage show, we now have the moose head fall off the wall on top of Basil. Much more believable and funnier too.

So now Basil is in hospital, being told to rest. He says he has to go back to the hotel as he's badly needed there.

Sybil: No you're not. It's running beautifully without you.

Basil: Polly can't cope!

Sybil: Well, she can't fall over waiters, or get herself jammed under desks, or start burglar alarms, or lock people in burning rooms, or fire fire extinguishers straight in her own face. But I should think the hotel can do without that sort of coping for a couple of days, what do you think, Basil . . . hmmm?

Louis Mahoney
Doctor Finn

In 'The Germans' we meet Doctor Finn, who tends to Sybil's toenail, and – once he has his fire extinguisher / saucepan accident – Basil's head as well!

Gambian-born British actor Louis Mahoney made the perfect casting for the doctor, perhaps in part because he originally moved to England from Gambia to study medicine. Leaving behind medicine to pursue acting at the Central School of Speech and Drama, Louis started his career in rep before joining the Royal Shakespeare Company as one of the first Black actors in the company.

By the time of his casting in 'The Germans', Louis was already a veteran of dozens of BBC and ITV productions, from *Z Cars* and *Doctor Who* to *The Professionals*. Later work saw him in the role of Jake, a regular on *The Lenny Henry Show*, and take to the stage as part of the original cast of Alan Bennett's *Allelujah!*

In addition to his acting career, Louis was an activist and campaigner and for many years represented African-Asian members on the council of Equity, the actors' union.

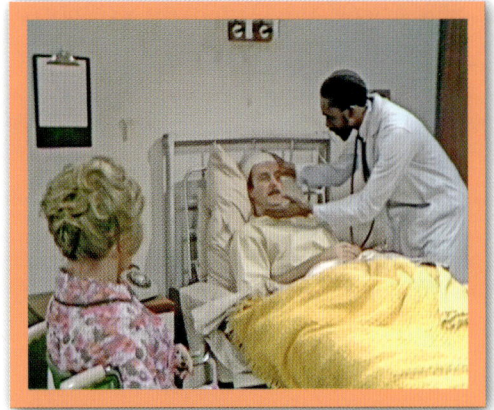

(The doctor comes in)

Doctor: What?

Basil: Oh, hello, doctor.

Basil pretends he's going to sleep, but escapes and rushes back to the hotel, where Polly is already greeting the first German arrivals. To establish before he meets the Germans that he is not himself, he has an exchange with the old ladies.

Miss Tibbs: We don't think you're well, Mr Fawlty.

Basil: Well, perhaps not, but I'll live longer than you.

Miss Gatsby: You must have hurt yourself.

Basil: My dear woman, a blow on the head like that . . . is worth two in the bush.

Miss Tibbs: Oh, we know . . . but it was a nasty shock.

Basil: Mmmmmmmm . . . would you like one? (hits bell) Next, please.

(Two men and two women come down the stairs)

Basil: (a hoarse whisper) Polly! Polly! Are these Germans too?

Polly: Oh yes, but I can deal . . .

Basil: Right, right, here's the plan. I'll stand there and ask them if they want to drink something before the war . . . before their lunch . . . don't mention the war! (he moves in front of the guests, bows and mimes eating and drinking)

2nd German: Can we help you?

Basil: (gives a startled jump) Ah . . . you speak English.

2nd German: Of course.

And we know what happens next. Basil simply can't avoid mentioning the war. A mention of the word 'prawn' and he's talking about Eva Prawn. And when he asks about 'hors d'oeuvres' he continues 'which must be obeyed at all times' and clicks his heels.

And it turns into one of the most iconic of *Fawlty Towers* sequences. People find it extraordinarily funny.

But why? It's a simple idea – a man can't stop talking about the war, to a group of decent, friendly, well-meaning Germans who were school children during the war.

Yes, there are some very good jokes – 'hors d'oeuvres', for example. But why the hysterical laughter?

Above left: Basil returns to the hotel and has a rather abstract exchange with Miss Tibbs and Miss Gatsby.

Below: Polly sees what is going to happen and makes herself scarce . . . just as Basil is about to perform his utterly mad German routine. We actually worked out the funny walk climax in 'The Germans' on the day of recording.

Several points:

1. Basil is not taunting the Germans. The very opposite! He is trying very hard not to. But he keeps harping on about the war because the Germans have triggered an obsession with avoiding the subject to the point where he thinks someone has mentioned Goering when they've said the word 'herring'. If Basil was deliberately trying to goad them, it would change the comedy completely, and although some people would laugh, it would have a very different feel to it – a very uncomfortable, unpleasant one. Unfortunately, the tabloid press sometimes saw the scene as 'sticking it to the Germans'. From our point of view, that could not have been more wrong. We were, in fact, sticking it to the kind of British person who could not see how Germany had changed after the war and were hanging on to stereotypes that had been outdated for thirty years.

2. I suspect that a lot of the notoriety of the German scene was to do with English people's dread of being embarrassed – which can mean that they find other people's embarrassment funny. From the start, Basil's behaviour is beyond embarrassing. Polly's reactions are terribly amusing as she tries to pretend she's not there. But he manages, in a short and intense exchange, to drop every conceivable brick, while trying to make the Germans feel welcome and at home.

3. And finally, his obsession with the war is so overpowering that he finishes by doing a spectacular goose-step because he knows they are a bit upset, and he's hoping the goose-step will CHEER THEM UP!!! Any time someone's effort to succeed ends in complete and utter failure, it's funny provided that the person who fails IS NOT UPSET. The biggest reaction in *Monty Python and the Holy Grail* is the Black Knight scene, where a human being has his arms and legs chopped off. Because the Black Knight is not even DISAPPOINTED. He just goes on goading King Arthur, as though he's on top.

Even when a doctor arrives to take Basil away, he is convinced that he has behaved impeccably, and the fault lies with the Germans' lack of sense of humour. The episode ends when he is knocked out again by the moose falling on his head – nice to bring the moose back to end the show (with the Major still talking to it).

The German Guests

The six German guests who give the episode its title . . . weren't actually all from Germany!

Willy Bowman (dressed in green in the episode) was born in Berlin in 1915 and went on to appear as a prison gangster in *Porridge* and a crime lord in Tim Burton's *Batman*.

Nick Kane played the bald-headed German guest who is seen in the reception scene. Nick was a German actor, with a limited screen CV; *Fawlty* seems to have been his only major role.

Despite his impressive accent, **Dan Gillan** was from Brentford, and had previously played a policeman in *Coronation Street*.

Lisa Bergmayr, **Thelma Horrocks** and **Barbara Bermel**, were also natives of the capital and regular BBC extras.

'I'VE NEVER SEEN ANYONE NOT LAUGH AT THIS!'

9.

REACTION TO THE FIRST SERIES

I'm glad 'The Germans' was the last transmitted episode of the first series ('Gourmet Night' was actually the last to be recorded!). It allowed us to go out with a bang! Albeit not a very loud one. Despite the beating of the car, the moose and the goose-step, the first series of *Fawlty Towers* didn't make that big an impact.

Although there was generally a friendly reception, the media were relatively restrained. I read a very accurate description of it in Graham McCann's excellent book, *Fawlty Towers: The Story of the Sitcom*. Graham, who also wrote the foreword to this book, was a lecturer and fellow at King's College Cambridge, and so is a cut or two above the average newspaper critic. As we are all sensitive to criticism, I thought I would get a more neutral, balanced account of the press reaction that I would write myself. Graham kindly agreed to be plagiarised:

The imminent arrival of this brand-new series seemed barely to register on the journalistic agenda. In stark contrast to the far more competitive and media-savvy marketing style of today's television networks, which trail and trumpet each new offering so strenuously over such a lengthy period that the unfamiliar appears almost overfamiliar by the time it finally reaches the screen, the BBC in 1975 preferred to

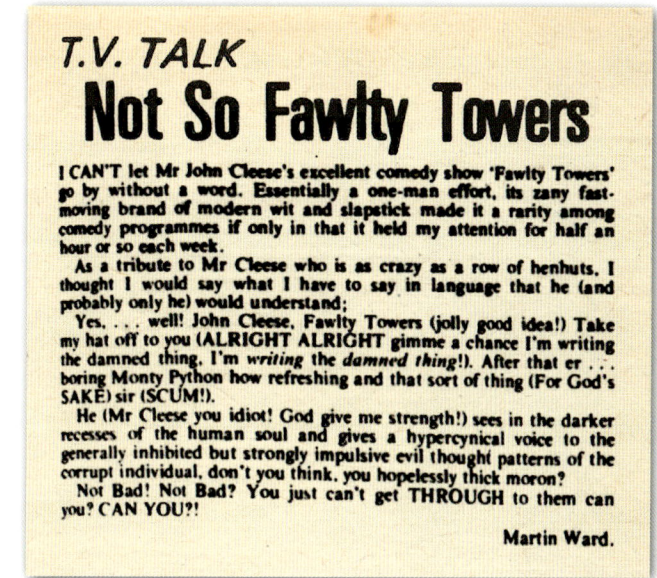

T.V. TALK
Not So Fawlty Towers

I CAN'T let Mr John Cleese's excellent comedy show 'Fawlty Towers' go by without a word. Essentially a one-man effort, its zany fast-moving brand of modern wit and slapstick made it a rarity among comedy programmes if only in that it held my attention for half an hour or so each week.

As a tribute to Mr Cleese who is as crazy as a row of henhuts, I thought I would say what I have to say in language that he (and probably only he) would understand;

Yes, . . . well! John Cleese, Fawlty Towers (jolly good idea!) Take my hat off to you (ALRIGHT ALRIGHT gimme a chance I'm writing the damned thing, I'm *writing* the *damned* thing!). After that er . . . boring Monty Python how refreshing and that sort of thing (For God's SAKE) sir (SCUM!).

He (Mr Cleese you idiot! God give me strength!) sees in the darker recesses of the human soul and gives a hypercynical voice to the generally inhibited but strongly impulsive evil thought patterns of the corrupt individual, don't you think, you hopelessly thick moron?

Not Bad! Not Bad? You just can't get THROUGH to them can you? CAN YOU?!

Martin Ward.

leave *Fawlty Towers*, like most of its other debut series, to tiptoe onto television, and patiently await discovery. There were no big magazine interviews (apart from one two-page feature in the *Radio Times*, which was somewhat compromised by the fact that the author had not yet seen the show), nor any high-profile advertising campaigns or advance screenings, and even the television pages in most of the national newspapers provided nothing more than the most cursory of references to the show's initial appearance. Tim Ewbank, previewing the day's schedules in the *Daily Mail*, did, to his credit, describe *Fawlty Towers* as the 'most promising' of the evening's few new attractions, and an anonymous writer in the *Observer* declared that it

Above: *Daily Express, 31 October 1975.*

Below: *Aberdeen Evening Express, 19 September 1975.*

JOHN CLEESE describes "Fawlty Towers," his new series starting tonight (BBC 2, 9.0) "low comedy with fast movement."

He wrote it with his wife, Connie Booth, basing the idea on an hotelier he met during filming for "Monty Python's Flying Circus."

John plays Basil Fawlty, proprietor of Fawlty Towers, an hotel in Torquay. Although nominally in charge, Basil is totally under the organising thumb of his wife, Sybil (Prunella Scales).

They are aided by Manuel (Andrew Sachs), a trainee waiter from Barcelona, who, on a good day can speak six words of English. Polly (Connie Booth), an art-student, hovers around at meal times to help out and earn enough to get herself through university.

In the first episode Basil tries to improve the class of the hotel's clientele with remarkable results.

Too much of a one-man show

by JACKIE DYASON

IN addition to BBC-1's Dad's Army and The Liver Birds, our Friday night comedy diet now includes BBC-2's **Fawlty Towers**, a series written by John Cleese and his wife Connie Booth, in which they also star, with Prunella Scales and Andrew Sachs.

Cleese plays the zany, eccentric proprietor of the hotel Fawlty Towers, and Prunella Scales plays his nagging wife, who obviously really does all the work. The opening episode (Friday, September 20, 9pm) showed us Cleese, anxious to improve the class of his guests, being taken in by a con-man posing as a rich peer (Michael Gwynn), and being saved in the nick of time from parting with his coin collection by the CID man (Robin Ellis) and the waitress (Connie Booth).

This simple storyline gave ample opportunities for some slapstick comedy interspersed with some Monty Python-like nonsensical dialogue at which Cleese is so clever. For example, Cleese tries to tell the non-English-speaking waiter (Andrew Sachs) to carry some suitcases upstairs in execrable Spanish — until the waiter finally gets the message at the same instant as Cleese decides to do it himself — so they both pick up the cases at the same moment and get tangled up.

Another funny moment occurred when Cleese, on the phone and trying at the same time, rather offhandedly, to get Lord Melbury to fill in the register hears that Melbury is a peer, whereupon he abruptly says "Go away" to the telephone and slams it down. Not very funny on paper perhaps, unless one is tuned in to the acquired taste of Cleese humour.

This was basically the trouble with the piece. There were some exceedingly funny moments, and John Howard Davies' direction kept up a good pace, but the story became rather banal when Cleese was off the screen. Although the rest of the cast were competent enough, the central character was far too necessary to the overall concept for it to be anything other than a rather obvious vehicle for him.

Unfortunately, I was left with the overall impression that if the viewer hadn't already acquired a taste for Python-type comedy, this attempt by John Cleese to broaden his appeal would leave them cold. On the other hand, for those of us already converts, it did provide an opportunity to see a very funny man without the sometimes incomprehensible self-indulgencies of the later Pythons.

If the rest of the series develops the potentialities of the situation without laying too much emphasis on the central character, to the exclusion of other opportunities for comedy in the scripts, it will be very entertaining and a pleasant way of spending half-an-hour on Friday nights.

Above: A one-man show? Really! *The Stage*, 25 September 1975.

Right: Basil – always trying to please?

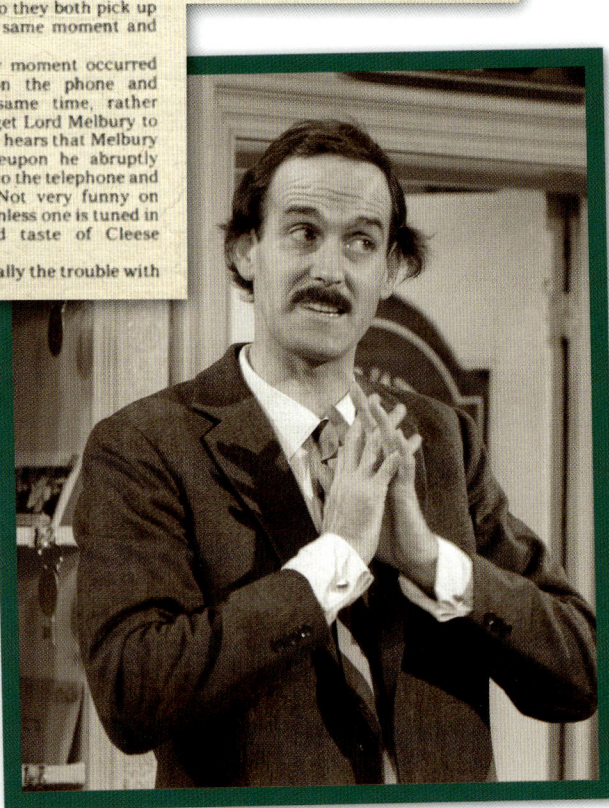

was 'not to be missed by JC fans', but that was more or less the highlight of the pre-publicity.

The first episode, therefore, went out on air rather quietly at 9.00 p.m. on Friday, 19 September on BBC2. There were only three channels in those days in Britain, and Friday nights were, unofficially, the best and most competitive night of the week as far as comedy was concerned. BBC1, for example, had *Dad's Army* (which at that stage was consistently attracting more than 12 million viewers and was considered to be more or less right at its peak) scheduled at 8.00 p.m., followed by another well-established sitcom, *The Liver Birds*, at 8.30 p.m.; ITV meanwhile, was showing Larry Grayson at 8.30 p.m. and a lavish, hour-long *Stanley Baxter Picture Show* special at 9.00 p.m. Thus, faced with the twin daunting challenges of 'follow that' on BBC1 (a completely unfamiliar sitcom having to impress immediately after the screening of two extremely familiar ones) and 'beat that' on ITV (relying on curiosity to lure some viewers away from the unusually high production values of Stanley Baxter's very popular sketch show – which one paper described, rather over-excitedly, as 'one of the major events of the year on television), the first edition of *Fawlty Towers* ended up faring as well as could have been expected. It pulled in a decent enough audience for that time slot on BBC2 (1,868,500 – compared with the 7,726,500 who watched the news on BBC1 and the 11,059,500 who tuned in to Stanley Baxter on ITV), but nonetheless, a relatively modest number of viewers for a show with a real ambition to flourish on mainstream television.

Series One Location Filming

Most of *Fawlty Towers* takes place within the confines of the hotel itself (or in the car park just outside it), the perfect pressure-cooker environment for the magnificent farces to unfold . . . However, during the first series, three episodes called for the characters to briefly venture away from the the hotel . . .

'A Touch of Class'
The *Fawlty Towers* crew filmed the sequence where Polly leaves the branch of Lloyds Bank on 17 December 1974 on Cookham High Street in Berkshire. Production documents reveal that in getting permission, Lloyds Bank were promised that their image would not be 'tarnished in any way' by the programme!

'Gourmet Night'
The scenes where Basil frantically drives his red Austin Countryman to and from the restaurant were all filmed in the London borough of Harrow. The location used for André's restaurant was on Preston Road (where Plato's restaurant was redressed by the art department and the proprietor Theo was paid £20 for his trouble!) . Nearby Mentmore Close would enter comedy legend as the location where Basil's car breaks down and he decides to give it a 'damn good thrashing!'

'The Germans'
For the establishing shot of the hospital where Sybil is having her toenail removed, Northwick Park Hospital in Harrow was used. The crew filmed this shot on 23 July 1975 – the same day all of the 'Gourmet Night' locations were filmed! The BBC donated £30 to the hospital trust in gratitude for allowing the filming.

It was a strange kind of success. In certain circles, among certain people, *Fawlty Towers* had quickly established itself as a favourite topic of conversation, with scenes analysed, characters interpreted and catchphrases (such as Basil's 'Coh!'; Sybil's 'Oh, I know . . .'; Manuel's 'Que?'; and 'Don't mention the war!') repeated on countless spontaneous occasions. Innumerable schoolchildren, office workers, undergraduates, politicians, taxi drivers, builders, caterers and even (and in some cases especially) hotel managers, waiters and chambermaids could be overheard referring to it, and laughing about it, from one week to the next. On the printed page, however, the series had left only the faintest of traces.

The subsequent dearth of reviews for *Fawlty Towers* was, therefore, more or less inevitable, as, in addition to these common problems, the show also had the 'misfortune' of being screened on a Friday – and all British national daily newspapers preferred to use their Saturday editions to showcase the weekend schedules rather than recall the previous evening's output, thus, anything shown on a Friday, regardless of its worth, tended to be ignored by the vast majority of the national critics (and, as the arts pages of the Sunday papers went

Above: 'The Germans' was the only episode of *Fawlty* to not start with a shot of the hotel. The story actually started in Sybil's hospital room.

to press on Friday afternoons, anything shown that night stood less chance of a mention than anything else in any other slot during the week). To make matters worse still, most of the 'quality' broadsheet papers still regarded television, as a potentially 'proper' cultural subject rather than an occasional source of distraction or controversy, with a certain degree of suspicion, considering most of its output to be evanescent and relatively trivial, and thus what critical TV columns existed were by no means guaranteed a daily, or even a weekly, space alongside those that covered the more established areas of the arts.

Fawlty Towers, as a consequence, was never going to register very strongly on the critical radar, because such a radar barely existed. Oliver Pritchett, however, did, to his credit, manage to review the pilot episode the following Monday in London's *Evening Standard*: he remarked that he had found the plot 'thin and obvious', and suspected that all of the other storylines in the series were similarly destined 'to take second place to the manic performances of John Cleese'. He concluded on a slightly more positive note by declaring that, although the first half-hour had been 'a bit frantic in its pursuit of laughs', he, 'would still award it a tentative three stars (out of five) and promise to return'. That, in fact, was more or less that as far as the initial national coverage was concerned, but a few fleeting comments did pop up on the preview pages at the end of that opening week.

The *Daily Express* was especially enthusiastic, with Douglas Orgill recalling the debut as 'hilarious' and asserting that, although he doubted that the next instalment would be able to 'retain the full

impact of the first one', if it turned out to be 'three quarters as good it will suit me'. The *Daily Mirror*, on the other hand, was far from complimentary. According to its previewer – a journalist by the name of Tony Pratt – the opening show had been 'almost a one-man effort' by Cleese and there was 'certainly room for improvement'. Beneath these comments was the following depressing conclusion:

'MIRROR VERDICT: Long John is short on jokes.'

It was a snap judgement that certainly niggled: John Cleese saw the clipping, saved it, and would still be referring to it more than thirty years later.

Another critique that cut deep came from Richard Ingrams, the then-editor of the satirical magazine *Private Eye* and most definitely not an admirer of John Cleese (nor, it seemed, of anyone associated with the Monty Python troupe). Relishing the opportunity to slip in the knife as an occasional TV critic, he proceeded to dismiss the show – not only in print but also in the presence of countless of Cleese's comedy contemporaries – as laboured, banal and unfunny. Cleese was so irritated by the gleeful severity of the attacks that he would wait patiently for the chance to exact his revenge (which, eventually, he would via a sly little gag during the second series in the episode 'The Kipper and the Corpse').

Above: Mr Ingrams (Charles McKeown) with his 'inflatable friend' in 'The Kipper and the Corpse'... A character who shares his name with a *Private Eye* reviewer!

Opposite page: Me and Pru at a press event shortly after the first series was broadcast.

The second episode fared no better, in the sense that it came and went without provoking much published comment at all, but there were signs, by the Friday of the third instalment, that the series was beginning to acquire some influential admirers. Tim Ewbank, previewing 'The Wedding Party' in the *Daily Mail*, hailed the show as 'the best of the Friday laughs at present', while the *Guardian*, in a pithy aside, judged it to be 'highly amusing'. Slowly but surely, a few more viewers were being nudged in the right direction.

It would be wrong, however, to suggest that everything now being committed to print was uniformly positive. Indeed, by far the most substantial response so far, by Peter Buckman in the *Listener* magazine on 9 October, was actually fairly damning:

'Unfair though it may be to expect pure genius to drip always from Cleese's pen, he and his wife have given themselves pretty hollow characters to play, and they have some trouble stretching the thing over half-an-hour. Of the cast, only Prunella Scales, as the proprietor's nagging wife, brings any real depth to her part, and this makes her considerably more sympathetic than the monster she is supposed to be. Cleese, moreover, while being lovably manic, is not exactly a great character actor, and tends to do little more than vary his pitch from forte to fortissimo in his effort to flog matters along. Most regrettably of all, a large part of the funny business revolves around that venerable stooge, a Spanish waiter with faulty English. While not for a moment accusing Cleese and Booth of racism, jokes about dagos and wops horrified some Americans who were watching with me, and once this had been pointed out, I began to notice all sorts of racist jibes.'

Such a negative reaction, however, was far from typical at the time.

Midway through its run, for instance, the show was being billed by the *Daily Express* as the 'funniest' and 'most essential viewing of the week', and even the previously unimpressed *Daily Mirror* was now advising its readers to 'put [the show] on tonight's menu'. Clive James – probably the most insightful, as well as wittiest, of a new generation of TV critics – had been 'on holiday' when the sitcom had started, but he managed to note (after the third episode) that the show had 'several times had me retching with laughter' before his 'on holiday' sign reappeared. As a consensus started to take shape, so a growing number of other commentators prepared to commit an opinion to print. Peter Fiddick, for example, reviewed the penultimate episode ('Gourmet Night') in the *Guardian*, praising the show for being 'something out of a new mould', and applauding the cast for their willingness to 'cheerfully embrace a range of comic methods that stretches from

Pythonesque funny walks, through split-second slapstick, to comedy of manners'. Prunella Scales was the actor singled out for the warmest praise of all, with Fiddick saying of her performance: '[She is] a smashing actress at any time, [and is] having a ball as Mrs Fawlty, adopting a refined whine somewhere between Henry Cooper and Twiggy, and attacking Cleese at the level she finds him, which is usually just below the nipples.'

The broadcaster Joan Bakewell, writing in the *Listener* the following week, spoke as one of those who had been drawn to the show belatedly after being made curious by all of the positive talk: 'I have only recently caught up with *Fawlty Towers* and come to see what I have been missing. Considering how many different styles of humour it taps, it should fail. And it almost does: we laugh with relief that John Cleese and his cronies continually pull it off. There is rattling repartee, full blown custard pie stuff, funny chases and walks, comic stereotypes and hilarious Laurel and Hardy routines.' There were similarly positive observations, here and there, as the days went by, as well as welcome little asides in the odd diary column. The sitcom's impact remained far from spectacular, but at least it was acquiring a reassuringly positive profile: 'The critics,' as John Cleese would put it, 'began to quite like it.'

By the end of the run, they liked it a lot. On the morning of Friday, 24 October, when the series was about to come to a close, there was a considerable amount of admiration expressed for what had been witnessed over the previous few weeks, as well as, it seemed, a fair measure of genuine regret that the run was now on the verge

THE DAY MR CLEESE GAVE ANDREW A REAL GOOD BASHING...

THE Spanish waiter who had to bear the brunt of John Cleese's fury in BBC-2's **FAWLTY TOWERS** has some real life bruises and scars to remind him of the series.

Actor Andrew Sachs, who played the long suffering Manuel, said :

"John was brutal. In one programme he had to hit me over the head with a frying pan, which fortunately was padded. It was fine in rehearsals. He hit me very gently. But on the actual take he got carried away and gave me a real bashing. I thought I would never get up again."

In the final episode Manuel set the hotel kitchen on fire and ran into the lobby with his jacket smouldering.

"The fire was handled beautifully but the chemicals they used on my jacket soaked right through and burned my skin. It is healing up now but it will be a long time before I can go in the sun again."

In spite of that the series, he says, was great fun to work on and most of the time was spent with the cast falling about laughing.

"I only had to look at John's dead pan face and I burst out laughing," said Andrew.

He had good training for the series. For the past nine months he has been appearing in the hit comedy No Sex Please, We're British at London's Strand Theatre.

"I reckon to draw blood at least once a fortnight in that," he says. "I have to leap through a serving hatch and people throw heavy books at me. Once I thought my ribs were caving in but I am hardened to it now."

Andrew (45), who could easily be taken for a natural Spaniard in Fawlty Towers cannot speak a word of Spanish. He was in fact born in Germany and fled to England with his family during the war.

Married with three children, he has worked mainly in the theatre during his career but is now hoping to do more television.

"Another series of Fawlty Towers would be marvellous," he says.

JOHN CLEESE
— wielded a frying pan

of being over. As Douglas Orgill, one of the show's earliest and most consistently enthusiastic journalistic admirers, remarked as he previewed the final edition: 'What can one say about *Fawlty Towers*, except the week has to be arranged so that one doesn't ever miss it?'

There were already plenty of firm and passionate fans around, but there were also a surprising number of people who had never seen the show and knew precious little about it. It was often a matter of feet and inches: on the one side, a *Fawlty* fanatic, and on the other, someone who barely knew that *Fawlty* even existed.

Above: *The Evening Telegraph* had a lovely chat with Andy on 7 November 1975 . . . where he mentions his hopes for a second series.

SECOND SITTING

10.

BACK FOR MORE

Above: On set again at long last! Me, Connie and Andy on the hotel reception set for a promo shot (taken just before the recording of 'The Psychiatrist'). The original set had been in storage for four years and needed a bit of a make-over – notice the now straight 'PRIVATE' writing on the office door, for example.

I've always found that there is one aspect of show business that is rather sad – you work with people, and you get rather fond of them, and then you probably never see them again. I remember in 1980 making *The Taming of the Shrew*. We rehearsed it for six weeks (I was paid £300 a week!). The director, Jonathan Miller, the best I ever worked with, cast it with actors from all over Britain. And we became a real team and formed friendships and then we taped the show, and we went to a BBC room where there were nuts and crisps and had a drink and never saw each other again. Although you retain very fond memories . . . Show-business people work on projects, which have an end. There is no sense of continuity. So when we'd recorded

'The Germans', Pru and Connie and Andy and Ballard, and JHD of course, we hoped there would be another series, but we'd no idea when.

We would never have guessed it would take four years. And the reason was that Connie and I got divorced.

Amicably. We had been wondering for some time if we should stay together. I had moved out, then back in, then back out, then back in and then, in 1976, back out for the last time. But although we were living apart we remained close friends and in 1977 acted together in *The Strange Case of the End of Civilisation as We Know It*. I played a descendant of Sherlock Holmes, Connie a descendant of Moriarty, and the actor Arthur Lowe played a phenomenally dim descendant of Dr Watson. At the end Connie (alias Mrs Hudson) shot me, firing an impossible number of bullets into me. But I remained unmoved, and revealed that I had suspected Mrs Hudson all along and instructed Watson to load her revolver with blanks. As I (as Holmes) finished his triumphant tirade, the half-witted Watson apologises to Holmes for forgetting to load the blanks. Holmes discovers he has been riddled with bullets. And dies. But this in no way symbolised our relationship.

A year or so after this, the question of a second series arose and Connie and I toyed with it. I was worried that it might not live up to the standard of our first series, because the audience would remember only the best moments of series one, and that a second series would have to be better than the first, to be perceived as being equally as good. We also feared that as the audience got more familiar with the main characters, they would be able to anticipate the trajectory of the plot, and would be able to guess in advance where the comedy was coming from.

What a load of old cobblers! I don't know where these ridiculous insecurities were coming from. If *Cheers* could do 276 episodes for NBC, we could probably handle another six! However, my ludicrous anxieties had a beneficial outcome, because

Connie and I worked harder even than on the first series, in a mammoth effort to avoid an anti-climax. So, we spent most of 1978 just trying to get the six scripts right. We were both living in Holland Park and we usually wrote at my place. The writing took up so much of our lives that we even went on two holidays together with our daughter Cynthia and kept working there.

Two moments stick in my mind.

The first came while I was reading a psychology book called *I'm OK, You're OK* about transactional analysis, which had become a major topic after Eric Berne's *Games People Play* first came out. The basic idea is that we all operate more

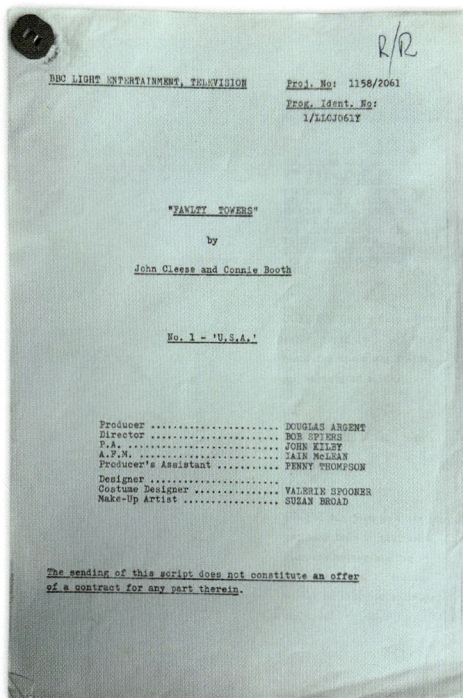

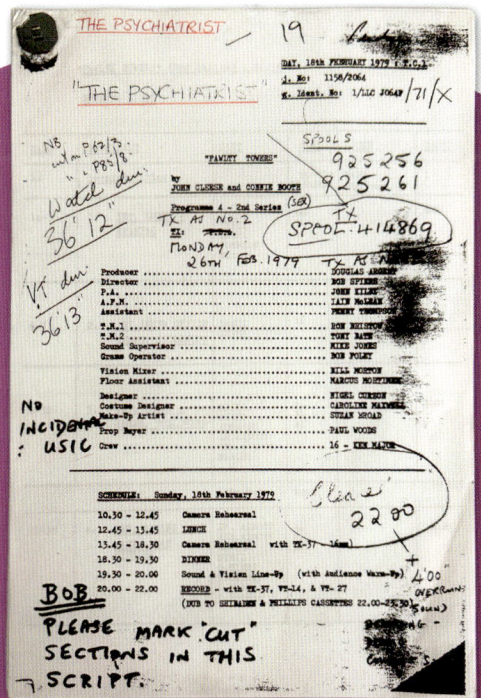

or less unconsciously, in three mental states: Parent, Child and Adult. I was reading about the characteristic behaviour and speech exhibited by someone who was stuck in his or her Parent role, and I suddenly realised it was a perfect description of Basil!

I showed Connie and we were both amazed that we had created a character by intuition alone, that exactly fitted the recognised psychiatric symptoms displayed by someone who lived most of their existence dealing with others as though they were their parent. It reminded me what Freud once said to the effect that artists and writers have some insights into the human constitution that were beyond the reach of professional psychiatrists.

The second moment came when Connie and I were having coffee with the woman who was the local guide for our travel agent. In search of comedy material, we asked her what was the most difficult kind of client that she had to look after. And she described someone who would become Mrs Richards in 'Communication Problems'. Just like that. Connie and I only had to add a hearing aid to the detailed description of a certain kind of older woman that our companion was laying out before us. This turned out to be someone who complained about everything, not in order to get the problem solved, but only to get a reduction on the bill. So Connie and I had been gifted a great idea for the first episode of the second series.

But, before we worked out that plot we'd learned that John Howard Davies could not direct the series, for the very good reason that he had been made BBC Head of Comedy. Not surprising when you consider that after the early Monty Pythons, he produced all of *The Good Life* series, a series of *Steptoe*, Frankie Howerd's *Whoops Baghdad* and *The Goodies*, including an episode that won the Silver Rose of Montreux ('Kitten Kong', 1972).

As Head of Comedy JHD commissioned *The Fall and Rise of Reginald Perrin*; *Yes, Minister*; *Only Fools and Horses* and *Not the Nine O'Clock News*. Beat that! And the most surprising thing is that this extraordinary run of successes was

Below: Sound Supervisor Mike Jones' copy of the camera script for 'The Anniversary'. In particular, the re-mounted recording, as the original had to be delayed a week, due to a BBC strike (see page 172).

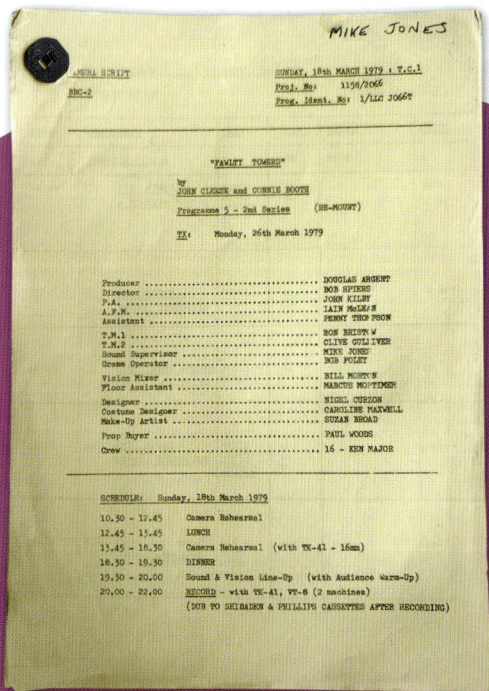

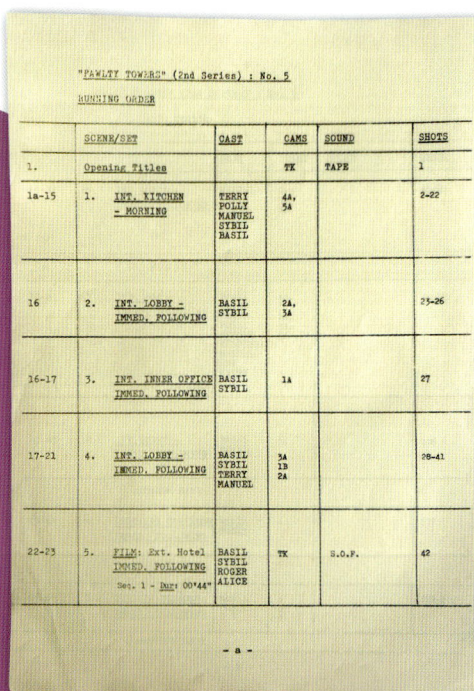

due to his impeccable instincts. When he was allotted to *Yes, Minister*, that series' writer, Sir Antony Jay, an old friend from *The Frost Report* with whom I'd founded the company Video Arts, called me for a quick assessment of JHD. I told him, 'Trust Johnny's instincts! They are pitch perfect. But pay no attention to his rationalisations. He can't do that bit!'

I think there is a deep, vitally important lesson here.

Comedy is not only hard to perform (as Henry Irving reminded us), it is extraordinarily complex. Every attempt to analyse humour is always only partial, because there are so many factors involved that no explanation can be really comprehensive. I have read theories about humour that include nothing about timing. It's like writing about cricket without mentioning there is a ball. I used to get into arguments about what was funny where people were using logic to win their point. Sorry, but logic doesn't tell us whether something's funny. It doesn't tell us if something tastes good either.

If you're any good at acting, every time you do comedy you are learning. And a lot of the learning isn't conscious. If you're practising your golf swing, you're learning what feels right. Westerners, whose culture is biased towards the left-hemisphere world of logic and verbal dexterity, neglect the non-verbal intelligences we have.

A story which illustrates this concerns a philosopher who decided one day that he should learn to swim, so he went and bought some swimming trunks and a couple of books about swimming. He put on the trunks and sat on the bank of the river. And being an intellectual, he read

Bob Spiers
Series 2 Director

Glasgow-born Robert Alexander Spiers swapped fame as a Scottish junior tennis champion for the theatre, and eventually a job at the BBC in 1967. Climbing the ranks in the light entertainment department, Bob made his directorial debut with *It Ain't Half Hot Mum* in 1975, before taking on one of the final episodes of *Dad's Army* in 1977.

With a reputation for keeping studio recordings running to schedule whilst simultaneously making inventive and creative decisions, Bob quickly became an in-demand comedy director. By the time he took the reins of *Fawlty* in 1979 (which won him a prestigious BAFTA award), he had already brought dozens of episodes of *Are You Being Served?* and *The Goodies* to the screen.

The 1980s would see Bob go freelance, working for ITV (directing *Press Gang*) and Channel 4. It was whilst directing *The Comic Strip Presents . . .* for Channel 4, that he would first work with French and Saunders, going on to direct dozens of the duo's episodes and later Jennifer Saunders' sitcom *Absolutely Fabulous* (which resulted in his second BAFTA!). In later years, Bob moved to Hollywood to direct *That Darn Cat* for Disney and returned to London to direct the Spice Girls in their blockbusting 1997 film *Spice World*.

Above: Dear Bobby, photographed many years after his stint at *Fawlty Towers*, at the Los Angeles, premier of his 1997 movie *Spice World*.

the books very quickly and retained all the information. And then he thought, 'Well, now I know how to swim, so I don't need to go in the water.'

If a basketball player is having an off-day, his teammates help him by shouting: 'Stop thinking!' A good comedian will slowly build up, at a largely pre-conscious level, a feeling for how to make something funny. JHD had that in spades, though he couldn't explain it! But he was promoted, so he had to be replaced by Bobby Spiers, who turned out to be a lovely, cheerful, well-organised, companiable head honcho, and, of course, another fucking Scot!

Douglas Argent / Producer

Essex-native Douglas Argent had already lived several lives' worth of adventures before taking on the *Fawlty Towers* producer's role in 1979. Second World War veteran, Argent was a navigator with the RAF's 84 Squadron. On one fateful mission in the Far East, his craft was shot down, and after a daring landing, Argent spent three years in a Japanese prisoner-of-war camp.

It was whilst in this camp that his youthful interests in theatre were awoken, and after safely returning to England, he went into the world of repertory theatre, and was later cast in several West End productions. By the end of the 1950s, Douglas had decided on a future in television, specifically behind the camera. Joining the BBC, he was drawn towards directing and eventually worked on some of the earliest television sitcoms: *Hugh and I* and *Till Death Do Us Part.*

Moving into the 1970s, Douglas took on the dual role of both producer and director of *Steptoe and Son* and *The Liver Birds*. It was this experience which stood him in good stead to work on *Fawlty Towers*, taking the series which John Howard Davies established four years previously and getting the complex machine up and running again. Funnily enough, Douglas's wife, actress Elizabeth Benson, appeared in the first series episode 'Gourmet Night' and later appeared again in 'The Kipper and the Corpse'!

Following his stint in the world's most famous fictional Torquay hotel, Douglas continued to both produce and direct. Notably he would instigate the long-running Windsor Davies sitcom *Never the Twain* for ITV, and away from comedy, he capped off his varied career by directing several episodes of *EastEnders* in 1991.

Above (L–R): Elizabeth Benson (Douglas Argent's wife) as Mrs Heath in 'Gourmet Night' and as Mrs White in 'The Kipper and the Corpse'.

Above right: On location in the car park of the Wooburn Grange Country Club, filming a scene for 'The Anniversary' (director Bobby Spiers in red). The owners had cleared a lot more of the trees when we returned in 1978, meaning we had to work even harder to maintain the Torquay illusion!

Opposite page, bottom right: Rehearsing a scene with our new chef, Terry (Brian Hall), in our updated kitchen set for 'The Anniversary', a well-thumbed camera script in the foreground.

Otherwise, Connie and I made just one change, which turned out to be a great success. We invented a chef. How we got through the first series without a chef is quite beyond me. It's bizarre, in retrospect . . . So it seemed the most natural thing in the world to create one. We always thought of him as a cockney, so when Brian Hall met us for the first time and told us that he worked as a London black cab driver when he wasn't acting, we were thrilled. And he fitted in perfectly. He'd done plenty of TV, of course, including appearances in BBC police drama *Softly, Softly*, but from day one he was there, being Terry, and no questions asked. Brian told me much later that when we'd first discussed how he should play Terry, I just said, 'The police are after him.' And that was all he needed! I love this story, as I think that a lot of introspection about a character's history doesn't add much to that character's funniness. I never heard Ronnie Barker talk about 'Method Acting'. In *A Fish*

Brian Hall / Terry

It is just as well Terry the chef wasn't cast for the first series of *Fawlty Towers*, as during the summer of 1975, actor Brian Hall was treading the boards as a member of the Royal Shakespeare Company in *Twelfth Night*!

Drawn into amateur theatre as a teenager, Hall was encouraged to pursue acting professionally. After leaving school he juggled shifts as a London cabbie before his professional career took off, appearing on stage in plays across the capital, bringing him to the attention of both the Royal Court and the RSC.

But as TV fell in love with the London underworld, Brian's authentic no-nonsense intensity meant it didn't take long before he found himself in demand, playing a revolving carousel of hard-boiled tough men and criminals across dozens of popular drama series from *Softly, Softly* in the 60s through to *Minder* in the 80s.

Perfectly cast as Terry, Brian would make a truly wonderful addition to the *Fawlty* cast in 1979, adding a cockney irreverence which complemented the various personalities of the established family of regular characters beautifully. Revealing a fantastic knack for comedic timing, Brian's work in *Fawlty* would lead to further sitcom roles throughout the 80s and 90s.

Called Wanda, Otto and Wanda have no pretence at a 'back story' and nobody has ever mentioned it! So farce in particular does not need any soul-searching during the rehearsal period.

In addition, it's very rare for a farce character to become introspective. I did once, during the second series, when Basil, sitting alone, asks, 'Was that my life?' and answers himself, 'Yes. Do I get another one?' This rarity worked well, for two reasons. One, it was very short and the pace picked up immediately. Two, it was television and could be shot in close-up. On stage, it would have died a death. So, my five-word direction to Terry was all that was necessary. After that, it was as though he'd been with us all along. (Incidentally, when Brian and I met, he was 42. I was 39!)

COMMUNICATION PROBLEMS

Above: The wonderful Joan Sanderson as Mrs Richards – one of the nicest people I have met in my life and the exact opposite to her character!

I'm very fond of 'Communication Problems'. First of all, there's the wonderful Joan Sanderson. I was in awe watching such a lovely person turn suddenly into a nasty old ratbag like Mrs Richards. From the moment she arrives at the hotel, she takes over the episode. She's very rude to Polly, who gets her own back by suggesting Mrs Richards discuss her query with Manuel.

Mrs Richards: Isn't there anyone else in attendance here? Really, this is the most appalling service I've ever . . .

Polly: Manuel! Could you lend Mrs Richards your assistance in connection with her reservation. *(to Thurston)* Now . . . *(she continues to give Thurston directions)*

Mrs Richards: *(to Manuel)* Now, I've reserved a very quiet room, with a bath and a sea view. I specifically asked for a sea view in my written confirmation, so please be sure I have it.

Manuel: Que?

Mrs Richards: . . . What?

Manuel: . . . Que?

Mrs Richards: K?

Manuel: Si.

Mrs Richards: C? *(Manuel nods)* KC? What are you trying to say?

Manuel: No, no – Que – what?

Mrs Richards: K – what?

Manuel: Si! Que – what?

Mrs Richards: C. K. Watt?

Manuel: . . . Yes.

Mrs Richards: Who is C.K. Watt?

Manuel: Que?

Mrs Richards: Is it the manager, Mr Watt?

Manuel: Oh, manager!

Mrs Richards: He is.

Manuel: Ah . . . Mr Fawlty.

Mrs Richards: What?

Manuel: Fawlty.

Mrs Richards: What are you talking about, you silly little man? *(turns to Polly)* What is going on here? I ask him for my room, and he tells me the manager's a Mr Watt and he's aged forty.

Manuel: No. No. Fawlty.

Mrs Richards: Faulty? What's wrong with him?

Polly: It's all right, Mrs Richards. He's from Barcelona.

Mrs Richards: The manager's from Barcelona?

Manuel: No, no. He's from Swanage.

I simply love this piece of nonsense, it is logical, after a fashion. It has to be: if it wasn't, it wouldn't work. It's the illusion of possible eventual understanding that keeps us listening and it finishes with Mrs Richards believing that Basil's last name is Watt. So, when she addresses him later, he thinks she's said 'What?' and replies

'I didn't say anything,' which sets them off again. When we gave Mrs Richards a hearing aid, we tried to make sure that the audience realised her hearing was rather selective. So, when she's discussing the sale of the house it becomes much better. I think there's no harm in getting fun out of the partial deafness that causes mishearing. I'm fairly deaf now and I've discovered I can always get a laugh if I repeat what I think someone has just said to me. But somehow, there would be nothing funny about someone who was completely deaf . . .

The other theme in the episode is Basil betting on the horse Dragonfly. This is fun simply because he has to hide it from Sybil. When she overhears Basil being given a tip about a horse, she warns him and he says, 'Yes, that particular avenue of pleasure was closed off some years ago,' which every night on stage gets a big laugh, much bigger than I would ever have expected! So now we have the essential

Below: In room 22, Mrs Richards has some complaints.

I apologise for the back-cloth, it really stinks, doesn't it! Try not to notice it, don't look at it! I shouldn't have drawn your attention to it really?!

God knows what it was. Basil has to get everyone to swear secrecy about Dragonfly. Easy with Polly, just achievable with the Major, but well-nigh impossible with Manuel.

Here's a communication problem with Manuel that we prolonged longer than usual:

Basil: Manuel, Manuel.

Manuel: Your horse, it win, it win!

Basil: Ssh!! . . . Manuel . . . *(putting his head close to Manuel)* You know nothing. *(Manuel is puzzled)* You know nothing.

Manuel: You always say, Mr Fawlty. But I learn.

Basil: No, no, no, no . . .

Manuel: I get better.

Basil: No, you don't understand.

element of a farce: a secret which must not be revealed. The whole plot now revolves around two different wads of money: Basil's winnings on the horse, and money that Mrs Richards insists has been stolen from her room, but which in fact she left in a shop in town while she was buying a large china vase.

Polly and Basil play through the variations of this, and it gets quite complicated after the shop owner delivers the vase and Mrs Richards' 'stolen' money, left behind in a glove. Basil has his moment of glory, 'For the first time in my life, I'm ahead!' – which inevitably means that things are not going to end well.

Connie and I always felt conflicted as we invented yet another roadblock for Basil. At the moment we realised what it was going to be, we would hop with glee and laugh our heads off, and then, as we started to type it out, we would suddenly feel sad and ache with sympathy for him, like we were inventing disasters for a real human being. It seemed as though there was something lovable about him. . . although

Manuel: I do.

Basil: No, you don't.

Manuel: I do understand that.

Basil: Shh . . . you know nothing about the horse.

Manuel: (*doubtfully*) I know nothing about the horse.

Basil: Yes.

Manuel: Which? I know nothing?

Basil: My horse, nitwit.

Manuel: Your horse, 'Nitwit'.

Basil: No, no, Dragonfly.

Manuel: It won!

Basil: Yes, I know.

Manuel: I know it won, too.

Basil: What?

Manuel: I put money on for you. You give me money. I go to vetting-shop . . .

Basil: I know, I know, I know.

Manuel: Why you say I know nothing?

Basil: Oh. Look . . . look . . . look . . . you know the horse?

Manuel: Witnit? Or Dragonfly?

Basil: Dragonfly. There isn't a horse called Nitwit. You're the nitwit.

Manuel: What is witnit?

Basil: It doesn't matter . . . look . . . it doesn't matter . . . Oh . . . I could spend the rest of my life having this conversation. Please try to understand before one of us dies.

'Communication Problems'

(aka 'Theft' and 'Mrs Richards')

SERIES 2 EPISODE 1

Recorded: 28 January 1979 (TC8)

First transmission: 19 February 1979

Guest stars: Joan Sanderson (Mrs Richards), Robert Lankesheer (Mr Thurston), Johnny Shannon (Mr Firkins), Bill Bradley (Mr Mackintosh), George Lee (Mr Kerr), Mervyn Pascoe (Mr Yardley)

Uncredited: Gary Dean (Hotel Guest), David Melbourne, Jane Watts (Hotel Guest Couple), Peter Caton (Taxi Driver), Rosina Stewart (Hotel Guest not in finished programme).

It's a long scene, but it holds, because every time we think it's ended – or at least every time Basil does – it doesn't. And Basil's determination to make absolutely sure Manuel says that he knows nothing about the horse makes it all the funnier when he pleads with him to tell Mrs Richards that he does.

Meanwhile, there's the usual *communication problems* with the Major, too. He can't remember anything that's happened recently, and when he finally does – 'Fawlty, you did give me that money. You won it on that horse!' – Basil's whole edifice of lies collapses.

Right: 'Fishwife! Fly! Fly! Flying Tart! No, no, no, it got off to a flying start, and it's name . . . was Dragonfly!' – Polly attempts to decode Basil's mime. Some pure Whitehall farce!

And finally, there are the confrontations with Mrs Richards: 'Do you have a hearing aid? Would you like me to get it mended?', 'the Hanging Gardens of Babylon', 'May I suggest you find a hotel closer to the sea – or preferably in it', 'Is this a piece of your brain?' and 'I shall visit you in the small hours and put a bat up your nightdress.'

Yet when I watch the episode, it seems a little bit short – as though it wasn't really a full episode. Perhaps it's because Mrs Richards is the only big role apart from the regulars. Perhaps it's because the plot, despite small complications, is basically

Right: George Lee's Devon-accented delivery man returns (after appearing in 'The Builders' four years previously) to deliver Mrs Richards' vase.

Below right: A Chinese famille rose style scroll-shape porcelain vase – just like the one Mrs Richards (almost) had!

a simple one – 'Rude guest gets the better of Basil'. Perhaps there are few visual moments, except Polly trying to remember the horse's name while Basil tries to mime it. Perhaps . . .

One last comment. There's a really major mistake right at the very end. The BBC crews were so effortlessly efficient throughout both series that it may seem graceless pointing out the one mistake they made. At the very, very end, when Sybil sees Basil counting his winnings, and the Major says, 'You won it on that horse,' just as Basil is handing the vase to Mrs Richards, the shot of Basil is wrongly framed, because it shows Sybil and 95 per cent of Basil. The 5 per cent that can't be seen is Basil's left hand and the vase he is holding in it. So, when he screams

Joan Sanderson
Mrs Richards

With her hearing aid firmly switched to the 'off' position (to save the battery), the English Riviera braces itself for the queen of miserliness, as Mrs Richards comes to town . . .

In a meticulous performance laden with fast-paced dialogue and dozens of examples of comic misunderstandings, Joan Sanderson is truly spectacular in 'Communication Problems'.

In contrast to her character on screen, Joan was a lovely person and a warm presence both in rehearsal and on set as she infused Mrs Richards with every ounce of the thrifty intolerance written into the script.

Elocution classes led to Joan losing her native Bristolian tones and in their place developing a strong upper-class accent. Added to this, Joan's height and

powerful acting chops led her straight into playing commanding female figures.

On screen, Joan memorably starred as Doris Ewell in school-set sitcom *Please Sir!* Shortly before taking on Mrs Richards, she stole the show in an episode of *Rising Damp* as a protective mother.

For *Fawlty Towers* fans, 1981's *The Great Muppet Caper* is well worth watching – I had the great pleasure of working alongside Joan as her on-screen husband in a wonderful dinner scene . . . with Miss Piggy looking on!

and drops the vase, we don't see it fall. We cut to a wider shot, but the vase had already landed. Knowing the huge laugh that the smashing of the vase gets every night at the Apollo, it's a shame that moment isn't preserved on videotape. But the big question is, 'Why didn't we do that shot again?' I've no idea, and no one else can remember. Two possibilities: one, we'd run out of time. Exactly two hours after we started recording, they pulled the plug, regardless of whether we'd finished the actual show. Two, the BBC couldn't afford a spare vase.

'THAT COST £75!'

JOHN CLEESE'S TOP FAWLTY TOWERS MOMENTS

7

THE PSYCHIATRIST

But if 'Communication Problems' seems a bit slight, I can hardly believe how much Connie and I crammed into 'The Psychiatrist'!

There are three different plot lines, which interweave and finally come together in a grand finale, where Basil learns that the woman in Mr Johnson's room is in fact his mother, causing Basil to crouch down and hide his head in excruciating embarrassment, only to be observed by the psychiatrist and his doctor wife, who have throughout the episode seen Basil in a series of moments when he appears completely insane. I like the downbeat punchline too, when the psychiatrist says firmly, 'I'm on holiday.'

Apart from the two doctors and Mr Johnson, we also have Raylene Miles, a beautiful and very sexy Australian girl, staying at the hotel on her own, with whom Basil gets more and more entangled in a number of apparently sexual encounters where his behaviour is innocent – though nobody would believe so.

Let's start with the doctors. Their arrival shows how terribly impressed Basil is by the professional class. (I remembered from my early years in Weston-super-Mare how the lower middle class treated doctors with exaggerated reverence, rather as though they were a higher form of life.) Basil gets rather over-excited.

Sybil: Thank you, Mr Abbott. *(she takes another look at the card)* Oh, Doctor Abbott, I'm sorry.

Basil: *(freezes for a split second)* Doctor?

Dr Abbott: . . . Yes.

Basil: I'm terribly sorry, we hadn't been told. (*Dr Abbott looks at him questioningly*) We hadn't been told you were a doctor.

Dr Abbott: Oh.

Basil: How do you do, doctor. (*He offers his hand; Dr Abbott shakes it briefly*) Very nice to have you with us, doctor.

Dr Abbott: Thank you.

Sybil: You're in room five, doctor.

Basil: And Mrs Abbott, how do you do. (*He shakes hands with her*)

Dr Abbott: Dr Abbott, actually.

Basil: . . . I'm sorry?

Dr Abbott: Doctor Abbott.

Mrs Abbott: Two doctors.

Basil: You're two doctors?

Mrs Abbott: Yes.

Basil: Well, how did you become two doctors? That's most unusual . . . I mean, did you take the exams twice, or . . . ?

Dr Abbott: No, my wife's a doctor. . .

Mrs Abbott: . . . I'm a doctor.

Basil: You're a doctor too! So you're three doctors.

Dr Abbott: No, I'm just one doctor. My wife is another doctor.

Sybil: (*ringing the bell pointedly*) Manuel? (*Basil is silenced; to the Abbotts*) Your room is at the top of the stairs along to the left.

Basil: Oh I see! You see, I thought, when you said you were two doctors . . . (*Manuel comes running in from the kitchen*) Manuel, would you take the doctors' cases up to number five, please. (*He shows the way, then follows them up the stairs, Manuel comes behind with the cases*) Yes, this way please, doctors . . . Yes, when you said you were two doctors I thought perhaps you were a doctor of medicine, perhaps a doctor of archaeology. . .

And this is before Basil discovers that the doctor is also a psychiatrist! As these shows were all set in the 1970s I need to explain.

Fifty years ago, British ideas about psychiatry and any form of psychological therapy were pretty primitive. I remember my mother saying to me, 'People only go to a psychiatrist if they are mad.' It was OK to be physically ill, because that was all right. No shame in that. But the idea of having psychosomatic symptoms was not OK because that meant there was something wrong with your brain. And that was morally dubious and definitely carried a stigma. And if you consulted a psychiatrist about a mental health problem, that was something to keep out of the press. So, knowledge of psychological ideas was, to put it mildly, scanty. It was assumed that 'shrinks' had strange, wizard-like powers and would see into your inner life while talking to you,

Below: Sybil is captivated by Mr Johnson, played by my friend Nicky Henson. I asked Nicky if he could do this part as I am so rude to the character throughout the episode, and I wanted to invite an actor in who really knew that I loved him! And of course, playing Johnson was perfect for him.

when, as Robin Skynner said to me, 'You're just trying to get a drink.'

This meant that the average person treated these people with suspicion and needed to be kept at a safe distance. So when Basil tells Sybil, 'They've got photographic memories!' it's not much of an exaggeration. And the one thing people did know was the name Sigmund Freud, and he said everything was about sex. And from my Westonian upbringing, I know there was no subject more embarrassing, and capable of excruciating discomfort, than that.

Sybil: Why are you getting so upset?

Basil: I'm not . . .

Sybil: You liked him when he arrived . . .

Basil: Look . . .

Sybil: And then just because you find out he's a psychiatrist you get all . . .

Basil: I'm not bothered by that. I'm not . . . I'm not bothered by that. If he wants to be a psychiatrist that's his own funeral. They're all as mad as bloody March hares anyway but that's not the point. Look, look! How does he earn his money? . . . He gets paid for sticking his nose . . .

Sybil: Oh, Basil . . .

Basil: No, I'm going to have my say . . . into people's private . . . um . . . details. Well, just speaking for myself, I don't want a total stranger nosing around in my private parts. Details. That's all I'm saying.

Sybil: They're down here on holiday. They're just here to enjoy themselves . . .

Basil: He can't.

Sybil: Can't what?

Basil: He can't tell me anything about myself that I don't know already. All this psychiatry, it's a load of tommy-rot. You know what they're all obsessed with, don't you.

Sybil: What?

Basil: You know what they say it's all about, don't you . . . mmm? Sex. Everything's connected with sex. Choh! What a load of cobblers . . . *(He goes into the dining room).*

. . . where the doctors have been discussing how difficult it is for hoteliers to take holidays. So when Dr Abbott asks him 'How often do you manage it?' Basil's worst fears are confirmed. After a moment's shock Basil says, 'Two or three

Nicky Henson
Mr Johnson

With his captivating charms from Colchester hanging around his neck, the charismatic ladies' man Mr Johnson's stay at Fawlty Towers was designed to make Basil's blood boil.

To play a suave hotel guest in 'The Psychiatrist' with an eye for the opposite sex, Connie and I brought in Nicky Henson. Nicky was a dear friend from my earliest days on television, when we both worked on the first series of *The Frost Report*, back in 1966.

Nicky's winning looks and natural way of working with the camera saw him work on everything from *Minder* to *Inspector Morse* via *Vera Drake* – always with a trademark swagger. His starring role in *The Bawdy Adventures of Tom Jones* is well worth investigating.

Nicky was also married to Una Stubbs (who would later appear in this series' 'The Anniversary') before amicably separating in 1975.

times a week actually', which causes confusion among the doctors. Of course, the whole episode is about sex – or sexual attentiveness. This moment tells us all about Basil's feelings about psychiatrists – fear of their 'powers', his obsession with their obsession with sex, and his distaste for what they do professionally – sticking their noses into other people's private . . . things. Sybil enlightens him on what they were actually talking about, pushing his embarrassment up another notch or two.

When Connie and I constructed any episode, our basic plan was to wind Basil up. Confusion is the principle of all farces, and the reason why great farce gets bigger laughs than any other kind of comedy. Remember, as Daniel Goleman says, stress makes you stupid, so the more that the protagonist is stressed, the more unwise his decisions get. He may have several options, and if he took the most sensible one, the farce would end! The worse his choice, the deeper the pit he is digging for himself and the more ridiculous his behaviour and the plot can get. At the beginning of an episode, Basil looks relatively normal. As we pile on the pressure, the more wound up he gets. If he had greeted the Germans in the first five minutes of that episode, he would have handled them more sanely. So Connie and I built up Basil's stress level very carefully.

At the beginning of 'The Psychiatrist', Sybil is flirting with Mr Johnson, who is the type most likely to irritate Basil – shirt open to the waist, medallions, leather jacket and a cocky, laid-back manner. Basil makes some monkey references; Sybil says Mr Johnson is rather attractive.

'The Psychiatrist'
(aka 'Sex')

SERIES 2 EPISODE 2

Recorded: 18 February 1979 (TC1)

First transmission: 26 February 1979

Guest stars: Nicky Henson (Mr Johnson), Basil Henson (Dr Abbott), Elspet Gray (Mrs Abbott), Luan Peters (Raylene Mills), Aimee Delamain (Mrs Johnson), Imogen Bickford-Smith (Girlfriend)

Uncredited: Kevin Hudson (Boy), Mercedes Burleigh, Derek Suthern (Hotel Guests)

Basil: Attractive?

Sybil: You know, easy and amusing and charming.

Basil: Charming, eh – well he's certainly covered in charms. I've never seen so many medals round one neck in my life. He must be the bravest orangutan in Britain.

And so the bickering has started, and we're only on page 2 of the script. Then the Abbotts arrive and after they go for a stroll, he needles Sybil by saying what an attractive woman Mrs Abbott is. Then Johnson insults Torquay! He refers to a guide to Torquay as 'one of the shortest books'. Basil is now spoiling for a fight.

Below: Australian actress Luan Peters' brilliant performance as Raylene Mills in the Room 7 light switch misunderstanding . . as Sybil is about to walk in at precisely the worst moment!

Basil: Are you dining here tonight? Here in this unfashionable dump.

Mr Johnson: . . . Well, I wasn't planning to.

Basil: Not really your scene, is it.

Mr Johnson: I thought I'd try somewhere in town. Anywhere you'd recommend?

Basil: Well, what sort of food were you thinking of – fruit? Or . . .

Mr Johnson: Is there anywhere they do French food?

Basil: Yes, France, I believe. They seem to like it there, and the swim would certainly sharpen your appetite. You'd better hurry, the tide leaves in six minutes.

Later that evening, while the Abbotts are having dinner, Sybil converses with them and Basil decides to join in.

Basil: My great-grandfather on my mother's side was a doctor, and so it was always felt I might . . .

Sybil: Run a hotel. Are you both in general practice?

Mrs Abbott: No, I'm a paediatrician.

Basil: Feet?

Mrs Abbott: Children.

Sybil: Oh, Basil.

Basil: Well, children have feet, don't they? That's how they move around, my dear. You must take a look next time, it's most interesting. *(To Dr Abbott)* And you, doctor? Are you a . . .

Dr Abbott: I'm a psychiatrist.

Basil: Very nice too. Well, cheers. *(He sips Dr Abbott's port, then realises what he's done.)* I'll get another one.

Next, we bring real sexual attraction into Basil's life in the form of Raylene Miles, a beautiful, sexy young Australian woman who has arrived at reception. Basil is obviously smitten and desperately trying to hide it, but in reaching for a light switch he inadvertently fondles Raylene's breast, just as Sybil enters the room. Next, he hears a young woman's voice coming from Johnson's room and realises that he

Basil Henson
Dr Abbott
Elspet Gray
Mrs Abbott

The Abbotts are both left suitably disturbed by their perplexing encounters with Basil Fawlty.

Basil Henson was educated at Sandhurst and served as a Major in the Second World War before he pursued his love of the stage. By the time he was cast as Dr Abbott, Basil was well known for his frequent gripping performances at the National Theatre. A later acting highlight saw Basil appear in a production of *The Merchant of Venice* opposite Dustin Hoffman in London's West End and on Broadway.

It is a testament to Basil's professionalism that he rehearsed and played the part of Dr Abbott in 'The Psychiatrist' whilst in the midst of severe back pain in the days leading up to the making of the episode.

Scottish-born Elspet Gray was another talented stage performer, well known for her appearances in the popular Whitehall farces of the 1950s and 60s (another *Fawlty Towers* inspiration). 'The Psychiatrist' made wonderful use of Elspet's excellent pace and comic timing.

Alongside many noted TV roles (including a memorable guest spot in the Second World War Two drama *Tenko*), Elspet made a fantastic queen in the very first *Blackadder* series and became well-known to younger viewers as Lady Collingford in *Catweazle*.

has smuggled a girlfriend in there. Basil challenges Johnson, who denies it, but orders a bottle of champagne anyway. Basil is so wound up by now that he spends the rest of the episode trying to prove there's a girl in Johnson's room. However, Sybil believes he's obsessed with the Australian girl in the next room.

At one point, he gets Manuel to help him put up a ladder so he can look into Johnson's room and confirm the unallowed guest, but when he reaches the top, he finds himself peering into the Abbotts' room. Sybil thinks he was trying to look into Raylene the Australian's bedroom and is so furious that she banishes Basil from their bedroom and he has to spend a sleepless night in a cupboard. In a final effort to convince Sybil of his innocence, he challenges Johnson, who admits he does have a woman in his room. Basil's triumph is short-lived, as Johnson's girlfriend has now left – so the woman turns out to be Johnson's mother. Everyone leaves, but Basil is so humiliated he

crouches down and pulls his jacket over his head, just as both doctors arrive in time to see this extraordinary sight.

The ladder sequence is the best comedy we ever did on film. (These sequences were all shot before the series was recorded.) The scene is beautifully lit, so that huge shadows of Basil and Manuel are projected onto the side of the hotel. As Basil climbs, we cut to Johnson and his girlfriend toasting each other, then back

Above: 'I didn't know she was in here. I just came in to check the walls' – psychiatrist Dr Abbott (Basil Henson) hears the commotion coming from Raylene Mills' room and investigates.

Below: With Manuel's help, Basil climbs up to look into what he believes to be Mr Johnson's room … I love the shadows here, beautifully set up by the lighting team.

to Basil getting to the top of the ladder, and then (in the studio) to me appearing at the window and looking in. Then the camera pulls back, slowly revealing Mrs Abbott and then her husband, staring in astonishment at Basil – this is my favourite moment of the episode – who then pretends he's checking the window, using a gesture he has used throughout the episode when he has been caught doing something he shouldn't be doing. In the movement, he overbalances the ladder backwards, and, cutting back to the exterior film, we see the ladder land on the grass.

Finally, the last moment, as the Abbotts stare at the weird sight of Basil with his jacket on his head impersonating a cockroach, derives from something I learned in 1963! I was watching the first – and best – Pink Panther film and there was a scene at the end where some open cars with pantomime animals in them were driving around a small Italian village square. An elderly man came out of a bar and sees this bizarre sight. He stared and then went back into the bar. We assume he was thinking, 'May as well have another drink.' But, no. He came back out again with a chair, placed it carefully, and sat down to watch. The audience now saw the absurd carnival scene through his eyes. It made it much funnier.

So, the last image, Basil's beetle impersonation, becomes funnier as it's observed by someone, especially a psychiatrist. And especially one who has already categorised Basil as 'clinically insane'.

Below: Mortified by the embarrassment of the reveal that Mr Johnson's mother is staying with him, Basil becomes a cockroach, as the Abbotts look on in puzzlement.

WALDORF SALAD

Above: Basil attempts to appease the Hamiltons (Bruce Boa and Claire Nielson), who have driven five hours and now want to eat . . . This epsiode is all about service and complaining!

Below: A Waldorf Salad! – 'It's celery, apples, walnuts, grapes . . . in a mayonnaise sauce!'

After all the scenes in the previous episode, where Basil makes himself ridiculous in full view of the psychiatrists, 'Waldorf Salad' is a very simple tale. It's all about bad service, and people complaining about it, culminating in an uprising by the guests, and Basil's ingenious response. So, we start with a classic example of bad service:

Basil rushes by on his way to a table where Mr and Mrs Johnston sit. Mrs Johnston has a half-finished prawn cocktail in front of her. Mr Johnston has a finished melon.

Basil: Have you finished?

Mrs Johnston: Er, yes . . .

Basil starts to collect the plates.

Basil: Thank you.

Mrs Johnston: Er, my wife . . .

Basil: Yes?

Mrs Johnston: I think those prawns might be off.

Basil: Oh, I don't think so.

Mrs Johnston: Well, they do taste rather funny.

Basil: Well, no one else has complained.

Mrs Johnston: Well, I really do think they're off.

Basil: But you've eaten half of them.

Mrs Johnston: Well, I didn't notice at the start.

Basil: You didn't notice at the start?

Mrs Johnston: Well, it was the sauce, you see. I wasn't sure.

Basil: So you ate half to make sure?

Mr Johnston: Look, my wife thinks they're off.

Basil: Well, what am I supposed to do about it . . .? Do you want another first course?

Mrs Johnston: No thank you.

Mr Johnston: You're sure?

Mrs Johnston: No, really, I'll just have the main.

Mr Johnston: *(to Basil)* Well, we'll just cancel it.

Basil: Cancel it? Oh, deduct it from the bill, is that what you mean?

Mr Johnston: Well, as it's inedible . . .

Basil: Well, only half of it's inedible apparently.

Mr Johnston: Well, deduct half now, and if my wife brings the other half up during the night, we'll claim the balance in the morning.

In this case the guest, played by the superb Terence Conoley, fights back. Re-viewing this scene reminds me that in the 1980s a famous London hotel chain used the *Fawlty Towers* episodes to train their staff! Most guests are like the two middle-aged ladies who are complaining to each other about the food. One says, 'I don't know how they get away with it.' The answer appears immediately, as Basil arrives at their table and asks, 'Everything all right?' and both ladies force a smile and say, 'Yes! Very nice. Thank you.'

Basil is being very rude, and, bearing in mind what I said about the need to wind him up, it's clear that he has already been wound up, for he is racing around trying to serve all the other guests while Sybil is leaning on a chair and droning on at length about the importance of beauty in life to a solitary guest who is trying to read his newspaper.

Basil: *(coming by carrying several things)* Busy this evening, isn't it.

Sybil: *(to Mr Libson)* I'll tell you a few of my favourites . . .

Basil: I said it's busy this evening.

Sybil: I'm talking to Mr Libson, Basil.

Below: Terry cleverly negotiates with Basil over the overtime request to cook for the Hamiltons . . . Until Basil realises Terry isn't actually going to a nightclass, but on a date . . . Brian Hall was so good at this part, he is just so right.

Basil: Good. Well, that's a help.

Sybil: I'm sure you can cope.

Basil: Oh, yes I can cope. Coping's easy. Not pureeing your loved ones, that's the difficult part.

(He's about to deliver the two plates of lamb to Mr Johnstone, who is relieved that the moment has at last come. However, the reception bell sounds.)

Sybil: *(to Mr Libson)* Did you know Bideford bridge has all different . . .

Basil: There's someone at reception, dear. Shall I get it?

Sybil: Yes.

Basil: It's my turn, is it? Fine. Oh yes! So it is. Funny, it's been my turn for fifteen years. *(He manages to get the door to the lobby open, still holding the plates)* Still, when

I'm dead it'll be your turn, dear – you'll be 'it'.

But Basil doesn't realise that all his discontented guests need is a leader – who happens to have just arrived at reception with his wife. They get off to a bad start, too, with Mr Hamilton, an extroverted American, complaining about the British weather and cars driving on the wrong side of the road. Worse, he wants dinner, and Basil explains that the kitchen has just closed. But Mr Hamilton has an idea.

Mr Hamilton: *(pulling out a wad of notes)* How much of this Mickey Mouse money do you need to keep the chef on for half an hour? One. . . two . . . twenty pounds, uh? Is that enough?

Basil: *(pauses to think, then)* I'll see what I can do.

Mr Hamilton: Thank you.

Below: Sybil and Basil discuss the finer points of making a Waldorf Salad. 'What's a Waldorf, anyway? A walnut that's gone off?'

JOHN CLEESE'S TOP FAWLTY TOWERS MOMENTS

9

'WHAT ARE YOU DOING? WHAT DO YOU MEAN, YOU'VE
BURNED IT! HOW COULD YOU FORGET ABOUT THEM?'

Basil hurries to the kitchen but gets in a squabble with Terry about payment for working late, and finally Terry refuses the offer and leaves. In *The Complete Fawlty Towers*, where the scripts of all the episodes are printed in full, the story so far – up to Terry leaving – has occupied 8 pages. The next scene, where Basil has to serve the Hamiltons and prepare their dinner, takes 14 pages. It's the longest

scene anywhere in both series! Just Basil trying (with very little 'help' from Sybil) to give the Hamiltons dinner . . . During the course of which, Basil learns that a 'Screwdriver' is not a screwdriver, that there are no Waldorfs in a Waldorf Salad and that Harold Robbins' books are not American pornographic tripe. Mr Hamilton learns that Basil doesn't have any celery because this Wednesday the delivery man may have fractured his arm, and that all these mistakes can be blamed on the chef, who Basil is pretending is still in the kitchen.

Finally, when Basil goes into the kitchen to shout at Terry, yet again, Mr Hamilton has had enough, and follows him. When he opens the swing door, he sees Basil swearing at an empty space, while playing the role of the non-existent chef. After about twenty seconds Basil sees Mr Hamilton watching.

Basil: (*Smiling welcomingly*) Mr Hamilton, may I introduce Terry who . . . (*indicates the empty space, then jumps*) Where did he go? (*to Hamilton*) Where's he gone? Did you see him?

Mr Hamilton: Maybe he went to get something to eat.

He leaves the kitchen decisively and goes to his wife in the dining room.

I simply love the fact that Basil, caught in the most outrageous lie, still tries to keep it going, like when he looked for the duck in his raspberry trifle. The desperate hopefulness is both insane and rather touching.

And Basil continues to insist that Terry must have just left before Mr Hamilton arrived. Hamilton silences him.

Bruce Boa
Mr Hamilton

An aggrieved guest who spars with Basil, before starting a full-on insurrection in the hotel – there had never been a visitor at Fawlty Towers quite like Mr Harry Hamilton.

Before acting entered his life, Canadian-born Bruce Boa studied theology at the University of Western Ontario, and played professional Canadian football. It wasn't until a tour of Central America and Europe that the possibilities of acting took hold of Bruce.

Settling in Britain in 1960, his marvellous voice and good looks soon saw him became one of 'the Americans' in British film and television. Bruce juggled James Bond films with small-screen guest roles as the ready-made, perfectly crafted character from the other side of the pond. Amongst other silver-screen hits, he will forever be part of cinematic history as the Rebel general in the 1980

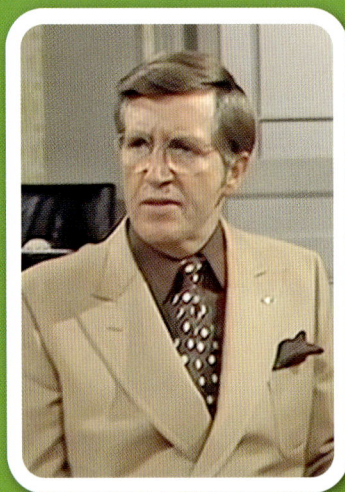

Star Wars sequel, *The Empire Strikes Back.*

Bruce's powerful scene-stealing performance as Californian visitor Mr Hamilton in *Fawlty* is no small feat, considering that he only had five days to learn the lines and prepare for the studio recording.

Despite airing third, *Waldorf Salad* was actually the first episode recorded for the second series, so in this episode the team were all still getting back into their wonderful rhythm from 1975. Thankfully Bruce made a great addition to the cast to kick-start this second run.

Mr Hamilton: Do you think I don't know what's been going on out there?

Basil: Oh – it's a bit of a debacle, I'm afraid . . .

Mr Hamilton: I'm talking about you taking twenty pounds off me to keep the chef on, letting him go, cooking the meal yourself and then pretending he's still out there.

Basil: Oh, that.

Mr Hamilton: Yes, that. And I'd be interested to know what you've got to say about it.

By this time some guests have gathered within earshot. They include the Major, Mr Arrad and Misses Tibbs and Gatsby.

Basil: *(to them)* Good evening.

Mr Hamilton: I asked you a question!

Basil: Yes – I'm sorry that your meal has not been fully satisfactory this evening . . .

Mr Hamilton: *(addressing the guests)* Hah! What I'm suggesting is that this is the crummiest, shoddiest, worst-run hotel in the whole of Western Europe.

The Major: No! No! I won't have that! There's a place in Eastbourne . . . what's its name . . .?

Mr Hamilton: *(to Basil)* And that you are the British Tourist Board's answer to Donald Duck.

'Waldorf Salad'

(aka 'USA', 'The Americans')

SERIES 2 EPISODE 3

Recorded: 21 January 1979 (TC1)

First transmission: 5 March 1979

Guest stars: Bruce Boa (Mr Hamilton), Claire Nielson (Mrs Hamilton), Norman Bird (Mr Arrad), Stella Tanner (Mrs Arrad), Terence Conoley (Mr Johnston), June Ellis (Mrs Johnston), Anthony Daws (Mr Libson), Beatrice Shaw (Miss Gurke), Dorothy Frere (Miss Hare)

Uncredited: Mark Kirby, Elaine Payne (Hotel Guests)

Basil: No, look, I know things have gone wrong this evening, but you must remember that we've had thousands of satisfied customers . . .

Mr Hamilton: All right, let's ask them, eh?

Basil: What?

Mr Hamilton: Let's ask them. *(to the spectators)* Are you all satisfied?

And emboldened by the American's example, the guests Basil treated so badly in the opening scene finally speak up.

Mr Johnstone: I think this is probably the worst hotel we've ever stayed in.

Claire Nielson
Mrs Hamilton

Sassy, strong and faultless, Mrs Hamilton has fully become accustomed to her new life under the Californian sun, the place where 'fresh orange juice pours like running water.'

Claire Nielson made for a wonderful Mrs Hamilton in 'Waldorf Salad'. In a part which could easily be swept away by all the blustering dialogue given to her husband, Claire very subtly adds to the frustration of service at Fawlty Towers.

After relocating to London from her native Scotland, Claire quickly became a TV comedy stalwart, as a regular on *The Dick Emery Show* as well as appearing in many sketches in *The*

Two Ronnies. She could also apply herself to drama in the likes of *Upstairs Downstairs, Pie in the Sky* and *Taggart*. During the 1980s, Claire took a break from acting to read English at King's College, Cambridge.

Later years saw Claire continue her TV work, opposite Richard Briers in *Monarch of the Glen*, and write a novel, along with several books on parenting.

Mrs Johnston: Yes it is. The service here is an absolute disgrace.

Mrs Arrad: I agree.

Mr Hamilton: You do?

And they all pile in with their complaints until Basil too has had enough.

Basil: This is typical, absolutely typical . . . of the kind of . . . *(shouting)* ARSE I have to put up with from you people. You ponce in here expecting to be waited on hand and foot, well, I'm trying to run a hotel here. Have you any idea of how much there is to do? Do you ever think of that? Of course not, you're all too busy sticking your noses into every corner, poking around for things to complain about, aren't you. Well, let me tell you something – this is exactly how Nazi Germany started, you know. A lot of layabouts with nothing better to do than cause trouble. Well, I've had fifteen years of pandering to please the likes of you and I've had enough. I've had it. Come on, pack your bags and get out!

And of course this is the moment when Sybil arrives. Basil explains what's going on.

Basil: Well, let me put it this way, dear – either they go or I go. *(Sybil just looks at him)* Right! Come back everybody. My wife's had a better idea. Come on back. I'm going instead. Well, goodbye dear. It's been an interesting fifteen years but all good things must come to an end. *(kisses her)* I hope you enjoy your new work here, helping run a hotel. Goodbye, Major. Goodbye, ladies, give my regards to Polly and Manuel. Bye, dear.

He stalks out through the main doors. Outside it is pouring with rain. He keeps going but after a few yards comes to a halt and stands there getting soaked. He looks up and thinks . . . Basil comes back in.

Basil: Hallo dear, I'm back.

Sybil: What do you want, Basil?

Basil: A room, please. Number twelve is free, I think. I'd like breakfast in bed at half past nine in the morning, please, that's eggs, bacon, sausage and tomato, Waldorf salad washed down with lashings of hot Screwdrivers . . .

And what happens next? Thank God this is the end of the show, so we don't have to solve that problem. As I've already said, you can always get a bit silly at the very end of an episode, because you don't have to follow it. Another thing I like about the end of an episode? Answer: you can start the next episode as though nothing has happened! Which is how we start the next episode where a guest actually dies!

Above: 'I'm suggesting that this place is the crummiest, shoddiest, worst-run hotel in the whole of Western Europe!' – Mr Hamilton's insurrection in full swing! Note dear Terence Conoley to the left of me as Mr Johnston (who was last seen without a hairpiece as Mr Wareing in 'A Touch of Class').

Below: Filming on location outside the Grange in the pouring rain, with the BBC rain curtain set up above me.

THE KIPPER AND THE CORPSE

Above: Sybil and Terry prepare the day's breakfast whilst Basil checks the date on the newspaper.

Below: Mr Leeman (Derek Royle, far left) is dropped off by his friends, Miss Young (Pamela Buchner), Mr Zebedee (Raymond Mason) and Mr Xerxes (Robert McBain). Derek Royle was a highly experienced farce actor, who played a fantastic dead body in this story. Make-up also did a tremendous job making him look so ill!

The problem with writing about 'The Kipper and the Corpse' is that it contains more visual, or physical comedy than any other episode. It's a truism in film and television that executives don't want to read scripts. The best a writer can hope for is that they will skim the script and notice two or three verbal jokes. But to expect them to read the stage directions and then to visualise the actions described in detail is futile. They won't and probably can't. So, I have the same problem. It would take paragraphs to describe to you all the physical comedy,

and you're going to skim them all. But the answer is simple. Watch it!

It's one of my three favourite episodes (along with 'Basil the Rat' and 'The Psychiatrist') and if you don't think it's really funny, you won't have bought this book, and so you won't be reading this. But I'll pick out a few points. There are only three plotlines. The main one was suggested to me by an old friend, Andrew Leeman. He was a successful restauranteur, but he started his training at the famous Savoy Hotel (established 1889). In search of comic material, I asked Andrew, 'What was the worst problem they had to deal with at the Savoy?' And without batting an eyelid, he answered, 'Getting rid of the stiffs.' So that was an episode all but written. Classic farce plot: something to hide! The second plotline is the doctor who wants his sausages. We managed to get Geoffrey Palmer to play Dr Price, so we knew that those scenes were going to work, as Geoffrey was a truly superb comic actor.

And the third plotline is a nasty, yappy little lapdog who bites Manuel and Polly, who poisons him with lashings of Tabasco. The dog fades out of the story with his owner asking for a vet. Connie and I always tried to bring all the plotlines together at the end of an episode, but we failed here. But I'm fond of the exchange at the opening of the show, when its proud owner tells the Major, 'It's a little shih-tzu' and the Major replies, 'And what breed is he?'

The first scene introduces the corpse-to-be, Mr Leeman (named after my friend Andrew), and we establish that he is being dropped off at the hotel by three business colleagues, whom we will see later. Mr Leeman is not feeling well, and he asks if he could have his breakfast in bed. 'Kippers?' Sybil suggests. 'Yes, thank you,' Leeman replies and makes his way upstairs. The next morning, Basil delivers the breakfast without noticing Mr Leeman is dead. He was earlier concerned that the kippers Terry was cooking were past their eat-by date, so when Polly reports Mr Leeman's death he panics, believing that the kippers may have poisoned him. When Polly points out that the corpse is cold, Basil is so relieved that he is still celebrating when Dr Price arrives.

The next scenes are all about 'getting rid of the stiff'. This is complicated by: one of the old ladies, Miss Tibbs, who sees the dead body and faints – not once, but on two separate occasions; by a couple, who are trying to get into their hotel room, where Basil has hidden the body in their wardrobe; and finally, after Dr Price has

forbidden the staff from keeping the corpse in the kitchen, by them concealing Leeman in a laundry basket that is waiting to be collected. Dr Price still wants his sausages, but when he goes back into the dining room, Manuel is clearing away the breakfast things from the doctor's table. One of my all-time favourite scenes ensues:

Dr Price puts his hands on the tablecloth, just as Manuel tries to remove it.

Dr Price: Leave it.

Manuel: No, I take it.

Dr Price: Leave it.

Manuel: No, no, is not time, please. *(Dr Price starts moving salt and pepper from an adjoining table)* No, no, no, please.

Dr Price: I'm sitting here.

Manuel: Is no lunch till twelve.

Dr Price: I'm still having breakfast.

Below: Manuel and Dr Price brilliantly dance around the dining table. It was such a pleasure to welcome Geoffrey Palmer to the cast of 'The Kipper and the Corpse'. I adored Geoffrey, it was a joy to work with him many times.

10 JOHN CLEESE'S TOP FAWLTY TOWERS MOMENTS

'WOULD YOU BELIEVE IT? I GET HIM HIS BREAKFAST, I TAKE IT ALL THE WAY UPSTAIRS, I LAY IT IN FRONT OF HIM, HAND HIM HIS NEWSPAPER, I TIDY THE ROOM, DRAW THE CURTAINS, GUESS WHAT HE SAYS? – NOTHING!'

Manuel: . . . Is finished . . . all gone . . . breakfast kaput.

Dr Price: *(sitting)* I'm having sausages.

Manuel: *(confiscating the cruet)* Is not allowed.

Dr Price: Put that back. Look, I'm a doctor, I'm a doctor and I want my sausages.

Manuel: I tell you, is finished. Bye-bye, please, bye-bye.

Dr Price rises, he gets salt and mustard from another table. As he returns, Manuel pinches his knife and fork and darts off. There is no other cutlery around.

Dr Price: Now look.

Manuel: Is finish.

Dr Price: *(getting really angry)* Give those to me. *(pursues Manuel round the table)* Come on, come on.

Manuel: No, is no possible.

They circle the table. Basil comes in from the kitchen.

Basil: Is everything all right?

Manuel: He want to eat now.

Dr Price: I've been trying to sit down, he keeps moving things from my table.

Basil: I'm so sorry.

Dr Price: He doesn't seem to understand that I haven't finished breakfast.

'The Kipper and the Corpse'
(aka 'Death')

SERIES 2 EPISODE 4

Recorded: 11 February 1979 (TC8)

First transmission: 5 March 1979

Guest stars: Geoffrey Palmer (Dr Price), Mavis Pugh (Mrs Chase), Richard Davies (Mr White), Elizabeth Benson (Mrs White), Derek Royle (Mr Leeman), Robert McBain (Mr Xerxes), Pamela Buchner (Miss Young), Raymond Mason (Mr Zebedee), Charles McKeown (Mr Ingrams), Len Marten (Guest).

Uncredited: Harry Fielder (Laundry Van Driver), Joe Santo (Mate), Julia La Rousse (Redhead), Maureen Stevens (Double for Miss Tibbs), Richie Sandrock, Reg Woods, Audrey Kirby, Tina Winter, Garth Watkins, Jeff Howard (Hotel Guests).

Basil: Manuel? Manuel, let me explain. *(He pokes Manuel in the eye)* You understand? Good. *(to Dr Price)* They'll be with you in just a couple of minutes.

I love when they circle the table, with Manuel holding the tablecloth as though it's a matador's cape. This is great acting by two of the very best.

Below: Andy, Derek and I doing some great stuff with the laundry basket. Derek Royle did some truly fantastic acting as the corpse, which in something as physical as this is a very difficult thing to do. In one of the scenes where we carry him I can remember we caught him on the side of the set, but Derek didn't make a sound or movement.

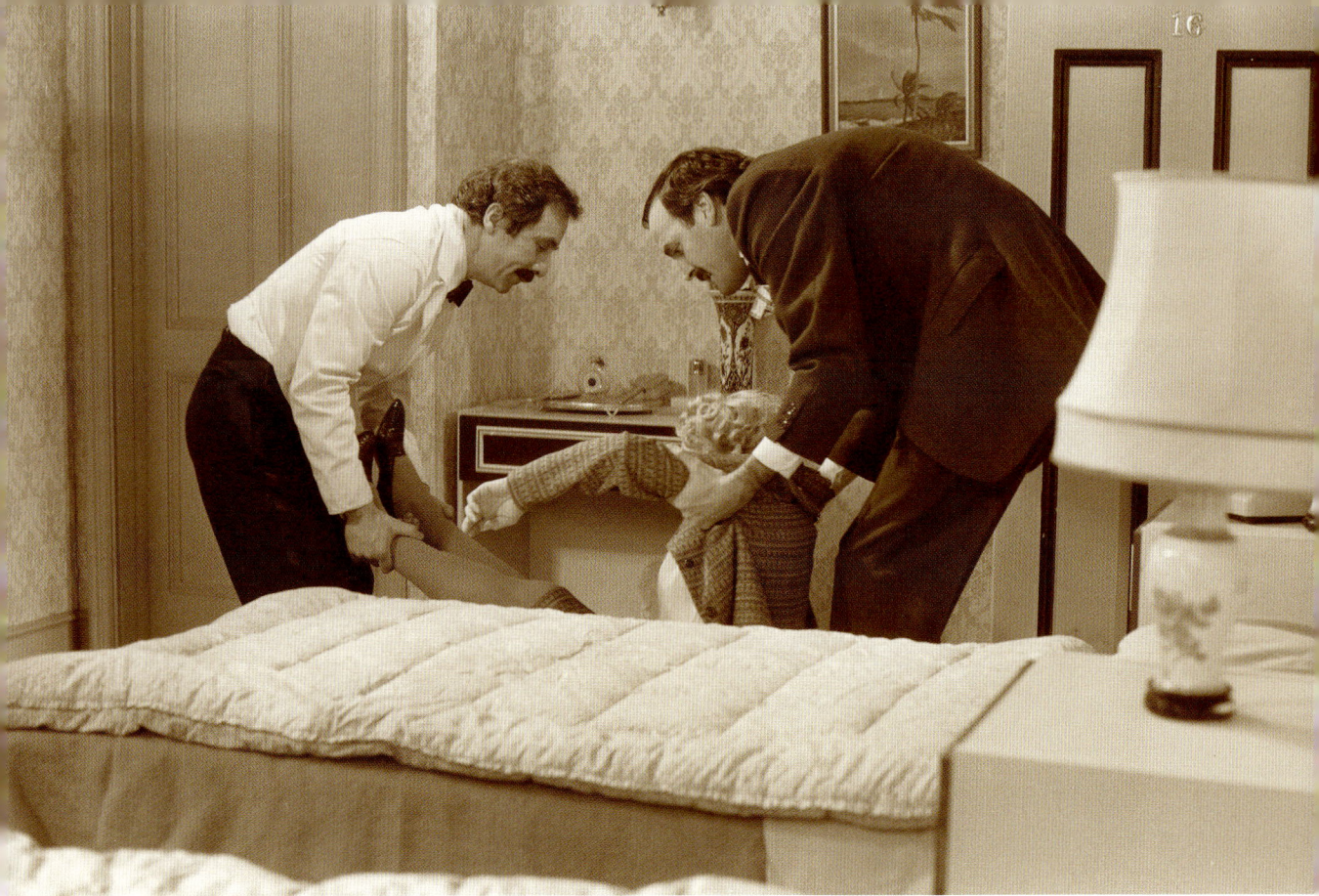

Above: Poor Miss Tibbs is lifted up by Manuel and Basil, after being knocked out by Polly! Bless Gilly Flower, this was the biggest moment she had in the series and she performed it brilliantly. This particular photo is from a cutaway shot we rehearsed and recorded, but it was edited out of the final epsiode.

When Basil enters the lobby again, he doesn't notice that the laundry basket has mysteriously moved its position. He finds Leeman's three business colleagues there, waiting to take Leeman to the meeting.

Miss Young: We've come to collect him.

Basil: (*Realising they must be the undertakers*) You've come to collect him! I'm sorry, I didn't realise. Modern dress.

Miss Young: What?

Basil: Your dress is very modern, I didn't realise women did it.

Miss Young: Did what?

Basil: Ssh (*points down at the basket*).

Mr Zebedee: He's downstairs?

Basil: (*quietly*) No, no – in the basket.

Mr Xerxes: . . . I beg your pardon?

Basil: He's in the basket.

Miss Young: In the basket?

Basil: Yes. (*to a passing guest*) Hallo.

Mr Xerxes: What's . . . what's he doing in the basket?

Basil: (*with a minimal shrug*) Well . . . not much.

Mr Xerxes: What are you talking about?

Basil: Don't you believe me? Look. Look. (*He opens the lid a little; they hesitantly look in; he glances round and opens it more; they look in and look at Basil, mystified; he looks at them, looks in the basket,* and reacts with horror. Polly comes downstairs.) Oh my God! He's gone! Where is he?

Polly: (pointing into the basket) Fresh laundry.

Basil: They've taken him! (Basil, Manuel and Polly rush outside, the laundry van is pulling away . . .)

Basil: Sorry to keep you. (He and an increasingly flagging Manuel drag the basket in and park it by the desk) It's all right. It's all right. We sorted it out. He's in this one.

Xerxes and company stare at him.

I think this is one of the funniest situations Connie and I ever wrote. Three people come to collect a colleague to take him to a meeting, and to begin with they are told he is being kept in a basket and then, when it turns out that he is not in the basket, the hotel owner goes and gets another identical basket and claims he is in this basket instead.

At some point lunacy like this has to be sorted out, and Sybil arrives to take care of Leeman's colleagues. Basil and Manuel have to take the body back upstairs, but terrify two guests and have to bring it down again and put it back in the basket. But Manuel is exhausted.

Manuel: Can't lift.

Basil: Come on!

Manuel: Too tired.

Basil: There's somebody coming!

Manuel: Mr Fawlty, I no want to work here any more.

Basil: Open the basket.

Manuel: No.

Basil: Open the basket! (Manuel opens the basket)

Basil: Now inside. (Manuel starts climbing inside it) Not you!

Manuel: I quit.

Basil: Get out.

Manuel: I on strike.

Basil: I'm warning you . . .

Manuel: I stay here. Is nice.

Basil: (nearly berserk) You see this . . . (indicating Mr Leeman) You're next!

Below: Mr Leeman's friends arrive at the hotel to pick him up . . . A fantastic piece of misunderstanding, as Basil assumes they are from the undertakers!

Below right: 'Look, I'm a doctor and I want my sausages!' – Geoffrey Palmer's Dr Price finally gets what he wants!

Opposite page, top right: A fantastic shot with me leaning up against the hat rack, hiding the corpse of Mr Leeman! Here we can see the episode's other guest stars: Mrs Chase (Mavis Pugh), and Mr and Mrs White (Richard Davies and Elizabeth Benson).

Sybil emerges with the business people and ushers them towards the entrance. They see Basil who is standing defiantly in front of the hat rack, trying to disguise the fact that he has stacked Mr Leeman on the umbrella stand part of the hat rack behind him. But Basil doesn't know that Mr Zebedee hung his hat on the rack when he first arrived, and it can't be retrieved now without revealing the dead body of their colleague.

Mr Zebedee now approaches the hat stand.

Basil: Yes?

Mr Zebedee: Could I get my hat?

Basil: Your hat?

Mr Zebedee: Yes. It's just the...

Basil: Yes, I'll have it sent on. Do you have a card with your address? I'll send it on.

Mr Zebedee: Well . . . could I just get it?

Basil: Well, do you have to have it now?

Mr Zebedee: Yes.

Basil: Well, supposing you lose it? It's very windy.

Mr Zebedee: I'd like to have it.

Basil: *(sighs at the basket)* Oh, right . . . Manuel! Manuel! *(the others look alarmed)* He's in the basket. He is . . . *(Polly comes downstairs)* Polly, would you get Manuel out of the basket, please.

Astonishment as Manuel emerges from the basket.

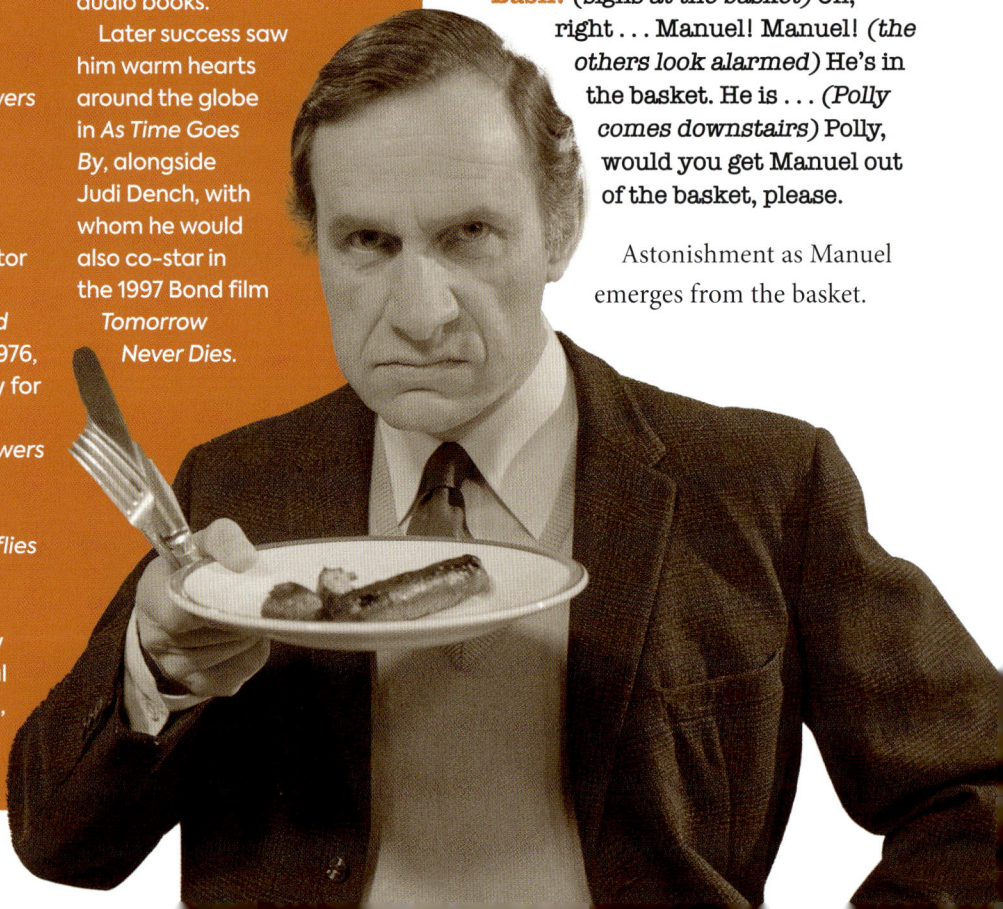

Geoffrey Palmer / Dr Price

We find out two things about Dr Price in 'The Kipper and the Corpse': he is a medical doctor, and he has a healthy appetite . . . Swept up in Manuel's mayhem at the dining table, the no-nonsense doctor has one focus: sausages!

With his impeccable comic timing and understated delivery, Geoffrey Palmer made for another perfect addition to the *Fawlty Towers* visitors book.

Cutting his teeth on the stage, Geoffrey gradually built up a career as a dependable character actor across film and TV. His big break came in *The Fall and Rise of Reginald Perrin* in 1976, revealing a natural affinity for studio comedy.

His casting in *Fawlty Towers* came just weeks after the first series of Carla Lane's bittersweet classic *Butterflies* aired – which became a smash hit.

Over the years, Geoffrey became the quintessential sitcom screen Englishman, able to convey so much with just a glance or the carefully judged raise of an eyebrow.

Big-screen appearances in *A Fish Called Wanda*, *The Madness of King George* and *Mrs Brown* brought him to a wider audience. Beyond the screen, Geoffrey's dulcet tones effortlessly lent gravitas to countless adverts and audio books.

Later success saw him warm hearts around the globe in *As Time Goes By*, alongside Judi Dench, with whom he would also co-star in the 1997 Bond film *Tomorrow Never Dies*.

He and Polly now try to identify Mr Zebedee's hat. This takes some time, and Miss Tibbs arrives to complain to Basil about her recent experiences. Dr Price appears, complaining that his sausages are off and should have been eaten last week. Miss Tibbs suddenly sees the body and screams. Other guests come running. Chaos.

Basil: *(seeing Sybil)* Ah, there you are, dear. You do look nice. Ladies and gentlemen . . . ladies and gentlemen . . . *(calling out through the main door)* Laundry's ready . . . *(to his audience)* Ladies and gentlemen, there have been a lot of cock-ups this morning, you all deserve an explanation, and I'm happy to say that my wife will give it to you. Thank you, thank you so much.

He gestures extravagantly towards Sybil. The throng turns towards her; he leaps into the basket and pulls the lid down. Two laundry men come in, pick up the basket and carry it out. Sybil is surrounded by the throng, all complaining noisily. The Major comes downstairs and sees the corpse.

The Major: *(to Mr Leeman)* What's going on, old boy?

Outside, the basket is loaded on the back of the van, which drives off. Sybil's voice wafts after it.

Sybil's: Basil! Basil! Basil! . . .

Below: The laundry van pulls away as the credits start to roll . . . A really nice gag to end things on. Eagle-eyed viewers (those who can read a spot of reverse writing) might notice the curved metal 'Wooburn Grange Country Club' sign in the background!

THE ANNIVERSARY

Above: Basil attempts to make some conversation with his and Sybil's old friends. Left to right, Virginia (Pat Keen), Alice (Una Stubbs), Arthur (Robert Arnold) and Roger (Ken Campbell).

Below: Me on set holding a newspaper with a headline that mentions the BBC strike which held back the recording of 'The Anniversary' by a week.

'The Anniversary' was recorded at the BBC TV Centre, on 26 March 1979. It was supposed to have been recorded the week before, but a BBC executive hit a rigger. That is, a middle manager at the BBC got into an argument with a rigger, who is someone who helps erect sets for TV shows . . . and punched him. So, there was an immediate strike. And I was delighted, because we'd already started rehearsing 'The Anniversary' and when the recording was moved on a week, it meant we had several extra days' rehearsal; and it was so enjoyable being able to rehearse without the usual pressures – trying to learn and rehearse 140 pages in four days – with the result that the acting in this episode was, I think, the best we ever had in an *Fawlty Towers* episode. Connie's performance was inspired, there

was perfect teamwork from the six guests, Manuel's rivalry with Terry showed a hilarious indignation we'd never seen before . . . and Sybil, showing her real vulnerability for the first time, was superb.

In fact, the only person whose performance was not top-class was me. But more of that later.

The only problem the strike brought us was the need to replace my old friend Julian Holloway, who we'd cast as Roger, and who had an unbreakable commitment on the 26th. But we managed to get Ken Campbell, whom the *Guardian* called 'unclassifiable'. I'd seen him in his bizarre and utterly wonderful *Ken Campbell Road Show*, and I'd spent time with him after that. He once told me that God had created the universe 'for the purpose of humour'. And his performance as Roger was quite divine . . .

Anyway, when I re-watched 'The Anniversary', I was shocked to realise that it was quite different in tone from the other eleven shows. But first, let's examine the plot, which is again very simple.

Last year, Basil forgot his wedding anniversary, and Sybil clearly gave him a hard time about it! So this year, he decides to play a practical joke on her. He pretends that he's forgotten it again. He invites guests and gets Manuel to prepare a special paella, but he acts towards Sybil as though he's forgotten. It's an almost affectionate act, as he is looking forward to the moment when she realises that he's remembered after all. But . . . Sybil is so upset by his subterfuge, that she finally just walks out. Just like that! And the three couples start arriving and, of course, can't wait to see Sybil. Now, Basil could just explain, and her friends would be disappointed, but basically they'd understand.

But this is not Basil's modus operandi. He must never admit that he's made any kind of mistake, that there's ever been any kind of cock-up. (Also, this is a farce, so there has to be a secret that the protagonist must cover up.) So, he has to start lying about why Sybil isn't there to greet them. And his lies get even worse than usual.

Alice: What's the matter, Basil?

Basil: Nothing . . . Nothing.

Alice: With Sybil.

Basil: Oh, with Sybil.
Oh . . . quite a bit actually.

Alice: Oh dear.

Basil: No, no, she's fine. She's absolutely fine . . . well, I mean she's feeling dreadful, but she'll live and that's what counts in the long run, isn't it. Ha ha.

Alice: Well, I'll pop up and see her then.

Basil: Oh, you don't want to bother with that.

Alice: Oh, but she's up there on her own, I'm sure she'd like a little company.

Basil: Uh-huh.

Alice: I know I would.

Basil: Well, you wouldn't if you looked at her. You know, she's very swollen up. You know . . . (he indicates the eyes) . . . And she looks fairly . . . you know what Sybil's like about her appearance.

Alice: Oh, don't be silly, Basil, she won't mind me seeing her.

Basil: (restraining her) Oh she would! I think she would.

Basil: Well, she's having a bit of a sleep . . . you know.

Alice: Well, she can sleep all day, Basil, she won't mind me just . . .

Above: A photo from the original exterior location scene with Una Stubbs as Alice and Julian Holloway as Roger . . . We had to reshoot this whole exterior sequence when we cast Ken Campbell as the new Roger for the remounted recording.

Happily ever after

In 'The Hotel Inspectors', it is revealed that Basil and Sybil have been married 12 years, and that they bought the hotel in 1966 . . . In 'Waldorf Salad' it is mentioned that they have been together 15 years . . . and they were due to celebrate this during the events of 'The Anniversary' on 17 April... This all suggests that the Fawltys were married in 1963, thus buying the hotel after three years of matrimony!

Basil: No, but she's . . . lost her voice.

Alice: Lost her voice?

Basil: Gone . . . just like that.

Alice: Basil, has the doctor been?

Basil: Nuts?

Roger: (*sotto voce*) They've had a row. She's refused to come down.

Basil: Um . . . you were just asking about the doctor.

Alice: Yes.

Basil: You see, he hasn't been yet.

Polly comes in from the lobby.

Alice: Ah! Hallo, Polly.

Polly: Oh, hallo, Mrs Tarry.

Alice: Isn't it a shame about Mrs Fawlty.

Polly: Isn't it – I'm afraid the doctor says she's going to have to be quiet in bed for a couple of days.

Basil: Yes, but the doctor hasn't actually been yet, Polly . . . I don't know who you were thinking of . . .

Polly: But that man this morning . . . he looked like a doctor.

Basil: Yes, yes, he did actually, yes, that's true . . . but he wasn't.

Finally, Basil persuades – no, bribes – Polly to dress up as Sybil and to lie in bed pretending to be her. This involves a wig and make-up and cotton wool in her cheeks . . . and a very darkened bedroom. When the friends come upstairs, Basil delays them until Polly is ready, and to pass the time he goes downstairs to get them some nuts. And Sybil arrives! She comes back to get her golf clubs. At this point, there is a very strange scene. I will return to it in a minute, because it has caused me to revise my opinion of the whole episode after forty-five years.

Anyway, Sybil leaves, upset and forgetting the clubs, and Basil runs back up to the waiting friends and finally allows them into the bedroom which he has kept so dark that they can hardly see and start falling over things. They speak with Polly, who waves and gestures that she cannot speak. Sybil's friend Virginia, who we have established is a nurse, insists on feeling Polly's glands, and Polly avoids discovery only by shoving her away, so that Virginia falls off the bed and injures herself. General astonishment.

The friends now return downstairs, and they assemble to say goodbye to Basil, so they can escape from this inexplicable experience. Then Sybil walks back in. She has had to come back for the golf clubs,

again. They all stare at each other until Basil, pretending that Sybil is not in fact Sybil, introduces his wife to her own friends as someone else, hurries her into the kitchen, and locks her in a cupboard. Then he goes back to the guests and ushers them out of the hotel. Basil (to Polly): 'Piece of cake.' He braces himself and makes for the kitchen. 'Now comes the tricky part . . .' Well, we're allowed to get really silly if it's right at the end, aren't we?

So, to go back to my feelings of shock when I re-watched this episode. It was because what Connie and I had written in this episode were moments when the audience feels real concern for Sybil, who reveals her unhappiness. For example, in the opening scenes, she is clearly really upset that Basil has forgotten the anniversary again. And when the audience

'The Anniversary'

Recorded: 18 March 1979 (TC1)

First transmission: 26 March 1979 (postponed from 19 March 1979)

Guest stars: Ken Campbell (Roger), Una Stubbs (Alice), Robert Arnold (Arthur), Pat Keen (Virginia), Roger Hume (Reg), Denyse Alexander (Kitty), Christine Shaw (Audrey).

SERIES 2 EPISODE 5

feels a character's real pain, it bothers them and they stop laughing. And I made a big mistake in the way I was playing Basil. I made him too cocksure, too arrogant, when playing that scene. Softer and slightly more amused would have taken the curse off it. As I performed it, he is a real asshole. The bickering between them is normally just a ritual, with very little real nastiness in it, and Basil's usual sarcasm is clearly due to the fact that Sybil isn't doing her share of the work running the hotel.

Below: Basil nervously looks on as his friends – now including Reg (Roger Hume) – wait outside his and Sybil's bedroom to wish her a happy anniversary.

'HELLO, DARLING, DON'T TRY AND SPEAK ...
WE THOUGHT WE'D COME WISH YOU HAPPY ANNIVERSARY.'

Above left: 'How extraordinary . . . How is the north?' Sybil arrives back at the hotel stunned by the scene in front of her, as Basil whisks her away. Note the BBC studio camera on the far left.

I think the next part of the show is funny, with Basil having to invent the dreadful and transparent lies, and bribing Polly to impersonate Sybil, but then I make the same mistake, only worse.

When Basil hurries downstairs to get some nuts for the friends to eat while they're waiting to get into Sybil's bedroom and Sybil returns, there is the most painful scene in the whole *Fawlty Towers* canon. She is really hurt and Basil has the chance to do something about it. He could have explained what had happened and taken her upstairs to surprise her friends . . . but he doesn't. He keeps going because he can't bear to lose face by revealing all his ridiculous lies. So, as Sybil says she ought to be leaving again, and clearly doesn't want to, he just says, 'Whatever you think is best.' So she leaves, even more upset than she was earlier. This time he is even more of an asshole than he was at the beginning, and Sybil's emotional pain is too uncomfortable to watch, and it doesn't feel the slightest bit funny any more.

A couple of examples of this rule about the audience being bothered by pain. I've already touched on the scene in *Monty Python and the Holy Grail*, when the Black Knight getting his arms and legs chopped off is the film's biggest laugh. Can you believe that? But it's because the Black Knight shows no pain, he's not even disappointed. In *A Fish Called Wanda*, a dog is flattened by a car – screams of laughter!

But in the first cut, the close-up of the squished dog had some blood and entrails. The laughter died in a moment. Complete silence. An audience can laugh at the *idea* of a flattened dog, but if reminded of the *reality* of it, the shock is too painful. So we simply replaced the bloody dog corpse with a dog-shaped raffia mat – pandemonium ensues!

Most of the time, Basil, after he's been wound up, behaves rudely and unkindly. But we don't hate him because we've watched him get so wound up and so we are able to sympathise with him to some extent, so long as he doesn't cause another character real pain (and when he makes the German woman cry, he's had a blow to the head). This misjudgement meant that I watched parts of 'The Anniversary' with discomfort and disappointment!

BASIL THE RAT

Above: This lovely little exterior scene set outside the hotel was the closest we came to actually filming inside the Wooburn Grange Country Club location.

After all the misgivings I had when I re-watched 'The Anniversary', I felt a rush of pure happiness as I watched 'Basil the Rat' again. It's really good!! I think it may be my favourite episode of them all. I've always felt that the top three were: 'The Kipper and the Corpse', 'The Psychiatrist', but I find I have even stronger warm feelings about the rat episode. First of all, it lasts 40 minutes! How on earth did we manage that? (Well, yes, there were some short rat shots that had to be recorded earlier, and about two minutes of film with Manuel going to the hut where he and Polly had hidden Basil (the rat),

but we still somehow recorded 37 minutes in the studio, in two hours. Then there's the title. If Manuel ever found himself a pet, of course it would be called Basil. So the subsequent misunderstandings follow effortlessly.

Then there's the fact that, apart from the health inspector and a young couple who appear in the last five minutes, there are no other guest actors. So all the funny stuff is performed by Manuel, Polly, Terry, Sybil and me. To see just how good Manuel, Polly and Terry are, is actually thrilling for me. This is probably the best script for Manuel, because it gives him more moods to play – pretending to be sad, standing up to Basil about Basil, alarm when he thinks his pet has been shot, frantically looking for him – and he is absolutely wonderful. So is Polly, desperate as usual to keep the show on the road, with those wide-eyed looks when she's trying out a lie. She never puts a foot wrong. Terry, who has created a whole character out of the small part of the chef, fits into the employee trio quite effortlessly. And Sybil's pretty good too. (And I'm also much better than usual, probably because Basil is at last frightened about something really important – the inspector closing the hotel down!)

But I haven't forgotten the young couple, with David Neville as the perfect upper-class twit of the year, getting superbly indignant and telling Basil off ('you grotty little man'), along with Sabina Franklyn as his unfairly rattled fiancée. And finally, the incomparable John Quarmby, first as the implacable bureaucratic threat, and, on his return, as the bewildered observer of top-drawer insanity as he arrives the next day to see Polly racing around with a large butterfly net, Basil is holding the rifle with which the Major has been shooting at the rat, and Manuel panicking that the owner of Fawlty Towers has been murdered. The way he just stands there, watching this, (like the old man with the chair in *The Pink Panther 2*), is . . . magnificent.

Years ago, I used to watch *Candid Camera*, and I learned a hugely important lesson. When people are utterly astonished

– as when a car turns out not to have an engine, or a snooker player's arm reaches out through a TV screen to retrieve a ball that has just come through the screen – anyone who sees this complete mystery … simply . . . stares. No expression. Not a single facial muscle moves. It's the purest blankness. And this is what John Quarmby does to utter faultless perfection. He just looks at the rat, and sits there motionless while Manuel drags the body of Basil Fawlty – who has obviously fainted – out of the dining room.

Top right: The Major takes up arms in the rat search! Note the bar's red walls for its second-series make-over.

Above: Basil takes a close look under Quentina (Sabina Franklyn) and Ronald's (David Neville) table in the dining room … much to Ronald's annoyance.

Below: Basil the Rat! The first reference to Manuel's pet 'hamster' was in 'The Germans', but in 'Basil the Rat', it is mentioned that Manuel has only had this particular pet for a year …

John Quarmby
Mr Carnegie

Liverpool-born RADA graduate John Quarmby has the honour of being the series' final guest star, as Mr Carnegie, the unflinchingly dedicated health inspector in 'Basil the Rat'. From his opening shot of sniffing a plate of raw meat on his hands and knees in the hotel's kitchen, to the absurd final moments of biscuit-tin-rat puppetry, John was sublime in the role.

After two decades in rep theatre he was no stranger to being caught in the middle of a farce. In 'Basil the Rat', Quarmby faultlessly delivers one of the longest single pieces of dialogue in the entire series with a meticulously delivered monologue of hotel failings.

Due to the knock-on effects of the BBC strike, production of 'Basil the Rat' was delayed by nearly two months, but fortunately John was still available for the later recording dates in May.

Another versatile TV face, away from fictional Torquay, John can be seen as a prison officer in *Porridge*, a fisherman in *Howard's Way* and a Lord in the lavish 1986 costume drama *The December Rose*.

The plot of 'Basil the Rat' starts simply. The secret that has to be kept from the inspector – that there is a large rat loose in the hotel – becomes a quest to avoid killing the inspector by poisoning him. This gives us ever more urgency than the usual secret-keeping. We start with Basil entering the kitchen and finding a total stranger examining the contents of the refrigerator. Basil's sarcasm is stilled by the man revealing that he is from the public health department.

Carnegie: These premises do not come up to the standard required by this authority. Unless appropriate steps are taken instantly, I shall have no alternative but to prosecute or recommend closure to the appropriate committee of the Council. Specifically, lack of proper cleaning routines, dirty and greasy filters, greasy and encrusted deep fat fryer, dirty, cracked and missing wall and floor tiles, dirty, marked and stained utensils, dirty and greasy interior surfaces of the ventilator hoods.

Basil: Yes, about the fat fryer . . .

Carnegie: Inadequate temperature control and storage of dangerous foodstuffs, storage of cooked and raw meat in same trays, storage of raw meat about confectionery with consequent dripping of meat juices on to cream products, refrigerator seals loose and cracked, icebox undefrosted and refrigerator overstocked. Food handling routine suspect, evidence of smoking in food preparation area, dirty and grubby food-handling overalls, lack of wash handbasin which you gave us a verbal assurance you'd have installed on our last visit six months ago, and two dead pigeons in the water tank.

Basil: . . . Otherwise OK?

He now tells them he will be returning tomorrow and if these have not all been corrected, he will be obliged to close the kitchen down. And he leaves. Polly, Terry and Sybil start working frantically to clean everything and Basil hurries upstairs to collect Manuel to get the pigeons out of the water tank. But when he enters Manuel's bedroom, he see an extra guest.

'Basil the Rat'

Recorded: 19 & 20 May 1979

First transmission: 5 October 1979

Guest stars: John Quarmby (Mr Carnegie), David Neville (Ronald), Sabina Franklyn (Quentina), James Taylor (Mr Taylor), Melody Lang (Mrs Taylor), Stuart Sherwin (Guest)

Uncredited: Peter Jessup, Suzanne Church (Hotel Guests)

SERIES 2 EPISODE 6

Basil: What is that?

Manuel: Is my hamster.

Basil: It's a rat!

Manuel: No, no, is hamster.

Basil: Well, of course it's a rat! You have rats in Spain, don't you? – or did Franco have them all shot?

Manuel: No, is hamster.

Basil: Is rat.

Manuel: No, I think so too.

Basil: What?

Manuel: I say to man in shop, 'Is rat.' He say, 'No, no, is special kind of hamster. Is Filigree Siberian

Opposite page: With his 'in mourning' black armband, Manuel sneaks out of the hotel's kitchen with a saucer of treats for Basil . . .

Below left: Manuel's Filigree Siberian hamster! The complexities of making this story meant for the first time we would spread the recording over two days with a pre-record non-audience studio day on the Saturday, where we did most of the complex bits with animals and puppets.

Below right: 'Basil the Rat' provided a look into Manuel's bedroom, suitably decorated with his guitar (last seen in 'Gourmet Night') and his 'hamster' . . . With its angled ceiling and walls, this room is tucked into the roof of the hotel. We see Basil walk from the regular first floor set then down a short hallway to another stairwell to get there.

hamster.' Only one in shop, he make special price, only five pound.

Basil: *(calmly)* Have you ever heard of the bubonic plague, Manuel? It was very popular here at one time. A lot of pedigree hamsters came over on ships from Siberia . . . *(he takes the cage)*

Manuel: What are you doing?

Basil: I'm sorry, Manuel, this is a rat.

Manuel: No, no, is hamster.

Basil: Is not hamster. Hamsters are small and cuddly. Cuddle this, you'd never play the guitar again.

After it is made clear to Manuel that they can't keep Basil in the hotel, Polly volunteers that she has a friend in town who will look after him. Manuel and Polly carry the cage down to town, to leave Basil with the friend. The next morning the kitchen is looking spick and span in preparation for the return visit of the health inspector. Breakfast is being prepared but we see that Manuel is so depressed that his behaviour is almost unrecognisable. Naturally, this irritates Basil, who tries to change his mood. In an attempt to raise Manuel's spirits he claps him on the back.

Basil: Look, look . . . don't look at me with those awful cow eyes! Why don't you go to the cinema tonight? Why don't you and Polly go to the ice rink tonight. Why . . . why . . . why don't you cheer up, for Christ's sake!

Sybil: Basil.

Basil: I cannot stand this awful self-indulgence.

Below: Basil gives Manuel some well-intended supportive advice on dealing with depression.

Sybil: Oh, leave him alone, Basil. He's just depressed.

Basil: Manuel . . . my wife informs me that you're . . . depressed. Let me tell you something. Depression is a very bad thing. It's like a virus. If you don't stamp on it, it spreads throughout your mind, and then one day you wake up in the morning, and you . . . you can't face life any more.

Sybil: And then you open a hotel. *(exits)*

Basil: We didn't win the war by getting depressed, you know.

I love this speech by Basil, because sometimes he must feel depressed himself, trying to run the hotel without much help, and enmeshed in a marriage which is often less than joyful. And the way he can avoid feeling depressed is to stay a bit manic. But other people's depression stirs up his own. It discomfits him. So, he finds Manuel's moping rather annoying.

And what I love even more is that the moment he hurries off, Polly goes to Manuel and tells him he's over-acting! Because then we know that the moping is all an act, and that Basil the rat is not far away, after all. And the audience doesn't have to be concerned about Manuel's sadness, if it's being faked (see my notes on pain in the previous episode!). Manuel smuggles some scraps out of the kitchen and takes them to Basil where Polly and he have hidden him in a little shed, but finds that Basil the rat has escaped.

Meanwhile, the Major is sitting in the bar, when he sees a rat on one of the tables, eating the peanuts. In a flash, the Major is off to get his gun. Basil catches sight of the Major as he returns to the bar but thinks he must be looking for a German – until the Major mentions his tail. Basil freezes. He realises what has happened, grabs the gun, puts it in the office, and goes into the dining room, where Polly is on all fours looking under a table. The truth is out!! And so, a Basil hunt begins. Basil, rummaging in the kitchen, finds some rat poison, and, taking a slice of veal, covers it with poison and leaves it on the floor by the fridge. Then he hears a shot, runs to the bar, and wrestles the gun from the Major. And now of course Mr Carnegie arrives, to see Polly running about with the butterfly net, and Basil wielding a gun.

Trying to ignore the madness, Mr Carnegie goes off to inspect the property. The Basil hunt continues, and Basil discovers that Terry has put the poisoned slice back with the other veal slices, which he is in the process of cooking. From then on, the activity and complications multiply so fast, it's pointless for me to describe them all. You couldn't take it all in.

Above: 'It's gone to London to see the Queen!' – Basil, Polly and Terry try to work out which piece of veal the cat has eaten . . .

Below: A delicious piece of veal . . . or perhaps it is veal subsitute?

11.

REACTION TO THE SECOND SERIES

After a bit of a break, the final episode of *Fawlty Towers* – my favourite, 'Basil the Rat' – was broadcast on Wednesday, 24 October, some seven months after the second series started. But just what had been the reaction to Basil's sophomore year on the television?

This time round, let's take a look at three most insightful audience research reports (an independent focus group was commissioned by the BBC at the time), alongside some equally insightful press cuttings…

'Communication Problems'
(Audience Research Department, 27 March 1979)

'There was an immensely enthusiastic response to this first programme in the new series of *Fawlty Towers*. Just over two-thirds of the sampled audience had seen all or most of the programmes in the previous series and they warmly welcomed its return. They clearly found the programme extremely amusing and enjoyable – "brilliant – I nearly split my sides laughing" – some describing it as one of the best comedy series ever. Its wit, hilarity and originality made it, in the words of one respondent, "the funniest programme in a long time – since the last series in fact." Just a few said that this first programme did not seem quite as funny as those in the previous series, but this was countered by others who regarded it as "one of the funniest episodes yet" and "excellent – well worth waiting for another series."

Above: Oh, and we won a BAFTA! Collecting the 1980 award for Best Light Entertainment Performance from Morecambe and Wise at the Wembley Conference Centre, Thursday, 20 March 1980.

Right: A few reflections on our second run in the *Sandwell Evening Mail* published on 24 February 1979.

Fawlty still towers over the rest

It was great to see the return of "Fawlty Towers" (BBC 2, Monday). What a joy to see the wonderful Basil Fawlty in a new story.

But wait. Is it my imagination, or has Basil mellowed just a touch? Was the plot just a little thinner than the last series? Was the deafness routine almost overdone with two characters misunderstanding? Was the brilliant Manuel still as funny?

To the last question, the answer is yes. Unfortunately, the answer is yes to the others.

But it is still head and shoulders above any comedy show on television today.

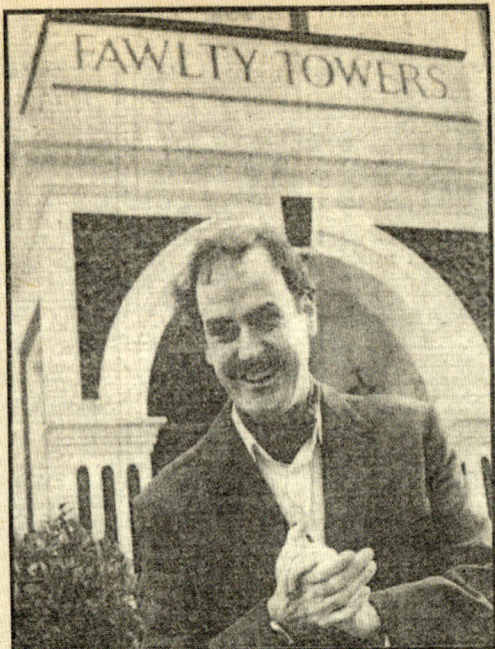

Above: A nice little interview I did with Tony Pratt for the *Daily Mirror* on 10 February 1979.

'Viewers could not find enough superlatives to praise Basil: "fantastic", "superb". The wonderful Andrew Sachs as Manuel and Jean Sanderson as the intermittently deaf and irascible Mrs Richards also drew a large amount of favourable comment. Indeed, the whole cast was considered "brilliant, very well cast and extremely amusing".

'The production, too, was thought excellent and "faultless" as always. This very favourable response to the programme is borne out by viewers' answers when asked if they intended to watch further episodes in this series, which were:

Yes, definitely	65%
Probably	22%
Possibly	9%
Probably not	3%
Definitely not	1%'

Series 2 – A General Review
(Audience Research Department, 9 May 1979)

'Respondents had greatly enjoyed this second series of *Fawlty Towers*. It was considered exceptionally amusing, entertaining and well written and, for many, was the most consistently funny show on television. Some did think the first series was better but they were most decidedly in a minority as nearly all thought this, in the words of one report viewer "a tremendously amusing programme".

'Although Basil was criticised by a few for what they felt was over-acting the majority considered him little short of brilliant ("he is absolutely fantastic"), Andrew Sachs as Manuel was also lavishly praised and there was general agreement that the whole cast was superb in its portrayal of the various characters, and that their team work and timing were excellent. The production, like all other aspects of the programme, was greeted with a great deal of enthusiasm and it was almost universally felt that the series had been first class entertainment.'

'Basil the Rat'

(Audience Research Department, 14 Nov 1979)

'Nearly all respondents were familiar with this show and indicated that they had enjoyed this edition a great deal. Indeed, many felt it was a first class comedy programme and thought that this was, perhaps, the best one of the series they had seen. They considered it particularly original, amusing and well performed, and the member of the sample audience who described the show as "altogether marvellous" appeared to be expressing the feeling of most respondents.

'It was widely thought that the characters in the programme were most original and quite different from the usual comedy stereotypes. The cast was regarded as excellent, with Basil, Sybil and Manuel's performances being frequently mentioned in a favourable manner. It was felt that all worked together extremely well and that the various characters complemented each other perfectly.

'The production, as with other aspects of the show, was also very highly regarded. It was considered slick and fast moving, keeping up the high standard set by previous editions. Many respondents took this opportunity to indicate their regret that this was apparently the last *Fawlty Towers* to be made but nevertheless looked forward to seeing the series repeated at some time.'

Above: Producer Douglas Argent collects the Situation Comedy Award for *Fawlty Towers* presented by BAFTA chair James Cellan Jones and HRH The Princess Anne at the Wembley Conference Centre on 20 March 1980.

Below: Ray Seaton in the *Wolverhampton Express and Star* thought *Fawlty Towers* 'might have lost its magic touch' on 27 February 1979!

Three faces of Basil Fawlty: "We laugh not because he is funny, but because we are expected to laugh."

Faulty folk-lore

RAY SEATON argues that Fawlty Towers has lost its magic touch

JOHN CLEESE was wise to wait a couple of years before starting a new series of Fawlty Towers, time enough for the comedy to become part of TV folk-lore.

It was a shrewd acknowledgement of the musical-hall advice: leave 'em wanting more.

The first series developed a taste; it whetted the appetite. The second series is likely to produce indigestible morsels. Cleese appears to have succumbed to his own mythology.

In the words of his own trade, there are unmistakable signs of his "going over the top." When in the first episode, he tore off his shirt behind the reception desk and beat his head on the counter, the action was more bizarre and self-indulgent than amusing.

When the hard-of-hearing old lady came to the desk to complain there was no paper in her room and was offered writing-paper, instead of a toilet roll, the comedy entered the broad channel of schoolboy howlers.

The strength of genuine comedy is the shock or surprise of recognition, a feeling of "I know what it's like — I've been there (or in that situation) myself!"

Cleese is said to have drawn the character of a brusque hotel proprietor from Donald Sinclair, former owner of the Gleneagles Hotel, Torquay, now living the life of Riley in Florida.

Luckless, volatile, irrational, irascible . . . The descriptive adjectives leap to hit Basil Fawlty between the eyes — and in the first series, Cleese maintained a sharp focus.

As if trying to go one better this time and make doubly sure that the character retains his comic grasp, he has enlarged on the angles, magnified the idiosyncracies and played up the foibles. The result is an air of frenetic determination to amuse, an assault on viewers waiting for Fawlty's re-emergence.

Like the clown who comes on to be greeted by an expectant audience, he indulges his mannerisms and goes off at a tangent before the script has prepared the way.

We laugh not because he is funny (which he is, occasionally), but because we are expected to laugh. Laughs are stored in a memory bank from the original series. There was really no need for John Cleese to work hard for renewed laughter. He had established the character and had only to reintroduce him. Instead, he is labouring the character's oddities.

The humour of Fawlty Towers is based on the reaction of Basil Fawlty to the embarrassments, problems and frustrations that come his way; more especially, to the assorted guests and staff of his hotel, who harass him.

Here, the new script is at its weakest, relying on stock characters from strip cartoons. The hard-of-hearing autocratic lady complaining about her room and the view in the first episode was a caricature specimen of her breed. To make the comedy effective Basil Fawlty should have delivered "the slow-burn," vainly trying to placate her, suffering her gladly . . . But Cleese's reaction was to explode straight away.

Another fault is to make the Spanish waiter a dumb cluck when it suits the script's purpose, as in not understanding a word said to him by the hearing-aid lady, and then responding in quite passable English at other times. Either he has a poor working knowledge of English or he hasn't: the script plays it both ways.

Fawlty Towers is a cut above other TV comedy, which only counterpoints the slothful quality of most situation comedies. But it does not justify the ecstatic acclaim it has received.

CHECKING OUT

Above: Pictured at the
Swallow Hotel in Newcastle
in 1978, doing a spot of
promotional work for our
second book of scripts
from *Fawlty*'s first series.

MOPPING UP!

NOTES, MERCHANDISE AND INTERNATIONAL REMAKES!

In this section, I thought it would be interesting to take a look at some of the wider aspects of *Fawlty Towers*. From the spin-off merchandise, the four attempts to remake the series for international markets and, to start things off, some chronologically arranged notes from production paperwork!

Don't let that last word put you off – this stuff is fascinating. Amazingly, for fifty years, a vast collection of the memos, letters and costings from the making of *Fawlty* in 1974–5 was kept in the BBC written archives centre. Well, for the first series anyway – most of the stuff from 1979 seems to have been unceremoniously shredded!

1974 – The Pilot!

Producer's Rough Estimates...

With the script delivered and budget agreed, on 15 September 1974, JHD wrote to the BBC Costings Unit with his estimates for the freelance creative fees for that December's 'John Cleese Pilot', (which would become the first episode of *Fawlty Towers*: 'A Touch of Class').

£600 – Ballard Berkeley
£500 – Connie Booth
£2,500 – John Cleese
£420 – Terence Conoley
£300 – Robin Ellis
£1,020 – Michael Gwynn
£450 – Andrew Sachs
£1,750 – Prunella Scales
£420 – David Simeon
£330 – Lionel Wheeler
£650 – Martin Wyldeck
128 – Ian Elliott
£64 – Gilly Flower
£128 – Julia Mellon
£192 – Patrick Milner
£64 – Oscar Peck
£64 – Annette Peters
£128 – Dennis Plenty
£88 – Gary Rich
£64 – Renee Roberts
£64 – Claire Russell
£128 – Pat Symons
£192 – David Waterman
£250. 25 – Dennis Wilson (Music)
£12,000 – Cleese and Booth (Script)

Total: £22,494. 25

Rehearsal Room Booking...

On 29 October, JHD booked rehearsal slots at the BBC Rehearsal Rooms in Acton for the pilot story, 'A Touch of Class':

Floor mark-up date: 16 December
Last rehearsal date: 22 December

Room 601 – BBC Rehearsal Rooms
7 days (+ ½) at £30
Total internal Cost: £225

JHD: Ticket Master...

On 30 October, JHD wrote a memo to the BBC Ticket Unit requesting tickets for the studio audience for the recording in December:

Could I please order 320 tickets for the John Cleese pilot programme called "Fawlty Towers" which is to be recorded in T.C.6. on Monday, 23rd December. We would like the wording to read as follows:

(White tickets with black lettering)

JOHN CLEESE starring in "Fawlty Towers"
By John Cleese and Connie Booth
Doors open 7.30 p.m.
Doors close 7.45 p.m.
Children under 14 not admitted.

A Research Trip to Torquay

On 18 November, JHD wrote to me regarding a little trip to Torquay:

Dear John, I enclose your ticket for Friday 22 November, and will meet you at the crash barrier five minutes before the train leaves. Actually there is no reason why I couldn't pick you up on the way if you want me to. We leave Paddington at 08.30 and arrive at Torquay at 12.08. We are booked back on the 16.01 from Torquay arriving at Paddington at 19.43. I will bring Spotlights with me and a polaroid camera and also one designer, namely Peter Kindred.

'Spotlights' refers to the actors' casting catalogue of faces – clearly good use was made of the long train journey!

First *Fawlty* Location Filming!

On 16 and 17 November, the first ever scenes from *Fawlty Towers* were shot – two days of location filming!

Monday, 16 November:

Artists and extras called at TVC for 07.00. A 30-seater coach to leave TVC for location at 07.50. Unit call: 09.00 on location at Wooburn Grange Country Club.

Prop Cars: Austin Allegro (Unmarked Police Car), Police Panda Car, 3.5 Rover

Catering: Coffee and sandwiches on location. Lunch: The Old Bell Inn, Wooburn.

Toilets, make-up and wardrobe room, telephone at Wooburn Grange.

Tuesday, 17 November:

Artists and extras called at TVC for costume and make-up at 07.00. A 30-seater coach to leave TVC reception at 07.50. Unit call: 09.00 on location outside Lloyds Bank, Cookham, Berkshire.

Catering: Coffee and lunch at the Copper Kettle.

Toilets, telephone, room for make-up and wardrobe, etc, at the Kings Arms, Cookham High Street.

....

Camera Script – Not Ready!

On 20 November, JHD's assistant Angela Sharp wrote a memo to the BBC printing department: *Just a note to let you know that the camera script for our programme 'John Cleese Pilot' on Monday, 23 December 1974 in TC6, will not be ready for duplicating until Saturday 21 December or early on Sunday 22 December. I should be glad if you could book this in for me. I will need 65 copies of it – and if possible would like six copies as soon as possible on the Sunday so that they can be marked up for the studio by the PA and AFM. Thank you.*

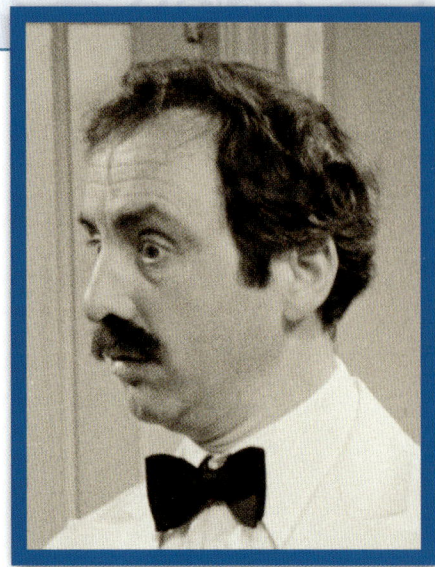

1975 – Series One

Andrew – we need you! . . . There was a spot of casting drama wrestling Andrew Sachs from his theatrical commitments for the recording of the first series. Here are some extracts from JHD's letters from Feburary 1975 to Andy's agent Richard Stone: *Andrew Sachs – It is imperative that we have an answer to his availability as soon as possible for the dates mentioned in August and September for the new series Fawlty Towers. John Cleese is in the position at the moment of postponing the writing of the series as he finds it impossible until the situation about Andrew Sachs is clarified. John tells me that he likes to write for the actor who is going to play the part and since we hope it is to be most successful, I am afraid I would like to ask you if you could release him on the following dates, August 7th, 14th and 21st and September 4th, and possibly the 18th. I know it is difficult, if not impossible, but it would add immeasurably to Andrew Sachs' career with both television and theatrical exposure.*

A letter from Miss Tibbs . . .
In March 1975, Gilly Flower and JHD exchanged some lovely correspondence:

Dear John, Please forgive me for writing to you but I have heard through the 'Grape-Vine' that you are producing some more episodes of "Fawlty Towers". Is there a slight hope that you may need the 'old ladies' again? I do so hope so as it was such a wonderful show and as people to work for you was just marvellous.

Dear Gilly, Thank you for your note. Yes we are doing a series of "Fawlty Towers" probably starting in August. As yet I haven't got the scripts although I imagine there will be something for you. I will let you know in due course.
Yours sincerely,
John Howard Davies

....

A letter to Prunella . . . On 30 June 1975, Angela Sharp wrote to Prunella with an update on the next five episodes of the first series:
I enclose herewith scripts for Fawlty Towers, *except for Episode Three they are complete except for the the cuts that will be made to bring them down to time. Episode three has not as yet got an ending as John Cleese has decided to tackle this on his return from holiday, but meanwhile I am enclosing the rough one.*

Grand Designs . . . Designer Peter Kindred wrote to JHD on 7 July 1975 with a complete breakdown of the studio sets required for the first series proper:

Recording 1: "O'Reilly"
VTR Sun 3 Aug

Lobby / Reception
As previous design from the pilot with additions. Front door to match film. Reception counters, doors to back offices, corridors, stairs and doors to Dining Room and Cocktail Lounge. Keep for Series. – 320 Man Hours

Dinning Room
As previous design. Keep for Series – 210 Man Hours

Cocktail Lounge
As previous design. Keep for Series – 190 Man Hours

Inside Back Office
As previous design. Keep for Series – 100 Man Hours

Corridor and Polly's Room
Once Only – 150 Man Hours

Drawing Room
Once Only – 150 Man Hours

Total Resources: 1150 Man Hours, £1150 Materials, £1200 Properties

Recording 2: "Sex"
VTR Sun 10 Aug
Stock Sets as Recording 1

Upstairs Corridor & Stairwell (New Set – Once Only) – 200 Man Hours

Kitchen (New Set – Keep for Series) – 100 Man Hours.

Bedrooms Opening on to Hotel Corridor (New Set – Once Only) – 200 Man Hours

Total Resources: 500 Man Hours, £500 Materials, £500 Properties

Recording 3: "The Inspector"
VTR Sun 17 Aug
Stock Sets as Recording 1
No New Sets Required

Recording 4: "Fire Drill"
VTR Sun 31 Aug
Stock Sets as Recording 1

Private Ward in Hospital (New Set – Once Only) – 100 Man Hours

Hospital Corridor (New Set – Once Only) – 100 Man Hours

Total Resources: 200 Man Hours, £200 Materials, £200 Properties

Recording 5: "Duck's Off"
VTR Sun 7 Sept
Stock Sets as Recording 1
Phone Backing and Additions to Kitchen set – 100 Man Hours

....

Recall to duty . . . On 11 July 1975, Angela Sharp wrote to Ballard Berkeley regarding his brief location scene for 'The Germans' (after the fire alarm goes off):
I enclose herewith a script for episode four of Fawlty Towers in which you will be playing the part of Major Gowen. We shall be filming Sc.13 on Tuesday 22 July and your call at Television Centre will be 08.30.

Series One Location Filming…

The location filming schedule for 21-23 July 1975 notes: *30-seater coach with artists and staff will leave TVC main reception for location at 08.45. The Unit call is for 09.30 on location at the Wooburn Grange Country Club.*

The document goes on to note the times for the artist to arrive at TVC for costume and make-up before departure. All male actors had 15 minutes to get into costume, the ladies 30 minutes, and Prunella Scales had 45 minutes!

Dressing Rooms – Sharing!

On 24 July 1975, Angela Sharp wrote a memo to Miss K. Knight to book TVC dressing rooms for the Sunday 3 August recording of 'The Builders': *Could I please book the following dressing rooms for artists appearing in the above programme:*

John Cleese (Star)
Prunella Scales (Star)
Andrew Sachs (Star)
Ballard Berkeley
David Kelly

Gilly Flower
Renee Roberts } *– Share if necessary*

George Lee
James Appleby } *– Share if necessary*

Michael Cronin
Michael Halsey } *– Share if necessary*

Barney Dorman
Pat Gorman } *– Share if necessary*

Tony Guyan – production
Dave Armour – warm-up artist

Fawlty Money:

On 30 July, a request was made to the BBC 'Money to be used in vision department' for:

10 x £1 Notes
Required by scripted Action

This money was requested to be used on set for 'The Builders'.

Pilot Insert…

On 11 August 1975, JHD wrote to Robin Ellis (undercover policeman Danny) regarding an insert scene written to go into the pilot programme to reflect Polly's change from a philosophy student to an art one:

Dear Mr. Ellis, I enclose herewith the re-write of the insert for the pilot programme which we will be recording on Sunday 17 August in TC8. Perhaps you would like to come along at 2.00 so that we can arrange make-up and wardrobe and then we will record your scene after we have recorded the main programme. Look forward to seeing you Sunday.

So two extra bits for 'A Touch of Class' (a total of 34 seconds!) were recorded after 'The Hotel Inspectors'. Eagle-eyed viewers may spot the joins as Robin's hair had to be dyed and pinned up and his jumper has lost its collar!

What if?

On 10 July 1975, JHD wrote to actor Richard Briers about a part in 'The Hotel Inspectors': *"My Dear Richard, I enclose a script from the new John Cleese series. The Part of 'Hutchinson' was written with you in the back of John's mind. I know it is cheeky asking you if you would like to play it, we would love to have you but will quite understand if you don't.*

Cribbins' way!

By 5 August however, JHD wrote to Bernard Cribbins (and the rest is history!): *Dear Bernard, Just to let you know that we start rehearsals on Tuesday, 12 August for episode three of Fawlty Towers, for which you are playing Mr Hutchinson. We are rehearsing in room 103 at the BBC rehearsal block.*

German lettering!

26 August 1975, JHD wrote to the BBC Graphics department detailing the on-screen captions required for 'The Germans': *Could we please have the following two captions, white lettering on black card size 20" x 24". Lettering to be bottom third:*

1. 'NEXT MORNING . . .'
2. 'WE WANT TO HIRE A CAR'

The Germans – Editing Notes:

The days immediately following the studio recording of 'The Germans' (on 1 September 1975), JHD and I reviewed all the recorded takes and JHD wrote up the below incomprehensible (!) notes for the VT Editor:

Opening titles and Sc.1. We redid the whole of Sc.1. + Opening titles again, but you said you would use some of the original. WE DID THIS RETAKE FOR TECHNICAL REASONS!

Shots 384-394, we did a retake of these shots after the end of the show. Use the 2nd retake.

Planned retake of the Moose's head falling on Manuel in the final scene. Use the 2nd one.

Guitar! On 2 September 1975, JHD had to make an urgent request in writing for a prop needed for the rehearsal and recording of 'Gourmet Night'.

This is to confirm my telephone conversation requesting a guitar for Andrew Sachs which he has to play in this week's episode of Fawlty Towers. *Could it please be delivered to Room 201 at the BBC rehearsal block at North Acton at 10.00am on Wednesday 3 September and be collected from TC8 on Sunday 7 September at 21.30. My apologies for this late request, and thank you for your help.*

Tickets… After the recording of 'Gourmet Night' on 7 September 1975, the audience house manager wrote to JHD with a breakdown of tickets issued and used for the 320 capacity TC8:

Producer: 80 Issued / 40 Used
TV Staff: 44 Issued / 35 Used
Sound Staff: 20 Issued / 14 Used
Public: 236 Issued / 174 Used
Total: 380 Issued / 263 Used

This means that there were 57 empty seats in the audience of 'Gourmet Night' – 57!

1978/9 – Series Two

BBC Contracts: On 6 October 1978, David Gower from the copyright department sent a memo to BBC brass:

Subject: Fawlty Towers *Series
I have an agreement in principle with the joint authors, John Cleese and Connie Booth for the above series at a joint fee of £4000.00 per script (to cover two performances). All further repeats and residuals are to be based on a notional fee of £2400.00 per programme.*

Getting the band back together …
On 3 January 1979, *Fawlty's* new producer Douglas Argent wrote to Prunella Scales with long-awaited details of the new series:

Dear Prunella, It was very nice to talk to you today, and once again, my apologies for not contacting you sooner. Herewith scripts for Episodes 1, 2 and 4. The re-write of No. 3 is being typed today. I do hope you like them. Your first call will be on 15 January, at Acton Rehearsal Rooms at 10.30 am. Bob Spiers will be directing. We are all looking forward very much to the series.

Series 2 Filming Booked: On 8 January 1979, newly appointed director Bob Spiers wrote to John Cleese with an update on the filming and recording:

Dear John, Filming for Episodes 3 & 4 will be on Tuesday, 30 January (Day) and Wednesday, 31 January (Night). If the industrial dispute has been fully resolved it may be possible to film both episodes on 30 January. Filming for Episodes 5 & 6 will be on Tuesday 20 February (Anniversary) and 21 February (Rat + standby day). As agreed, the weekly schedule will be as follows:

*Mon-Tues: Rehearsal
Wednesday: off for learning
Thurs: Rehearsal
Fri: Rehearsal (11.30am Tech Run)
Sat: Rehearsal (am only)
Sun: Recording*

Series 2 update from John: On 31 January 1979, I wrote to Bob Spiers with an update on the scripts for the second series and when the editing would fit in between making later episodes:

Dear Bobby, Did some calculations regarding editing deadlines. Hopefully by the end of this week we will have Mrs Richards finished and The Hamiltons nearly finished. During the two clear weeks between 18 February and 5 March we are going to have to finish editing the Hamiltons and also Sex and Death. This will give us four in the can taking us up to the fourth transmission on 31 March. So the fifth show (recorded 11 March) will have to be edited during the week we are rehearsing the sixth show in order that it can be transmitted on the 19th. I suggest the Wednesday and the Saturday afternoon.

A hotel full of tat! – *Fawlty Towers* merchandise!

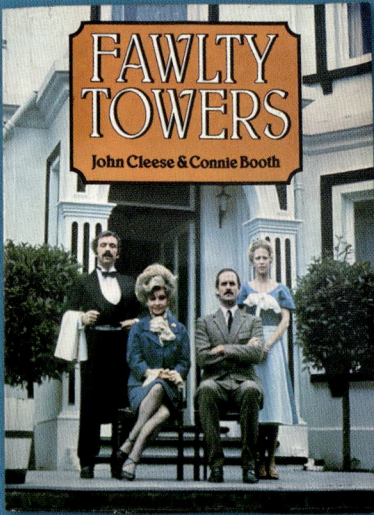

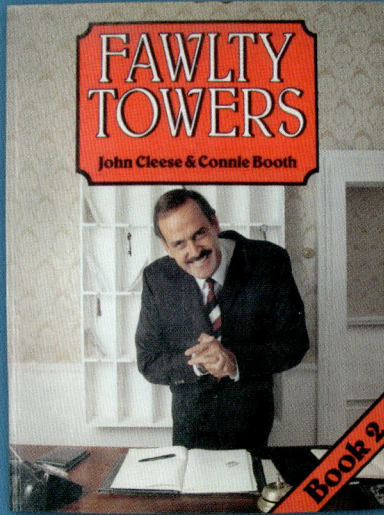

The timeless humour of *Fawlty Towers* has also become a reliable stocking-filler for almost as long as the series has existed, from script books to audio and video recordings of episodes … and even a model car!

For dedicated viewers, the wait between series of *Fawlty Towers* could be soothed by the release of two books of episode scripts (featuring specially shot cover photos!). The first, issued in 1977, consisted of 'The Builders', 'The Hotel Inspectors' and 'Gourmet Night', alongside snaps from key scenes. The second, *Book 2*, featured the rest of the first series. Later volumes collected all 12 scripts and proved to be a bit of a literary sensation, selling millions of copies and clogging up charity shops for decades!

Audio recordings of comedy shows were massive sellers for BBC Records, so *Fawlty* was soon added to the range, starting with a first release in 1979. This LP featured 'Mrs Richards' (the record's title for 'Communication Problems') and 'The Hotel Inspectors'. When this album proved a success, a further three followed, each consisting of two soundtracks

of television episodes, this time with newly recorded narration from Andrew Sachs (in character as Manuel) to explain the more visual moments from the story.

In the 1990s, these four LPs were also released on cassette and CD, where the final two episodes not originally issued on vinyl were now included.

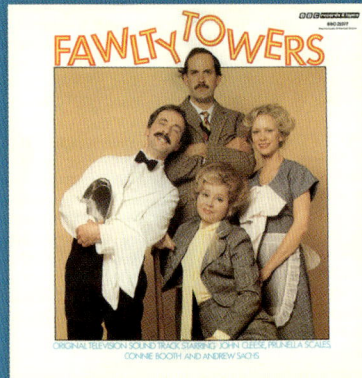

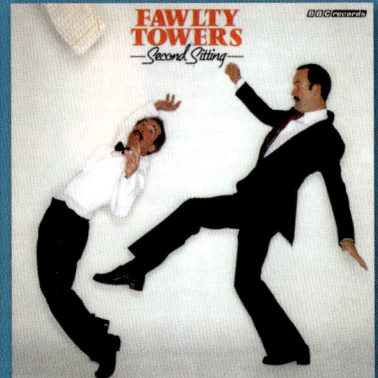

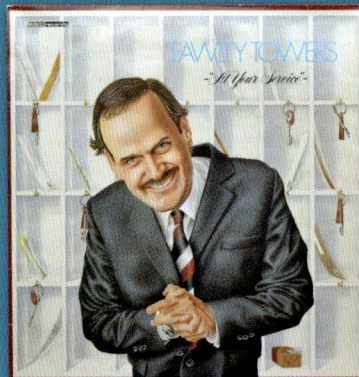

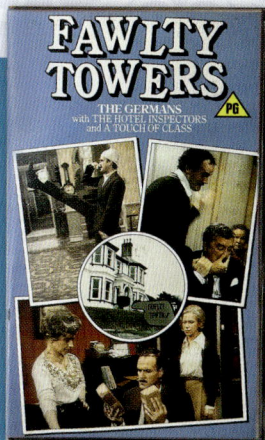

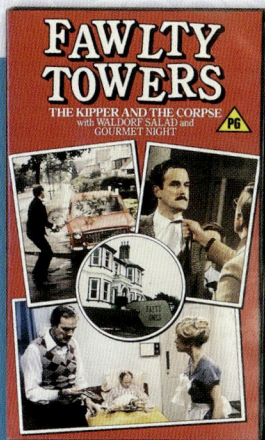

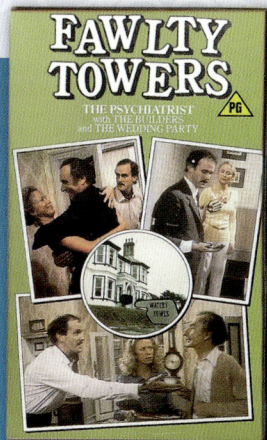

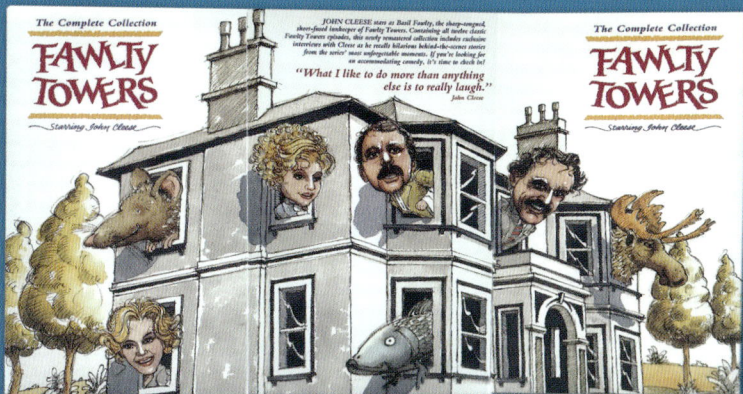

With the home video boom of the early 1980s, the BBC started packaging up classics from its archive with *Fawlty* being one of their first releases. Episodes from both series were jumbled up and thematically grouped into threes and edited together as one programme (with new credits comprising of all three episodes added at the end). Being the days just before satellite TV, this was the only way for viewers to watch the show for many years and they sold in bucketloads. Releases stateside featured some particularly stunning artwork.

With the advent of the DVD, the series was released again, several times! Later releases included a host of bonus extras, including commentary tracks along with 'making of' documentaries. For the most recent release on Blu-ray, all of the original location film elements from the second series were located and re-scanned – and it all looks like it was only filmed yesterday!

Amongst a treasure trove of other glorious goodies released, the dedicated viewer could actually play a *Fawlty Towers* computer game in 2000! But no collection could be complete without a miniature Austin 1300 die-cast scale model, complete with a suited Basil with branch, as seen in 'Gourmet Night'.

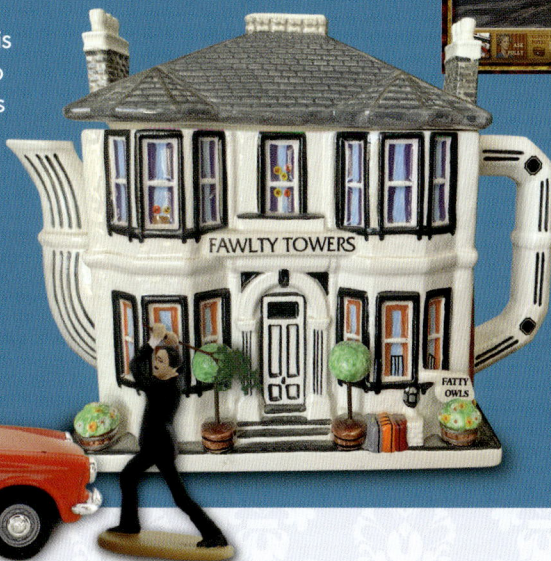

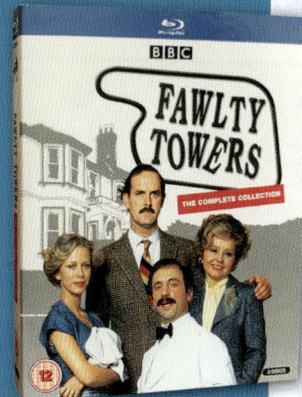

Fawlty Towers – International Remakes

Whilst the original adventures of Basil have been dubbed into dozens of languages around the globe (including a version for Spain where Manual became Italian!), there have been four attempts to completely remake the series for a foreign market …

Snaveley
ABC, 1978, pilot episode only

The very first remake of *Fawlty Towers* was made before the second series of the original had even been written!

Snaveley transferred the action from the English Riviera to a US highway motel. The character of Basil became Henry Snavely, played by popular American film actor Harvey Korman of *Blazing Saddles* and *Herbie Goes Bananas* fame, whilst the US take on Sybil was Gladys, with actress Betty White cast.

All of the international remakes of *Fawlty* would take a different approach to their Manuel equivalent. For *Snaveley*, the second-language-challenged waiter became an Albanian refugee, Petro.

For the story of their pilot, the ABC team took the British story 'The Hotel Inspectors' (with 'The Germans' wall-mounted animal head) and followed the basic plot and structure pretty faithfully. When it came to the dialogue, however, the American writers started from scratch and stitched many of their own gags around the framework of the British script.

Above: A climactic moment from 1978's *Snaveley* pilot, with Frank LaLoggia (Petro), Deborah Zon (Connie), Betty White (Gladys) and Harvey Korman (Henry Snavely).

Snaveley was made in the mode of a traditional American studio sitcom, of the kind which had been made since the 1950s. Here the humour is telegraphed for the audience – often with a knowing pause to allow a laugh. This results in the characters never really coming alive and the episode makes you very aware that this is a performance.

It seems almost cruel to make comparisons between *Snaveley* and 'The Hotel Inspectors'. The comic misunderstandings here have none of the frenzied pace and tension from the original.

Another important departure is that the dynamic between Henry and Gladys just isn't anywhere near as antagonistic as Basil and Sybil's. The leading couple in *Snaveley* feel no worse than Homer and Marge on a bad day!

There are some great lines however, such as when Gladys picks at Henry: 'You forgot to order toilet paper again', 'I didn't forget,' he replies. 'When you ration it, the guests don't waste it!' Elsewhere, a variation of one of the great lines from the original sneaks in – when a guest complains about an order Petro has taken, Henry replies: 'He's an Albanian refugee, you might as well give your orders to the cat!'

Despite some fun moments, however, the magic just wasn't there and ABC didn't take up *Snaveley*'s 25-minute pilot as a series.

Amanda's
ABC, 1983, 13 episodes

Despite the muted reaction to their first attempt, ABC were still keen to have another go!

This time the series was re-tooled as a vehicle for actress Bea Arthur, fresh in the minds of American viewers as Maude Findlay in the hugely popular *All in the Family* and spin-off *Maude*.

Bea played Amanda Cartwright, owner of the Californian beachside hotel, Amanda's by the Sea, which we soon learn is located nowhere near the sea! Amanda runs the hotel with her son Marty (Fred McCarren) who is fresh from 'Hotel Management School' – one of the recurring jokes in the series – and his spoilt wife Arlene (Simone Griffeth).

Joining them is Aldo, played by Tony Rosato, their Mexican waiter – although Amanda feels free to comment to guests the abstract Basil-esque line: 'You'll have to excuse him, he's from Toronto'.

Amanda is Basil re-made as a vibrant matriarch, very much in charge, but with an eyebrow raised at all the madness going on around her. The character never properly raises her voice, and all the high jinks that unravel around her just seem to mildly annoy her. There is certainly none of Basil's dramatic responses to disaster or class envy and self-reflection.

The opening episode once again roughly remakes 'The Hotel Inspectors', but seems to cherry-pick elements from several *Fawlty Towers* episodes, with a kitchen fire, talk of a special gourmet dinner and Amanda riffing on the 'Room View' scene from 'Communication Problems'.

In later episodes, the daughter-in-law conflict became another regular source of comedy, and Marty and Arlene suspect Amanda of having an affair with Aldo!

Additional comedy comes from Amanda's silent partner in the hotel, Clifford Mundy (played by Keene Curtis), who pours cold water on Amanda's new ideas. 'You're flirting with disaster!' he says on the eve of a new cabaret night at the hotel. 'I have flirted with worse!' she says.

The jokes are here, but none of it seems to fit together. The humour feels almost grafted on and not forming organically from any of the characters or the results of an unfolding story.

Coming off the back of Bea's previous series, *Amanda's* was given a lot of publicity in the press, but viewers swiftly slipped away. ABC pulled the plug on the series after 10 weeks, despite having three episodes already recorded ready to broadcast. Of course, reaching 13 episodes in any form beats *Fawlty Towers*' total tally so *Amanda's* certainly wins that accolade!

For Bea Arthur, she would soon bounce back in the comedy *The Golden Girls*, which also starred *Snaveley*'s Betty White, making *The Golden Girls* a kind of home for former *Fawlty Towers* remake survivors!

COMEDY PREMIERE!
Bea Arthur is back in funny business!
Outspoken as always. More outrageous than ever. Out to make you laugh as Amanda, the woman who runs a small hotel ...and everybody in it!
Amanda's
Check in for laughter!
7:30PM

Far left: The cast of *Amanda's*: Simone Griffeth (Arlene), Fred McCarren (Marty), Keene Curtis (Clifford), Bea Arthur (Amanda), Rick Hurst (Earl Nash) and Tony Rosato (Aldo).

LAUGH INN!

At the Whispering
Pines Hotel...
you can expect
fresh towels,
little soaps and
complimentary
insults!

john larroquette is

payne

new comedy

The
laughs
start
at

7pm

Payne
CBS, 1999, 9 episodes

It would be 16 years before another stateside version of *Fawlty* was attempted, this time by rival network CBS. This series went back to a married couple running a hotel, Royal and Constance Payne, played by John Larroquette (future star of *Boston Legal*) and JoBeth Williams. Together they run The Whispering Pines Inn, with their waiter Mo, of Indian descent, played by Rick Batalla, and Julie Benz as waitress Breeze O'Rourke.

The dynamic between Royal and Constance is once again more akin to a pair of wise-cracking spouses: 'Have you noticed that for each year of our marriage I start drinking earlier and earlier in the day – what is that about?' Constance says to Royal in an early episode.

The first story made, 'Pacific Ocean Duck', was the only one to be based on a *Fawlty* story, and essentially follows 'Gourmet Night' with (once again!) elements of 'The Hotel Inspectors' thrown in. The episode follows the plot of the original script with an incapacitated chef and an

Above: The cast of 1999's *Fawlty Towers* re-make *Payne*: Julie Benz (Breeze O'Rourke), JoBeth Williams (Constance Payne), John Larroquette (Royal Payne) and Rick Batalla (Mo).

unreliable car. In place of a branch to vent vehicle frustrations, however, Royal gets out of his car and watches as it rolls off a cliff!

John Larroquette is a natural at delivering comic dialogue, but the character of Royal comes over so smoothed out. This renders the whole thing rather lightweight. When the already thin plots are squeezed into 22-minute episodes (with scenes and dialogue around ad breaks written to keep viewer attention), none of it works, despite each episode opening with a close-up of the 'Whispering Pines' sign in various states of distress.

In one scene Miss Tibbs and Miss Gatsby's American equivalents tell Royal they are heading out to a nudist beach. Royal tells them, 'I'll alert the coast guard,' and a nearby Mo

(hoovering with an unplugged vacuum cleaner) asks Royal, 'Are they Lesbianese?'

Critics at the time were fast to make unfavourable comparisons between *Payne* and *Fawlty Towers*, with Canadian newspaper *The Globe and Mail* commenting, 'The visceral terrors of *Fawlty Towers* become simple misunderstandings. Nothing is wounding or dangerous, no one's going to snap and every problem is quickly resolved.'

Payne had all the hallmarks of a glossy sitcom of the era with fast cuts and quick musical scene breaks with exterior shots. Whilst stylistically things had a pinch of *Friends* about them, the viewing figures were anything but, with the series pulled after eight episodes (leaving one unbroadcast).

Zum letzten Kliff
RTL, 2001, pilot episode only

The most recent attempt to remake *Fawlty* was by German broadcaster RTL, and was without a doubt the version closest to the original.

Zum letzten Kliff (which translates as 'The Last Cliff'), was set on one of the northern German islands with Viktor and Helga Stein (another slightly more affable take upon Basil and Sybil) running the hotel, with their hapless Kazakh waiter, Igor.

Mirroring the original series, RTL made 'A Touch of Class' as their pilot story. It is fascinating to see the familiar moments from the British episode come alive in a different setting, with Helga's nagging requests for her husband to both 'write the menu and hang the painting' every bit as tedious as when Sybil first nagged back in 1975.

Other elements of *Fawlty*'s debut are given a contemporary twist, with clearly more modern-day German versions of con man Lord Melbury and undercover policeman Danny Brown. The episode's climax, however, sees Viktor Stein also echo perfectly a dumbstruck Basil holding two bricks in the hotel office. Elsewhere, the new version of Mr Wareing's progressively frustrated drinks order sounds even more angry in German!

What places *Zum letzten Kliff* apart from the trio of American attempts is a noticeably lower production budget. But this soon becomes a massive advantage, as the smaller, more contained sets (with fewer extras dotted about) allows focus to be purely on the characters and the flow of the story. Importantly, unlike any of the other remakes, *Zum letzten Kliff* actually feels like a farce, and you can see Viktor Stein's frustrations bubbling away before rising to boiling point by the crescendo of the episode.

With my endorsement (and I popped up on set to meet the cast and crew) and a fantastic German Basil in actor Jochen Busse, the performances and comic timing in this production were razor sharp.

The team had high hopes of remaking every original *Fawlty Towers* episode (though perhaps one of them would have needed some tweaking. . .), but sadly only the pilot was made, and the episode didn't impress the German television executives enough to commission a full series.

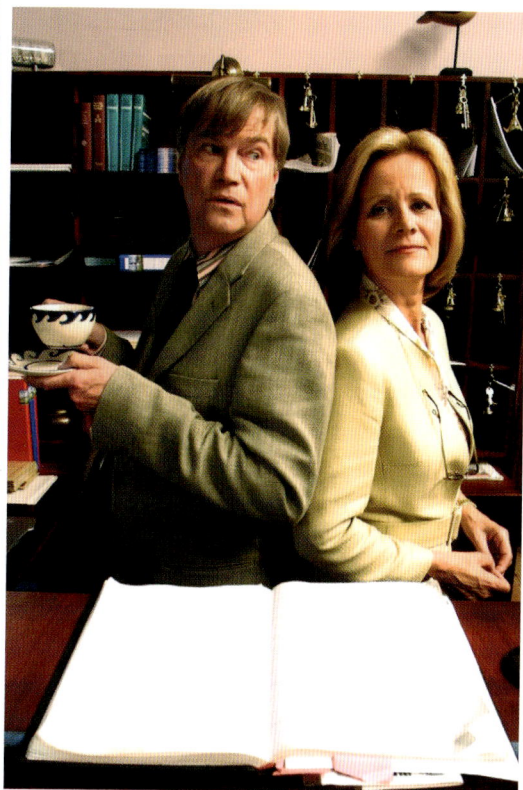

Above: The German incarnations of Basil (Jochen Busse) and Sybil (Claudia Rieschel) in 2001's *Zum letzten Kliff*.

Below: Me with Jochen Busse on the set of the German version of *Fawlty* in Cologne.

13.

BASIL'S LONG SHADOW?

People have asked me whether the success of *Fawlty Towers* opened doors for my showbusiness career. No! But it did shut a few. Let me explain . . .

About five years ago, a British journalist asked me, 'Why have you been in so few English films?' I was surprised by this. It had never struck me! But the more I thought about it, the more I realised: he was right! And I blame *Fawlty Towers*.

From 1967 onwards, I got the occasional day on a movie, mainly when Denis Norden had written the script and then recommended me. The 70s brought three Python movies, but I don't think the other Pythons ever saw an episode of *Fawlty Towers*. (They certainly never mentioned it.) So that was not a factor in my being cast in Python films.

And I now realise I was offered very few roles in English films or TV. Plenty of offers in America and the rest of the world, but not in good old Blighty. Simply because people who were making movies in England didn't want Basil Fawlty suddenly walking into a Jane Austen novel, or even a *Notting Hill*-style romcom.

In the decade after *Fawlty Towers*, I got the only great script I was ever sent, *Clockwise* by Michael Frayn, and a couple of small parts: *Privates on Parade* and *Yellow Beard*. After that I was offered four days on Bond, and two days on Harry Potter – both American-financed – and a wonderful small part in Kenneth Branagh's *Frankenstein*, where I was so heavily disguised that several of my friends didn't recognise me. Just as well, as nobody wants to watch Basil Fawlty being stabbed to death by Robert de Niro.

Why was it so different in the US? Because *Fawlty Towers* was hardly known there! You may remember that the *Fawlty* shows were of variable length. The shortest was 28 minutes and the longest was 35 minutes. The dear old BBC didn't care, bless them, but American commercial TV shows had to be exactly equal lengths – otherwise the advertisers got very upset that their ad did not go out at exactly the right time.

So *Fawlty Towers* was transmitted in America only on Public Broadcasting Service (PBS), which accounted for a measly 2 per cent of the viewing audience. 98 per cent of them only knew me – if they knew me at all – as one of those zany *Monty Python* guys.

So I appeared in many TV shows and movies, including: *Third Rock from the Sun*, *Rat Race*, *The Great Muppet Caper*, *Rudyard Kipling's The Jungle Book*, *Pink Panther 2*, *Clifford the Big Red Dog*, *Charlie's Angels*, *Scorched*, *Will and Grace*, *Entourage* and *Cheers*. No, in the USA, *Fawlty Towers* was not destroying my career!

Above: Getting to play some Hollywood gothic horror as Professor Waldman in Kenneth Branagh's atmospheric 1994 flick *Mary Shelley's Frankenstein*.

Below left: Me as eccentric hotel tycoon Donald Sinclair in Jerry Zucker's 2001 comedy film *Rat Race*. My character's name was of course a tip of the hat to Basil Fawlty's original inspiration from the Gleneagles Hotel.

Below: As the new Q in 2002, alongside Pierce Brosnan's 007 in the James Bond film *Die Another Day*. I had played R in the previous film, together with the original Q, Desmond Llewelyn.

VOTE POLLY

Above: Polly as the leader of the Liberal Democrats?!

Below: What could have been – Manuel in full matador regalia! In reality a 1976 publicity shot Andy did to promote the series.

People have heard rumours that I had an idea for a *Fawlty Towers* film. Yes, I did have an idea. But it was only an idea, never a serious proposition.

The idea was this . . .

Basil and Sybil have sold the hotel and retired. Manuel has gone back to Spain where, with his savings, he has opened a restaurant called El Ratto Basil. Polly has become the leader of the Liberal Democrats. Manuel invites the Fawltys to visit him in Alicante. They decide to spend their summer holiday in that part of Spain. They book the tickets. When they arrive at Heathrow, they experience every kind of frustration that can occur at airports: delays, miscommunication, changes, lack of information. After a few hours, Basil is at the end of his tether and involved in angry exchanges, when . . . their flight is called. Basil and Sybil board. They settle in and begin, finally to relax. All is well . . . until the plane is hijacked. (Remember, this takes place in the late 1970s.) Three terrorists order the plane to fly to Tripoli. Sybil wakes Basil up and he flies into an indignant rage, furiously arguing with the hijackers, who are rather thrown by his boldness. Basil grabs a gun, and the other passengers join in and overcome the hijackers.

Cheering and celebrating, the passengers thank Basil. He is the hero of the hour. The passengers sing 'For He's a Jolly Good Fellow' and Sybil gives him a kiss! The captain now makes an announcement, congratulating Basil, but regretting the plane now has to return to Heathrow. Basil loses it and, as he still has a gun, threatens to shoot the captain if he does not take everyone to land in Alicante. When the plane arrives, Basil, still a hero to the passengers, is arrested by the Guardia Civil and taken off to prison, where he spends his two weeks' holiday.

It'll never be made, believe me!

Recuerdo de ALICANTE

Sybil at the Hotel Gleneagles!

In September 2006, Prunella Scales was invited down to Torquay as guest of honour for the reopening of the Hotel Gleneagles – which was of course our original inspiration to write *Fawlty Towers* all those years ago. Suitably enough, Pru arrived in a red Austin 1100 – the same car as driven by Basil in the series.

A highly convincing and realistic mannequin dressed as Basil was also on hand, with a leafy branch ready for any car-thrashing required . . .

To Celebrate The Re Launch Of
HOTEL GLENEAGLES
The Inspiration for The BBC's
"FAWLTY TOWERS"
By Actress
PRUNELLA SCALES
On
September 18th 2006

As *Fawlty Towers* became more popular, I started getting scripts for TV commercials featuring Basil. None of them was any good because they all started with Basil being angry before anyone had wound him up, which makes him too dislikeable.

But after a mere 25 years, I received a script for Specsavers where Basil thrashes an innocent police car that looks almost exactly like his own. A very good idea. Unfortunately, after the usual ritual adulation the creative team decided they knew better than me how to make it funny, which was undeniably possible, but not statistically likely.

Consequently, the finished commercial is littered with small mistakes in the editing and the sound, and two huge ones,

namely the wig and the awful ending, where Basil runs away from the camera and then disappears by suddenly leaping sideways out of shot. I suggested that a van should pull out in front of him, which he would then run straight into – making the point that his eyesight was not very good, which seemed to me the whole point of the commercial.

Above: The final frame from the 2016 Specsavers *Fawlty Towers* advert.

Below: In 2008 Andy and I brought back Manuel and Basil for a delightful little sketch for *We Are Most Amused*, a comedy celebrating the 60th birthday of the Prince of Wales.

They were quite a self-confident bunch and when we finally contacted them, they claimed it was original in its own right, and, as evidence of this, they pointed out that the word 'Fawlty' was spelled differently to their show. I heard later that when someone else opened up a rival operation, the Dining Experience sued them for breach of copyright! Anyway, what hurt was that when people in Australia were asked if they'd seen our shows in the theatre, they said they hadn't gone 'because they'd already seen the other one.' And ours had Stephen Hall in it!!

So, due to Covid, it was seven years before Phil McIntyre decided the time was right to put the show on in the West End. Parts of this plan were straightforward. We could use the same set as Australia, same moves, which had been polished in Oz over a couple of months. CJay would be directing again and, of course, I would add the occasional note, so all we needed was . . . new actors. As in Australia, CJay

whittled down lots of hopefuls until there were three or four contenders for all the main parts. I was abroad, so I attended by Zoom, and was stunned by the sheer quality of what I saw. There were three absolutely top-class Basils, 2.5 Sybils, three Manuels and two Pollys. Any of them could have walked onto the West End stage and done the job superbly. I was overjoyed. A few weeks later, I returned to London and joined the rehearsals at quite a late stage, by which time it was in very good shape. CJay had drilled them so well, but I was still able to enjoy myself by suggesting a few final touches . . . Like: 'Do the bickering with a bit less bite, so it becomes more of a ritual than real sniping' or 'Try standing closer there' or 'Keep trying to get the wallet the whole way through the dialogue' or 'Try waiting longer before you do the line.' Or 'Smile more when you say that, so it's not so obvious that it's rude.'

Below: Me pictured with the West End cast we carefully assembled, during an early rehearsal.

It was such a lovely company too. Everybody liked everybody, which is a characteristic of CJay's productions, and so rehearsal was a process of play and discovery, not just 'running it', so that you won't make mistakes on the opening night. It helped that I laughed my silly head off all through the first run-through that I saw. I think the cast realised suddenly just how funny they were.

Meanwhile, I felt much more confident than one usually does. The script was bloody good (!) and the cast were doing it with real pace and skill. (Normally, rehearsal is 'just trying to make it work'. All I had to do was to make it work a little bit better.) Phil McIntyre told me later, that a lot of people in the theatrical world were very dubious about its success – 'it might be controversial'. 'Rather old-fashioned'. 'People will worry about Basil bullying Manuel.' 'The woke people will object to some of the attitudes.' Completely wrong. People loved it ('I haven't laughed like that for years').

This kind of carping is always with us. I showed a script of the *Wanda* musical that my daughter Camilla, John du Prez and I have written to some experienced producers, and this is what I heard: 'The modern audience will not accept a woman as manipulative as Wanda.' 'Wanda can't be seen to have orgasms when Otto speaks Italian.' 'You'll never get away with the stuttering.' 'The story is too dated.' 'The fish torture scene is too much for today's audience.' One producer said she ran an animal sanctuary, so she couldn't be connected to a film where small dogs are killed.

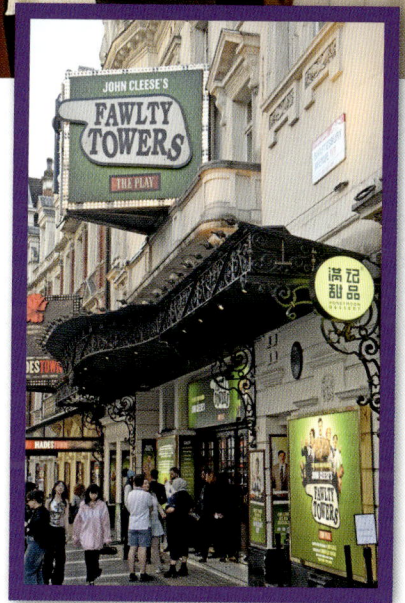

Above top: Basil (Adam Jackson-Smith) and Manuel (Hemi Yeroham) share a classic moment on the stage.

Above: Our original West End home, the Apollo Theatre on Shaftesbury Avenue.

Most of these objections were heard in 1987 when we were trying to get a studio to back *Wanda*. Eleven out of twelve Hollywood studios passed on it then. It is now regularly ranked as one of the funniest films ever made. It cost $7 million and made over $200 million. And no studio, in the US or the UK, would give us $3 million to make *Life of Brian*. I don't know why these people think they know what they're doing. Oooh. I feel better after that. So, anyway, I don't think I've ever felt much

happier (professionally) than when I saw the show on opening night. From my little box I watched most of the performance, but I couldn't take my eyes off the audience – it seemed years since I'd seen rows and rows of people rock with laughter like that. And the funny thing was . . . I was hugely content just to be a part of the whole show. I had no desire at all to be down there on stage. In fact, I was relieved Adam Jackson-Smith was down there as Basil, doing the really hard work.

I must acknowledge that the success of *Fawlty Towers: The Play* gave me enormous satisfaction. The moment when I looked down from my box and watched the audience, their eyes streaming with tears of laughter, was what they call 'a peak experience'! It involved everyone, the cast, the audience and all the people behind the scenes . . . a simple delight in the laughter we were creating. It didn't matter that the average age was about 65, it didn't matter at all that I was not down there performing, it didn't matter that no critic awarded us more than three stars the next day – all that laughter was undeniably . . . a good, happy thing.

But it did please me that the longer the run went on, the younger the audience looked. It was because parents brought their children, most of whom had never heard of *Fawlty Towers*, and their children told their friends that the show was just plain . . . FUNNY! So they came too. As I said, I'd noticed that even very young children laughed at *Fawlty Towers*, because they understand about people being frightened of each other. Many children also have extra sympathy for Manuel.

In retrospect, it seems surprising that the theatrical world was so doubtful that the show would succeed. But our producer Phil McIntyre told me that when he first approached theatre owners, the first question was 'Is Cleese going to be in it?' And when Phil told them 'No', they immediately lost interest. It didn't help when he produced good attendance figures from the Australia performances. Phil explained that he wanted to use a cast of excellent stage actors in order to achieve a longer run, but still none of them were interested. It was only when a play flopped at the Apollo that Nica Burns, the theatre owner, gave us a short 12-week run. Then, when the show proved so popular that you could hardly get a seat, the run was extended and extended for almost a year until we ran up against an unmoveable booking. So we took a break during that 14-week run, and then came right back into the Apollo, followed by an eight-month tour of the UK. Phil adds that, to their credit, ATC, Cameron Mackintosh and LW Theatres all told him they regretted missing out on the booking. The odd thing is that for once, I felt completely confident! Maybe I was being simple-minded but I knew the adapted script was very funny, and when I saw the quality of the actors during the auditions, I was thrilled, and strangely smug.

As my dear friend William Goldman, who was a great screenwriter, said in the best book ever written about Hollywood, *Adventures in the Screen Trade*: 'Nobody knows.'

Below left: Our incredible multi-level set as it appears in the West End production.

Below: The theatrical poster for the original West End run – what a cast!

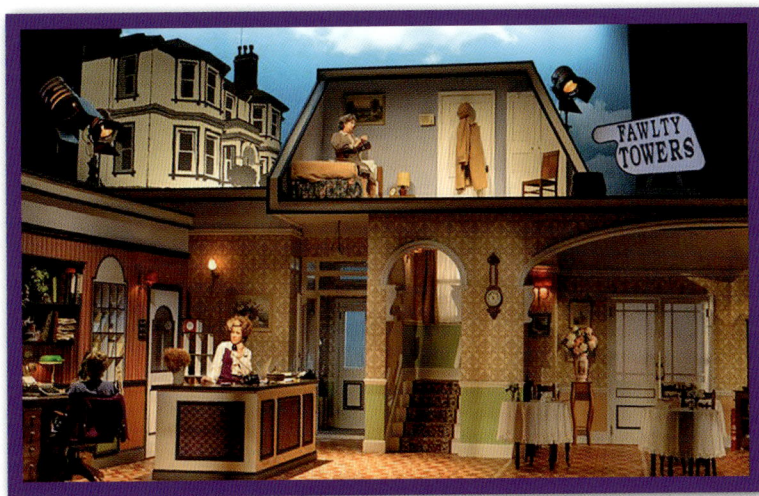

Caroline Jay Ranger / Director, *Fawlty Towers: The Play*

After a vibrant career as both a theatrical performer and a music video choreographer, CJay Ranger moved into directing and soon amassed a string of West End credits to her name. She was the perfect choice to bring Basil to the stage.

'Phil MacIntyre first had conversations with John in 2015, around the 40th anniversary — the idea of a *Fawlty* show was in the air. I had directed the *Monty Python* shows at the O2, and John had seen how I'd worked with those strong, incredibly creative, brilliant minds; I'd been on that learning curve already! John originally thought of a three-act play, in line with a traditional farce — I suggested amalgamating three of his favourite episodes. John immediately said these were "Communication Problems", including the Mrs Richards character and all her wonderful anger, frustration and disgust; "The Hotel Inspectors", with Basil fawning, begging, bowing to the wrong men — the spoon salesman and the upmarket seller of outboard motors; and then "The Germans", of course.

'The "spark" moment was when I realised we could set the play as if the events happened over a weekend, with all the different characters coming in and out, and we could swap in characters like Mr Walt, culminating in a marvellous finale, with all the characters present. As a director, I wanted to keep the spaces in the theatre alive. Once I suggested the weekend idea to John, we were off, and by January 2016 we had a draft together. I had moments of thinking, "What have I done?"! When you grow up with *Fawlty Towers*, it's in your DNA, and you want to do it justice. This is a show that has defined comedy for the whole world.

'In terms of the casting for the original production, we didn't want people who would copy. If we tried to do straight copies, we'd fail — so no impersonators. Instead, we went back to the original stories of the hotel owners, the Sinclairs. Donald Sinclair had been in the Merchant Navy during the war, one of only three men who survived the sinking of an entire ship. Mrs Sinclair was already running hotels while he was still at sea — she was super strong, super smart. You could imagine the hatred that would grow inside those people for these ultra-fastidious, pernickety, small-minded guests. And you can feel the strength in the writing — the mannerisms of those characters and their physicality are so well drawn. All the actors did their research, so that we had developed those characters fully, and only then did we let the actors watch the TV show. We knew the audience would smell a rat (!) if the characters hadn't come from an honest place.

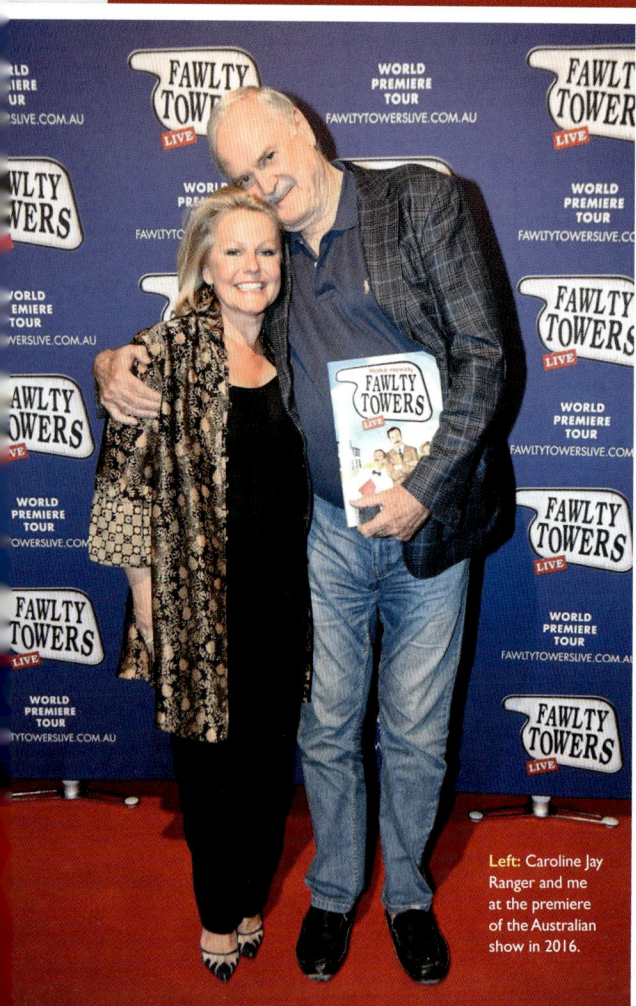

Left: Caroline Jay Ranger and me at the premiere of the Australian show in 2016.

Above: At the London press night for the play in May 2024. (L–R) Adam Jackson-Smith, yours truly, Anna-Jane Casey, Terry Gilliam, CJay and Michael Palin.

'In rehearsal, we adhered to every comma, every comedy beat, every breath that's in the script. We rehearsed for three weeks, then John came out for four days, for what felt like a masterclass. He spent one-on-one time with all the actors, and working with someone who knows his craft that deeply, who has complete dexterity with language, who can say, "If you are looking at him, it won't be funny, but if you're looking at her, it will," who can tell you how much pressure to give every exclamation mark, was invaluable. When you can sit back and watch someone in their flow, with that perfect comedy timing . . . John sprinkled gold dust on everything. John never stops asking questions, and he is always happy to change things – I've watched the show over and over again and it's still as funny,

and I think that is from John's sense of play, it's like being five years old, completely unprecious. And that lack of inhibition and freedom allowed me as a director to be free with his work, which is empowering and collaborative. Creatively, it leads to brilliant outcomes.

'Of course, we had to have intense attention to detail to create, in producer Lucy Ansbro's words, "a solid machine". All of the set work and prop work are carefully choreographed. Along with my associate, Denise Ranger, I spent hours finding the exact angle of the hotel desk to the audience, adjusting it millimetre by millimetre. The stage doors all open and close together, a character will slam something shut for emphasis and that will generate a laugh – none of this happens by accident. We went through every detail of the

set design, costumes and props – for example, even the fabric of Mrs Richards' dress needed to feel right. There are real trees off-stage to make the shadows that fall on-stage look right, there are 1970 TV lamps to give the right atmosphere. Those carefully considered, choreographed moments are all part of the audience's experience, even if they don't realise. We want them to feel like guests in the hotel. They'd first experienced the show at home, after all. We were lucky to get the Apollo Theatre, because the intimacy of that space worked so well. I'm really proud to say that that attention to every specific detail was adhered to by every member of the production team, creative team and all the actors, so we could deliver the best version of this adaptation, night after night, to exhilarated full houses.'

15.

A LIFE CALLING TO LAUGHTER

I was always drawn to comedy. I can remember listening to *Up the Pole* with Jimmy Jewel and Ben Warriss, *Much Binding in the Marsh* with Richard Murdoch, Kenneth Horne and Sam Costa, and *ITMA* with Tommy Handley, and also Jon Pertwee and Eric Barker and Arthur Askey . . .

'Listening' – as this was before we could afford a television. There were three in Weston-super-Mare, and one belonged to the father of a school friend, Reg Pinn, so we would drive down to the Pinns' on Sunday evening to watch *What's My Line* with Eamonn Andrews and Gilbert Harding. But it was on radio that I found *The Goon Show* in about 1954 at the age of 15. It became the love of my life, along with Bristol City FC and Somerset Cricket Club. It wasn't just that it was gloriously funny, it was liberating, making fun of things that we were supposed to take seriously, and hinting at a whole new, and rather subversive, view of our lives. All my contemporaries adored it too, and the morning after a broadcast, we would gather excitedly, feeling like a very special secret society, and talk through the entire 30 minutes, squealing and choking with laughter – just as many youngsters did in the early 70s, with *Monty Python*.

It was always this liberating effect, this re-jigging of horizon that excited me and drew me towards Spike Milligan and Michael Bentine, and plays at the Bristol Old Vic like N. F. Simpson's *A Resounding*

Below: Me, aged fifteen . . . and six feet tall already!

Below right: After comedy, the next two big loves of my life, Bristol City and Somerset Cricket Club.

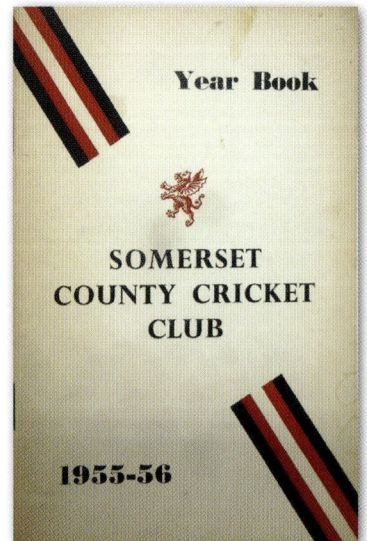

Tinkle and *One Way Pendulum* and even
surrealists like Ionescu, until I realised
they weren't funny. The next thrill came
at Cambridge when I stumbled upon a
matinee at the Arts Theatre of *Beyond the
Fringe*. To this day it remains the funniest
show I've ever seen. Peter Cook, Dudley
Moore, Jonathan Miller and Alan Bennett
with a parody of a Church of England
sermon that had the audience literally
screaming with laughter – extra volume
coming from the instant recognition that
we never had to respect this rubbish again.
'Life is like a tin of sardines. We're all trying
to find the key.'

So then I started spending my time at
the Cambridge Footlights Club, because
I really liked the members, and did a
bit of writing (and discovering I had
creative abilities, disguised for years by
studying Science and Law!). I finished up
performing in the Footlights annual revue
in 1962 and 1963, and the second show
was astonishingly good and we finished up
playing for five months in the West End.
And soon after, David Frost catapulted me
into British television, and in 1967, David
gave me a show with Graham Chapman
and Tim Brooke-Taylor called *At Last the
1948 Show* where we were able to do zany,
whacky, off-the-wall, crazy, goofy, madcap
comedy of the kind we'd always wanted to
try but didn't, because we were new boys
and people wouldn't let us.

Which led to *Monty Python*, etc, etc.
But I never thought of comedy as more
than entertainment and sometimes, as
with *Life of Brian*, entertainment that said
something important. But for the next
fifty years, I didn't question this Oxbridge,
rather snotty, somewhat condescending

attitude, when comedy was always viewed
as the poor cousin of real, important,
vastly superior 'Drama' with 'real straight
actors.' I admit, I rather forgot what
Jonathan Miller had said to me when he
directed me in *The Taming of the Shrew*
for the BBC. Discussing comedy, he told
me, 'Comedy was good enough for Mozart
and Shakespeare. So it's good enough for
me.' And then I went to the Sarajevo Film
Festival. I seldom go to film festivals. I
don't know why. I think they're rather fun.
Maybe it's because I'd be bound to run
into Terry Gilliam. And in Sarajevo they
told me about the civil war that broke out

Above: Me back in February
1967 with my fellow cast
mates from *At Last the 1948
Show*. Top row: me, Aimi
MacDonald and Graham
Chapman. Front row:
Tim Brooke-Taylor and
Marty Feldman.

when the old Yugoslavia collapsed in the 1990s. At one point, I was told, Sarajevo was under siege by the Serbs – for four years. Four . . . years! Four years during which the Serbs, up in the hills above Sarajevo in the valley below, lobbed shells down on its inhabitants, and with their telescopic rifles, shot people crossing the streets below. I asked them how they got through it. They told me they had found an underground car park, converted it into a cinema, and showed comedy films there every evening – many of them Python movies, I'm proud to say. But what stunned me was what they said next . . .

'After we'd laughed for a couple of hours, we all came out feeling better.'

They felt better although nothing had changed!

This meant that their laughter altered their mindset, so they were able to cope better with their terrible predicament.

I couldn't stop thinking about this.

And soon afterwards, I started attending Comic Cons! Which are exhausting, but very rewarding, because you get to talk to hundreds of fans, who turn out to be an extraordinarily nice, patient bunch, on the look out for a bit of fun. Many of them say 'Thank you for making me laugh all these years!!' A lot of the women say, 'Thank you for helping me to form my sense of humour,' but a startling number of both sexes say, 'Thank you for helping me through difficult times.'

Laughter is much more important to people's lives than the puritans realise. And today, I'm afraid, there's much less of it than there was.

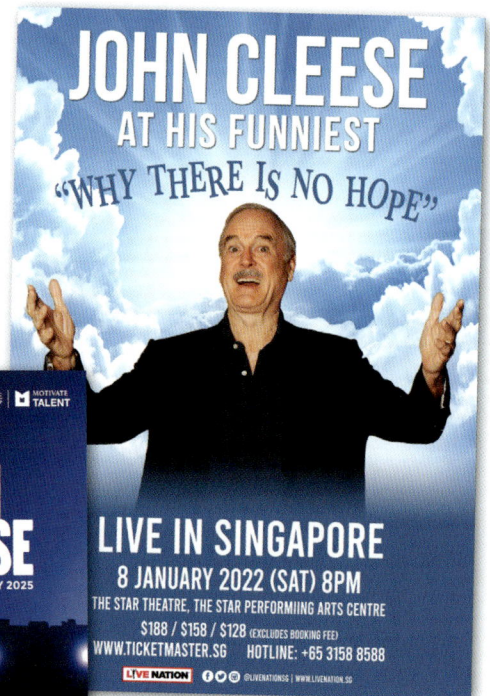

AN EVENING WITH
JOHN CLEESE
25 JANUARY 2025

JOHN CLEESE
AT HIS FUNNIEST
"WHY THERE IS NO HOPE"

LIVE IN SINGAPORE
8 JANUARY 2022 (SAT) 8PM
THE STAR THEATRE, THE STAR PERFORMING ARTS CENTRE
$188 / $158 / $128 (EXCLUDES BOOKING FEE)
WWW.TICKETMASTER.SG   HOTLINE: +65 3158 8588

AFTERWORD

Before we started on *Fawlty Towers*, I'd worked a bit with John on the film adaption of *Romance with a Double Bass* and the *Monty Python* 'King Ludwig' sketch. When he suggested we collaborate, John already had Basil's blueprint. We worked from 9 to 5 in John's study at our home in Woodsford Square. We both sat at his desk and he did the typing. The dialogue was his; I worked with him on developing the situations and the characters. Sybil, Manuel and Polly came fairly quickly and were effortless compared to the convolutions of the plots. We always mapped out the plots before John wrote any of his dialogue. On occasion, we'd improvise. In 'Gourmet Night', for instance, when John started swearing at his stalled car – 'And now he has to hit it,' I said. John mimed picking up a branch and started beating the imaginary car. We were both excited and laughing hysterically. It was a big moment. I'm proud of it.

Working out the logistics of, say, 'The Psychiatrist', where John looks for the light switch and puts his hand by mistake on the breast of a girl doing a yoga exercise, took ages to work out. The logistics to make the scene work were so intricate that I just couldn't keep up with it. I had to lie down until John finished the scene.

The work on *Fawlty Towers* was a wonderful catharsis for us both. The essence of collaboration, it seems to me, is chemistry, and our opposite family backgrounds blended well for comedy. John grew up in a household where chaos and hostility were stifled. In my house, with an alcoholic father, the hostilities were physical and voluble, often resulting in a police visit for disturbing the peace.

As an American working on this quintessentially English sitcom, I often felt out of my depth. But I knew Basil in my core, and John's dialogue brought him to such vivid life. Out of our disparate origins and skills, it seems we made something enduring which at the time we could never have imagined.

Connie Booth

ABOUT THE AUTHOR

For over 600 years (or thereabouts), John Marwood Cleese has delighted generations with an impeccable body of work. He has become one of the most highly thought of purveyors of rib-aching belly laughs, avant-garde walking practices and insightful musings upon the human condition – more often than not, providing all three services at once!

John was born in Weston-super-Mare in 1939, and soon took up the popular youthful pastimes of football, cricket and growing tall. Also at this time, his young ears would became attuned to the hilarious and vibrant world of captivating wit emanating from the radio . . .

Responsibility would briefly take hold in the form of Law at Cambridge University, but that institution's famed Footlights theatrical club lay in wait. Flanked by like-minded comedic souls, John soon found himself honing his craft, writing and performing comedy revues. By 1963, one such revue, *A Clump of Plinths*, became an unprecedented success at the Edinburgh Festival Fringe before moving to London's West End and touring internationally.

Now established, John never looked back and was snapped up as an in-demand performer and writer for radio and television. The popular satirical sketch show *The Frost Report* would give John his first taste of entertaining millions from the confines of a TV studio.

In the late 1960s, John co-founded the era-defining comedy troupe Monty Python, whose inventive blend of the absurd and the funny made their sketch show instantly cherished around the globe (leading to feature-film spin-offs, tours and a musical). It would be the success of *Python* which would open a door at the BBC to develop a pilot project with his then-wife Connie Booth. The resulting series, *Fawlty Towers*, was a masterpiece of farce, going on to be voted Britain's Best Sitcom several times over and becoming a beloved icon of the genre.

In the decades that followed, John would write and star in a host of feature films such as *A Fish Called Wanda* and *Fierce Creatures*, and be cast in a range of other films, embracing both comedic and more serious roles. At the same time, a company John co-founded – Video Arts – would become the world's leading producer of corporate training films.

In later years, John would continue to make welcome appearances across major feature films (from James Bond and Harry Potter to *Shrek*!) and shamelessly steal the show in any TV series he would guest star in. Recently, John has penned several best-selling books on his work and reflections on an extraordinary life. He tours regularly to packed houses around the world.